Equity & Trusts

Private Law Tutor Publishing

Foreword

Thank you for buying this book. The problem that I encountered when studying law is: knowing everything. There is so much to read and so little time to do it. If you skip some material, or a case you are none the wiser. So throughout my years teaching law I have devised a system and I am going to share this with you.

You may have encountered different methods or formulas to help when advising a client in a mock scenario. One of example is the *IRAC* method or another is *Celo*. These are well documented and you can read about these. I never used them, because I had a method in my head that worked. It was not until I started teaching that I spoke about it. I call my method the **"Fact Law Sandwich"**. Let me explain. If you are asked to advise a party as to their legal rights this is how you present it:

FACTS
GENERAL PRINCIPLE
LAW
APPLY TO FACTS

In **Fact:** simply state what you have been told, this why you can never be accused of not considering the facts. In **General principle:** you simply state what the general rule of the relevant issue is. You express it as if you are speaking to a child who has no knowledge of law. In **Law**: you state "using the authority of…..and you go on to state which statute or case helps prove your point. Lastly in **Apply to Facts**: you apply the reasoning of the case to your factual scenario. Your advice will sound and look structured and professional. The reason it is called the "Fact Law Sandwich", is because the advice contains two outer layers of facts that sandwich the principle and law in the middle.

This book is written to provide the student with a good knowledge of the most important cases on their study. It is written in a way to facilitate the Fact Law Sandwich method. I provide the general principle, the name of the case with full citation, the facts, the Ratio (the thing the lecturers say you always need to use), and application i.e. how the case should be applied. No other book provides this information at your fingertips. I hope you enjoy using it.

Contents
Private Law Tutor Publishing

Welcome/Introduction/Overview

This book provides you with basic information as a basis for you to form your own critical opinions on this area of law. Once you have mastered the basics, you will be inspired to question contract principles in your essays and apply them in mock client advisory scenarios. Again, for your convenience, we have also published a book which provides you with examples of how to answer such questions and how to apply your knowledge as effectively as possible to help you get the best possible marks.

This aid is a fully-fledged source of basic information, which tries to give the student comprehensive understanding for this module. However, it is recommended that you compliment it with the further reading suggestions provided at the end of each topic, as well as read the cases themselves for more in-depth information. This book provides an analysis of the basic principles of the law of Equity and Trusts. The following is a summary of the Book content:

- An introduction to Equity Law;
- An introduction to Trusts Law;
- What these areas of English Law seeks to achieve; and
- The legal-philosophical development of this area of law.

The aim of this Book is to:

- Provide an introduction to anyone studying or interested in studying Law to the key principles and concepts that exist in the Law of Equity and Trusts.
- To provide a framework to consider Equity and Trusts Law within the context of examinations.
- Provide a detailed learning resource in order for legal written examination skills to be developed.
- Facilitate the development of written and independent critical thinking skills.
- Promote the practice of problem solving skills.
- To establish a platform for students to gain a solid

understanding of the basic principles and concepts of Equity and Trusts, which can then be expanded upon.

Through this Book, students will be able to demonstrate the ability to:

- Demonstrate an awareness of the core principles of Equity and Trusts.
- Critically assess challenging mock factual scenarios and be able to pick out legal issues in the various areas of the law.
- Apply their knowledge when writing a formal assessment.
- Present a reasoned argument and make a judgment on competing viewpoints.
- Make use of technical legalistic vocabulary in the appropriate manner.
- Be responsible for their learning process and work in an adaptable and flexible way.

STUDYING EQUITY & TRUSTS LAW

Equity & Trusts is one of the seven core subjects that the Law Society and the Bar Council deem essential in a qualifying law degree. Therefore, it is vital that a student successfully pass this subject to become a lawyer. Additionally, a knowledge and understanding of the principles in these areas is needed in order to study other law subjects such as land, probate and Wills.

The primary method by which your understanding of the law of Trusts will develop is by understanding how to solve problem questions. You will also be given essay questions in your examinations. The methods by which these types of question should be approached are somewhat different.

TACKLING PROBLEMS AND ESSAY QUESTIONS

There are various ways of approaching problem questions and essay questions. We have provided students with an in-depth analysis in the question and answer series of books.

Chapter 1 - Introduction to Equity

INTRODUCTION

Equity represents one of the two main ramifications of the UK law system. On one side there is Common law, such as the law made by the judges in the Common Law courts. On the other side there is Equity, the law made by the judges in the Chancery courts. A clear understanding of the origins of Equity is essential in order to comprehend the principles on which it is based and the way those are applied. Concepts such as 'trust' must be illustrated in the light of the historical development of the subject.

WHAT HAPPENED IN THE VERY BEGINNING?

The origins of Equity lie in the Middle age. At the time in order to go to court an individual needed to be a 'free man' (Sir and Lord) and make sure that the case fitted into a particular range of claims, called 'writs'. Writs were templates that encompassed those claims considered deserving to reach the court. The purpose of creating writs was to prevent the courts to be flooded by undeserving cases. Furthermore, in 1258 the Proclamation of Oxford came into force with the aim to prevent the creation of further writs. Less potential claims were allowed to go to court. The society kept developing while the law fossilised.

Only one option was left to those not able to take their cases to court: The King. The King, as fount of all justice, had the power to override the writs and declare fair the consideration of a case even though it did not fall within the required categories. At some point due to the volume of claims, the King appointed someone to deal with this burden in his place, the Chancellor, traditionally the Senior Advisor of the King (someone that may be seen as the current Prime Minister). The Chancellor was usually a cleric, a religious person whose approach to the cases based on theoretical concepts such as justice, fairness and equity. The Claimant used to send his petition to the King in Council. The petition was addressed to the Lord Chancellor that examined the case. In time the Chancellor started building up a body of rules and Equity commenced to be more formalised. In order to balance the high degree of flexibility applied to the cases and guarantee more certainty, the Court of Chancery built up a proper legal system called Equity.

Equity has been created in order to mitigate the harshness of the Common Law. Initially it was a second option for those cases not able to have a cause of action before Common law courts under the writs. Afterwards it became an option to reach a more suitable remedy upon the facts of the case that Common Law would have not provided and a way to fill the gaps, internal to the Common Law system. The purpose of Equity was to achieve justice and fairness *ad hoc*, by looking at each case on its own.

As separated bodies of law, Equity and Common Law may reach different outcomes so that a conflict may arise. How could conflicts be resolved?

General Principle: Where there is a conflict between common law and equity, equity shall prevail (per Coke CJ).

Earl of Oxford's Case
Facts: Magdalene College sold a piece of land to Queen Elisabeth I. The land was later on sold to Mr Spinola. A statute, 13 Eliz c 10, provided that conveyances of estates by the masters, fellows, *any college dean to anyone for anything other than a term of 21 years, or three lives, 'shall be utterly void'.* It was thought transfer to the Queen would grant unimpeachable title. Spinola thought this, and so did Edward de Vere, the Earl of Oxford, who bought the land in 1580 and built 130 houses. John Warren leased a house through intermediaries. Then, Barnabas Gooch, Master of Magdalene College, claimed that he was able to lease the land to John Smith. Warren brought an action of ejection against Smith, but his lease expired before it was heard by court. Warren asked the question to be decided anyway. **Ratio: Equity is a modifier of the Common Law therefore whether a principle is established in Equity it has to be followed in Common Law.**

Per Lord Ellesmere LC "The office of the Chancellor is to correct man's consciences for frauds, breach of trusts, wrongs and oppressions of whatsoever nature and to soften and mollify the extremity of the law (...) When judgment is obtained by oppression, wrong and a hard conscience, the Chancellor will frustrate and set it aside, not for any error or defect in the judgement but for the hard conscience of the party." Application: The Court of Equity decided in favour of the Defendant, holding that he was entitled to relief.

The fundamental role exercised by both ramifications of the law and the potential conflict between the two have led to the introduction of the Judicature Acts 1873-1875. The Act has unified the civilian legal structure by creating one set of courts including both the court of Equity and the court of Common Law. Nevertheless, it is not that simple to transplant Equity and Common Law within one single system since they have been separated for several centuries. Two separate bodies of rules have been built up for years until the point that equity has, for instance, built a more sophisticated body of rules in relation to property rights with the introduction of trusts. Trusts are a property regime that is strictly related to the Equity system. They have developed out of the division of law and equity.

THE SIGNIFICANCE OF THE NINETEENTH CENTURY IN THE DEVELOPMENT OF EQUITY

During the Nineteenth century several important reforms were introduced in order to balance the presence of the two parallel law systems of Common law and Equity. The introduction of the Common Law Procedure Act 1854 permitted Common law courts to adopt equitable remedies next to the usual damages. The Chancery Amendment Act 1858 allowed the Court of Chancery to award the Common law remedy of damages next to the usual equitable remedies. The Judiciary Act 1873 and 1875 fused the two systems of Common law and Equity in one single administrative structure. More specifically, the purpose of the Act was '*the vesting in one tribunal the administration of Law and Equity in every cause, action or dispute which should come before that tribunal*' as Jessel MR stated in **Salt v Cooper** [1880] 16 Ch D 544 In order to prevent situations where courts might face conflicts between the two systems, Section 25 of the Judiciary Act 1873 established:

'Generally, in all matters not hereinbefore mentioned in which there is a conflict or variance between the rules of equity and the rules of common law with reference to the same matter, the rules of equity shall prevail.'

General Principle: '*There is only one court and the equity rules prevail in it*' (Jessel MR)(On the front cover of this book).

Walsh v Lonsdale [1882] 21 Ch D 9
Facts: The parties stipulated an agreement for the lease of a mill for seven years. The Claimant was let into possession. The agreement was stipulated without the adoption of a deed. In the agreement there was a clause establishing that rent would have been paid one year in advance whether the Defendant demanded. When Lonsdale asked the Claimant the payment in advance, he refused it and the Defendant distrained for the amount. The Claimant sued the Defendant on the ground of illegal distress and specific performance of the contract for the lease. **Ratio: The equity rules prevail and the maxim applied by the court Lord Jessel MR was equity looks on that as done that which ought to be done. Application:** Since Equity does not require compliance with particular formalities such as the use of a deed,

the court held in favour of the Defendant on the ground that he was entitled of the payment in law and in equity. The agreement between the parties had to be treated as equivalent to a contract for a lease under a deed.

General Principle: The purpose of the law is to reach fairness in the best interest of the parties, unhindered by the constraints of law or equity.

Federal Commerce and Navigation Ltd v Molena Alpha inc [1878] QB 927
Facts: Three ships got let to charterers for about six years. The agreement included the following clauses: i) the rent had to be paid twice monthly in advance. In default of payment the owners had the right to withdraw the vessel after notice; ii) deductions from hire were admitted. The charterers made deductions from hire without prior agreement with the owners. The ship-owners withdrew the charter by instructing the master not to sign any bills with the charterers. The latter read the owners' action as a repudiation of the charter and they sued them. **Ratio: 'During that time the streams of common law and equity have flown together and combined so as to be indistinguishable the one from the other. We have no longer to ask ourselves: what would the courts of common law or the courts of equity have done before the Judicature Act? We have to ask ourselves: what should we do now so as to ensure fair dealing between the parties?' as Lord Denning stated. Application:** The House of Lords held in favour of the charterers. The breach of the term of the contract made by the owners went to the root of the contract by depriving the charterers of their main benefit such as the issue of the bills which was essential to the charterers' trade. The Defendant's conduct was held to be a wrongful repudiation of the contract.

HISTORICAL AND CONCEPTUAL BACKGROUND

1. What is Equity?

The key points in relation to introduction of Equity can be encompassed in four categories:

- Until 1875 Equity was regulated by a different court such as the Court of Chancery.

- The main reason why Equity has been created was to mitigate the harshness of common law.

- Equity represents a distinct legal system

- Equity is based on an exclusive and a supplementary jurisdiction.

2. Development of Equity to the Judicature Acts

KEY DATES

1066   Norman Conquest

1154   Centralisation of Legal System under Henry II - Common Law Courts

1258   Expansion of Writ System restricted by Provisions of Oxford

14C   Petitions to King as "fountain of justice".

1473   Lord Chancellor issues decrees in his own name

c. 1500 Greater part of land in England held under uses

1529   Rules of Equity begin to develop leading to formality

1535   Statute of Uses – attempt to abolish 'uses' (early trusts)

1540   Statute of Wills – land could be left by will

1560   Lord Chancellor enforces "Use upon a Use" (see slide 11)

1615   Earl of Oxford's case: Dispute over common injunctions.

1616   James I resolves it in favour of Court of Chancery.

18C/19C Increasing rigidity of Equity. Delays become a scandal.

1854   Common Law Procedure Act

1858   Chancery Amendment Act ("Lord Cairns' Act")

1873/1875   Judicature Acts – common law and equity administered by single High Court and Court of Appeal

1882   Walsh v. Lonsdale - fusion applied in practice - the rules of Equity prevail

1925   Modern Trust replaces the "Use upon a Use"

Comprehensive Property Law Reform: "The 1925 Legislation"

EQUITY'S MOST CHARACTERISTIC INSTITUTION: THE TRUST

One of the main reason why Equity has been created lies in the institution of trust as a supplement of common law. During the 13th century, owners of lands left their properties to relatives or friends while abroad. The use of the lands by these individuals was identified by common law as legal ownership. Equity introduced a new way to look at this title. Lands were hold for the benefit of the real owner. Trust can be looked at as a modern version of the 'use'. Later on, the **Lord Chancellor applied the same institution to those circumstances where a person held a property for the benefit of a**

third party appointed by the first owner. The adoption of the device was extended to new situations. Holding land under a 'use' also had other advantages: typically to allow it to be inherited by persons other than one's heirs, and to avoid various incidents of feudal tenure.

EQUITY ACTS *IN PERSONAM* (AGAINST THE PERSON)

'Equity acts *in personam*' represents one of the leading maxims. By describing property rights as rights *in personam* the law means that the right can be exercised against the entire world. Those entitled of the right cannot be deprived by anyone. In the presence of a trust, the interest of the beneficiary (such as the person for whom the property is hold) cannot be compromised by anyone. No one but the beneficiary can claim the right over the property. According to Equity rules, there is only one person that may steal the right of the beneficiary over a property. This person is the so-called 'bona fide purchaser for value without notice' or 'Equity's darling'. Equitable interest may be lost in the presence of a persona falling into this definition.

The position was recently summed up well by Lord Millett, in [2012] CLJ 583 at 587-8:

"Equity creates proprietary interests in the beneficiaries by its ability to enforce the trustee's obligation to manage the trust property for their benefit, and to enforce the duty not only against the trustee himself but against his successors in title other than a bona fide purchaser for value without notice".

EQUITY AS A SUPPLEMENTARY JURISDICTION

It is fundamental to understand that Equity is not a completely separated system. It works arm in arm with the Common law system. For instance, when answering to the question 'who has legal title?', you will look at the Common law rules, since the beneficiary owns the trust property in equity and the trustee in law.

This appears clear when looking at the equitable remedy of injunction.

Example: A person keeps trespassing the land of Mr X. Prior to 1854, Common law courts would have dealt with the issue by awarding Mr X with damages. In order to obtain a different remedy, Mr X would have had to go through two separated processes: one at Common law courts, one at the Chancery court. What Mr X really wants is to prevent that person from trespassing. The remedy that would come from the Court of Chancery is the so-called injunction. The court would directly order the trespasser to stop.

NATURE OF EQUITABLE RIGHTS

Equitable rights are shaped on the basis of legal rights. This is well-illustrated by the following examples from the law of real property:

Legal	Equitable
Fee simple	Equitable fee simple
Legal lease	Equitable lease
Legal charge (mortgage)	Equitable charge
Easement	Equitable easement

THE EQUITABLE DOCTRINE OF NOTICE

Historically, the equitable doctrine of notice was extremely important, and applied both to land and personalty. By looking at its application in Land the doctrine is better illustrated. A person that buys a land subjected to a legal mortgage will still be bound by the legal mortgage. It does not matter whether he was aware or not of the existence of the legal mortgage over the land. Things are different in the presence of an equitable mortgage. A person that buys a land subjected to an equitable mortgage will not be bound by it if he was unaware of its existence. The theory is simple, but the doctrine became more elaborate.

General Principle: If the purchaser meets each element required by the doctrine of notice (legal estate, valuable consideration, lack

of notice and good faith) then they can ignore a prior equitable right, in that case a trust, even though the beneficiaries had been swindled by the (seller) trustees.

Pilcher v Rawlins <u>(1871-72) L.R. 7 Ch. App. 259</u>
Facts: Jeremiah Pilcher made a settlement under which three members of Pilcher's family were to stand possessed of about £8000 in trust for Jeremiah Pilcher during his life and after his death for his children. With the consent of Jeremiah Pilcher, the trustees were allowed to vary the investments and appoint new trustees. The Defendant was a solicitor appointed as trustee in relation to the £8000. The money represented a security of a mortgage deed. **Ratio: Equity has an interest in and a power over a purchaser's conscience. The bona fide transferee of the legal estate for value without notice of the equitable interest acquires the legal title in priority over the beneficiary. Application:** Three are the main types of notice available:

- *Actual Notice*

The purchaser was aware of the equitable interest before buying the property. Actual notice occurs even though a person forgets about a notice or is in possession of a document that notifies the equitable interest but he does not read it.

- *Imputed Notice*

Imputed notice occurs where the buyer was not personally aware of the equitable interest, but his agent (typically the solicitor) was. The buyer will be considered bound by the equitable interest.

- *Constructive notice*

A constructive notice comes into place when a purchaser did not actually know of the equitable interest, but either the legal estate purchaser fails to make any inquiries as to prior equitable interests, or where although he makes inquiries, these are taken to be insufficient.

General Principle: There are circumstances in which a high standard of inspection is expected. If this fails, constructive notice may be implied.

Kingsnorth Finance Co Ltd v Tizard [1986] 1 WLR 783
Facts: The Defendant was the sole owner of the matrimonial home. Mrs Tizard was granted with a beneficial interest. The couple started having problems and they got separated. Mrs Tizard left the house. She was at home every day to look after the two children. When required, she spent the night at the house since the husband was away to stay with the children. One day Mr Tizard mortgaged the property. When he applied for the mortgage he defined himself as a single man. The surveyor did the inspection of the house when wife and children were out. The inspector noticed signs of children, but he did not find anything in relation to the wife. Mr Tizard said that the ex-wife moved out months before. The Claimant made a loan offer and the Defendant accepted. When the Claimant tried to enforce their charge, the issue was whether the Claimant's legal mortgage was subject to the equitable interest of the wife. **Ratio: Physical presence becomes actual occupation even though a person has not exclusive or continuous and uninterrupted occupation of the property. It is surveyor's duty to properly verify how the house is used when informed of a marriage. Application:** The court found the Defendant not liable on the ground that the surveyor was under a duty to do more investigations once finding out about the presence of children.

Land Law today

Thanks to the introduction of the registration of lands, cases involving the doctrine of notice are fewer. The doctrine only applies in those circumstances involving pre 1925 restrictive covenants or equitable shares on unregistered land. The Land Registration Act 2002 protects equitable interests since registration represents a notification to the world. By consulting the land registry, a purchaser can find all the information in relation to a land.

MAXIMS OF EQUITY

Maxims represent a group of mottoes that encompass the principles on which Equity is based on.

- **Equity will not suffer a wrong to be without a remedy** -Where statute or common law does not provide for the remedying of a wrong; it is equity which intercedes to ensure that a fair result is reached.

- **Equity follows the law** -The principle is that statute will be obeyed.

- **Where there is equal equity, the law prevails** - Where there is no clear distinction to be drawn between parties as to which of them has the better claim in equity, the common law principle which best fits the case will be applied.

- **Where equities are equal, the law prevail** - Equity will favour whoever created their rights first. A mortgagee would be given priority over another mortgagee if he created his mortgage before the other.

- **He who seeks equity must do equity** - Whoever seeks equity must have acted entirely fairly themselves. A Court of Equity will not act in favour of someone who has, for example, committed an illegal act.

- **He who comes to equity must come with clean hands** - A person claiming rights under an agreement to which they are not complying with will not be assisted by equity.

- **Delay defeats equity** - Equity aids the vigilant and not the indolent. If a claimant allows too much time to elapse between the facts giving rise to her claim and the service of proceedings to protect that claim, the court will not protect her rights. The doctrine of not allowing an equitable remedy where there has been unconscionable delay is known as 'laches' (**Partridge v Partridge** [1894] 1 Ch 351).

- **Equality is equity** - It is ancient principle that *'equity did delight in equality'*.

- **Equity looks at the intent rather than the form** - Equity will give effect to the substance of any transaction rather than merely to its surface appearance **(Parkin v Thorold** (1852) 16 Beav. 59).

- **Equity imputes an intention to fulfil an obligation** - The principle assumes an intention in a person bound by an obligation to carry out that obligation.

- **Equity regards as done that which ought to be done** - Equity will consider that something has been done if the court believes that it ought to have been done. In **Walsh v Lonsdale** (1882) 21 Ch D 9, a binding contract to grant a lease was deemed to create an equitable lease even though the formal requirements to create a valid common lease had not been observed.

- **Equity acts *in personam.***

- **Equity will not assist a volunteer** - A trust operates on the conscience of the legal owner of the property.

- **Equity will not allow a statute to be used as an engine of fraud.**

- **Equity abhors a vacuum** - Equity will not allow there to be proprietary rights which are not owned by some identifiable person **(Vandervell v IRC** [1967] 2 AC 291).

- **Equity will not permit a person who is trustee of property to take a benefit from that property qua trustee.**

- **A trust operates on the conscience of the legal owner of the property** - The legal owner of a property will be obliged to hold it on trust for any persons beneficially entitled to it where good conscience so requires.

HOW THE LEGAL TITLE IS GOING TO BE USED?

The trustee plays two important roles thanks to the legal title received. First, he has to follow the trust fund itself by running, administering it in accordance with what has been dictated by the trust document. If there are multiple trustees, they all hold the property as joint tenants; they will hold the property together. Second, the trustee has to transfer the legal title to the beneficiary that will become the absolute owner of the property.

Summary

- Equity represents one of the two main ramifications of the UK law system. On one side there is Common law, such as the law made by the judges in the Common Law courts, on the other side there is Equity, the law made by the judges in the Chancery courts.

- The origins of Equity lie in the Middle age.

- The Claimant used to send his petition to the King in Council. The petition was addressed to the Lord Chancellor that examined the case. In time the Chancellor started building up a body of rule and Equity commenced to be more formalised.

- Equity has been created in order to mitigate the harshness of the Common Law.

Chapter 2 – Introduction to Trusts

Introduction

A trust is an equitable device created by Equity in order to transfer a property under the control of a trustee for the benefit of a beneficiary. The most common definition of trust has been given by A Underhill and D Hayton in the *Law of Trusts and Trustees* (16th Edition, Butterworths, 2002):

> *'A trust is an equitable obligation, binding a person (called a trustee) to deal with property over which he has control (which is called the trust property) for the benefit of persons (who are called the beneficiaries or cestuis que trust) of whom he may himself be one, and any one of whom may enforce the obligation.'*

The definition refers to the most commonly used private trusts. Nevertheless, it is important to mention at an early stage that charitable and private purpose trusts also exist. According to Section 1 of the Recognition of Trusts Act 1987, *'For the purposes of this Convention, the term trust refers to the legal relationship created inter vivos or on death by a person, the settlor, when assets have been placed under the control of a trustee for the benefit of a beneficiary or for a specified purpose.'*

The development of the trust

Trusts have developed out of the division of law and equity. **The settlor of property wishes to transfer this property to a friend for the benefit of a third party namely his children or wife (up to a hundred years ago women were not permitted to have property).** The original owner can execute a document of transfer, transferring the property to his friend the trustee, for his children. The dispute that would arise is whom the property belonged too? The document of transfer makes the friend the legal owner, but the original intentions of the settlor was that the friend nominally own and control the property for his children, the rightful owner.

The common law courts would examine the transfer document and hold the friend is the legal owner for all purposes, although the original intention of the settlor was the property is given for the benefit of the third party. The Equity/Chancery courts recognised this arrangement, that the property was not owned by the trustee but by the third party. Eventually the position of the chancery courts prevailed, the equity courts would enforce the trustee to act in the benefit of the third party and not for his own purposes. The beneficiary's right under the trust became known as the equitable and beneficial interest. The trustee is said to have legal title; this was seen through the common law courts that believed the trustee to be the legal owner of the property.

The nature of the trust

The trust involves an equitable obligation, which is imperative in nature.

"Stated in its simplest terms, a trust is a relationship which exists when one party holds property on behalf of another." Per Lord Nicholls, **Royal Brunei Airlines v. Tan** [1995] 3 All ER 97, at 103.

"A trust exists whenever the legal title is in one party and the equitable title in another. The legal owner is said to hold the property in trust for the equitable owner." Per Lord Millett, *Restitution and Constructive Trusts* (1998) 114 LQR 399, at 403.

"A trust is an arrangement in which one person, who is called the settlor, transfers property to another person, who is called the trustee. In so doing, the settlor directs the trustee to hold the property either for the benefit of certain persons or for the promotion of some purpose. If the trustee undertakes to carry out the direction, he becomes subject to a binding obligation which Equity will enforce." Professor Everton, *What is Equity About?* (London, Butterworths, 1970), at pp. 22-23.

Figure 1: this is a diagram showing the relationship of parties in a trust.

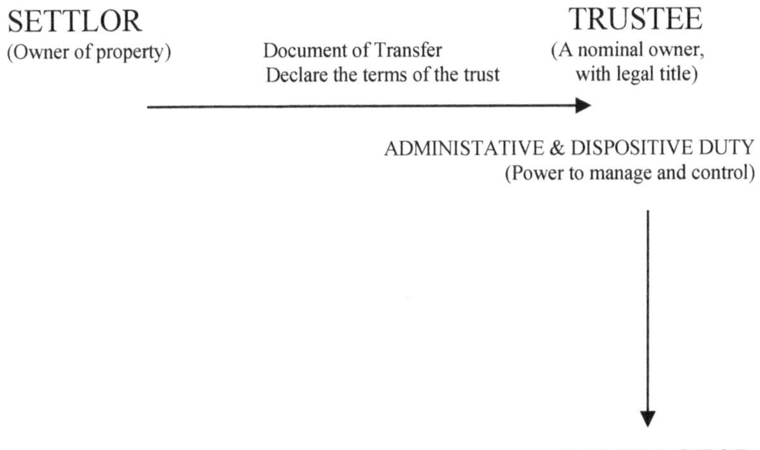

The settlor when establishing a trust of his property will transfer the property to a trustee. The transfer document will stipulate the trustee is the nominal or ostensible owner of the property, but the terms of the trust will state the trustee must hold the property for the benefit of the third party the beneficiary. The beneficiary is entitled to enforce his right under the trust against the trustee, this right is called equitable interest because it was originally the Chancery courts that recognised the third party's right.

The practical function of a trust

The crucial quality of a trust is a means of separating management and the right to benefit of property. Thus, a trust is a means for creating a separation of management and benefit to property. Contrastingly, Absolute ownership involves both these elements an absolute owner enjoys control and benefit.

General Principle: The creation of a trust can allow for the legal ownership and equitable benefit to be divided.

Vandervell v IRC [1967] 2 AC 291

Facts: Mr Vandervall was a rich businessman who wanted to save paying tax and attempted to create tax avoiding schemes. In 1958 Mr Vandervell instructed his trustees to transfer some shares they held for him to the Royal College of Surgeons ("RCofS") which was a charity. With an option in the transfer he could buy back the shares in the future for £5000. In 1961 the RCS had received more than £150,000 in dividends from the shares and Vandervell's trustees exercised the option to repurchase. The Inland Revenue claimed tax from Vandervell on the basis that he had not disposed of his interest in the shares for the period 1958 – 1961 because there was no writing. **Ratio: The House of Lords found that the option had created an automatic resulting trust for Vandervall and that therefore he retained an interest in the shares and had to pay tax on them. The RCofS could not have been taxed because it is a charity and was exempt from that taxation. House of Lords also stated obiter that where the legal and the equitable interest are intended to be transferred together there is no need for a separate written disposition of the equitable interest. Application:** Although the tax avoidance scheme failed and Vandervall was made to pay tax on the shares of the company, the case demonstrates the attempted splitting of ownership and benefit.

General Principle: There are four fundamental propositions that well illustrate the law of Trusts.

Westdeutsche Landesbank Girozentrale v Islington BC [1996] AC 669, HL

Facts: The case was in regard of an interest rate swap, a transaction where one party agreed to pay the other over a certain period interest at a fixed rate on a notional capital sum. The other party agreed to pay over the same period interest at a market rate on the same notional sum. Few years earlier the House of Lords held interest rate swap agreements void in the light of the Local

Government Act 1972. The argument between the parties arose when the Claimant sued the Council in order to recover £1,145,525 (including compound interest). The Council accepted to pay the money back under the void contract, but only including simple interest. The issue for the court was whether an equitable proprietary claim was available to the Westdeutsche bank in the present case. **Ratio: Lord Browne-Wilkinson listed four leading principles of trust law which are: (i) Equity operates on the conscience of the owner of the legal interest; (ii) A person cannot be a trustee of the property if and so long as he is ignorant of the facts alleged to affect his conscience; (iii) There must be identifiable trust property; and (iv) Once a trust is established, a beneficiary has a proprietary interest in the trust property, enforceable in equity against any subsequent holder of the property other than a purchaser for value of the legal interest without notice. Application:** The House of Lords held that there was no resulting trust so that the Council could only recover its money with simple interests since there was only a claim for recovery in common law.

Advantages of Trusts

- **Separation of income and capital** - The use of Trusts enables assets to be segregated from what belongs to the settlor. Trusts protect the so-called beneficiaries from the consequences of the settlor's insolvency. Whether the settlor becomes insolvent, creditors will not be able to access the properties of the Trust. Therefore, the trust is used for asset protection. These types of trusts allow large amounts of money to be held on trust, which accumulate substantial interest payments, which are to be paid to the benefactor. For example, money can be left to my friend on trust, to hold for my wife for life and then for my children. (This means the wife will receive the interest for life and then the children will get the money, when she dies). The separation of money and capital also allows future gifts – The mechanics of a trust allows a gift to be made which will continue on in the future over time.

- **Joint and collective ownership** - Trusts can be used to create concurrent or subsequent interests in land. Thanks to the use of Trusts the settlor may partition the asset for the benefit of several people. For instance, the settlor may leave a property to A for life with reminder to B. This means the property belongs to A for the duration of his life and then B will benefit from the property at the death of A.

Collective investment - Investment on the stock market in an efficient way requires large amounts of money far beyond what is available to most individuals. Thus a trust allows collective investment, which is managed by professional investment managers on trust. These managers are in control of the money they invest it and act in the best interests of the third parties, who in this type of situation may also be the settlor. The same works for investment and pensions, which works through the law of trusts.

Administrative convenience - The administration and management of a property by the trustee may be useful in those circumstances whether the beneficiaries have not a high level of financial and investment knowledge or whether the beneficiaries are young.

Tax avoidance - Trusts allow those using it to avoid or mitigate tax liability.

Rights relating to Trusts

- **Settlor's position**

The settlor is the person that creates the Trust and sets its content. The settlor decides the form of the trust, the beneficiaries and their interests and the trustee and their obligations. Before the creation of the Trust, the settlor must be the absolute owner of the property in question. He must hold the legal and beneficial ownership of the property. Once the Trust has been created, the settlor loses both the legal title and the beneficial interest. Once the settlor has determined the terms of the trust and transferred the property, he is unable to revoke the trust. He no longer enjoys any rights unless he has made provision.

- **Trustee's position**

The Trustee receives the burden of managing and administering the property under the trust for the benefit of the beneficiaries. Between the trustee and the beneficiaries there is a fiduciary relationship that basis on confidence, trustworthiness to act for the benefit of the beneficiaries and not for its own benefit. The trustee's administrative functions are really concerned with looking after the money. If it were a fund, this would include investing and re-investing the money. If it is a single item, the trustee must ensure proper state of repair and so forth. The trustee's dispositive responsibilities refer to making transfers and payments to the beneficiaries.

- **Beneficiaries' position**

Beneficiaries have equitable rights in the property and a beneficial interest in it. Beneficiaries may sue the trustee and any third party for damages for breach of Trust. They can get the property itself back or whatever has been substituted for, even if given to somebody else. Beneficiaries are entitled to assign the whole property or part of it to third parties. They may also terminate the trust by requiring the trustee to transfer the legal title of the property to them.

The nature of the beneficiary's rights

Personal and proprietary interests: In an example of the simplest type of trust a bear trust, where there is one beneficiary. Here the trustee function is to look after the trust property until it is ready to be transferred to the beneficiary in accordance with the trust instrument. In this type of case the nature of the beneficiaries' interest is one which is a form of ownership of the trust property. The beneficiary is said to have a propriety interest in the trust property.

Figure 2: a diagram demonstrating the distinction between a beneficiary's propriety interest and person right

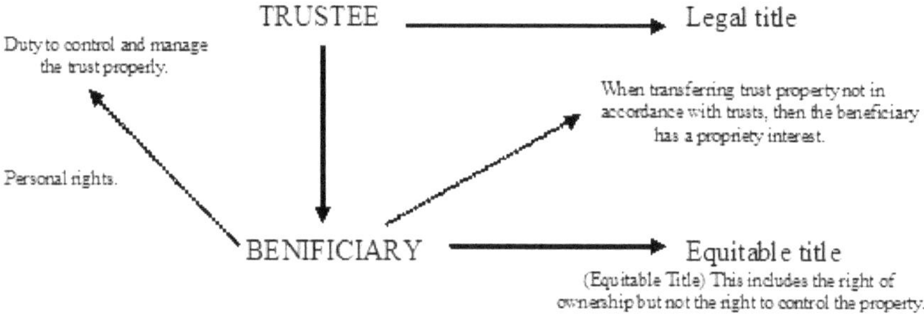

General Principle: The beneficiaries' interest is one which is a form of ownership of the trust property.

Vadim Schmidt v Rosewood Trust [2003] 2 AC 709

Facts: The settlor established two trusts in the Isle of Man with an Isle of Man company acting as trustee. The settlor died unexpectedly and intestate. The applicant sought access in both his personal capacity as heir to settlor and in his capacity as executor of the settlor's estate to documents in the possession of the trustee. The Court was unable to determine the proper construction of the gifts contained in the trust documents and hence was unable to determine whether the applicant had a proprietary interest in the trust property such as to entitle him to access the documents sought on the basis of the rule in **O'Rourke v Darbishire** [1920] AC 581. **Ratio: the court held that persons with a non-proprietary interest in a trust, such as the object of a trust power, may now seek access to trust documents, with such access now to be treated as a discretionary question for the court in the exercise of its inherent jurisdiction to supervise the administration of trusts. Application:** The Privy Council reformulated the basis upon which a person interested in a trust may seek access to trust documents; abandoning the rule previously thought to have been established in **O'Rourke v Darbishire** [1920] AC 581 that access is available to persons with a "proprietary interest" in the trust property.

The trustee has legal title of property while the beneficiary has equitable title. The equitable title is a form of ownership, referred to as beneficial ownership. The difference between beneficial ownership and absolute ownership is the absolute element of management and control of the property. The nature of ownership is that it gives rights, which are good against everyone, whereas a propriety right is only good against the other person involved. The trustee is under a duty to control and manage the trust properly this gives rise to a personal right to the beneficiary. Moreover, if the trustee transfers the trust property to a third party not in accordance with the trust instrument this then entitles the beneficiary to a claim to reclaim this property from the third party; this can be described as a propriety right. Thus the beneficiary owns the property but a beneficial ownership as opposed to absolute ownership.

General Principle: Beneficiaries are entitled to terminate the trust if they have attained the age of majority (over 18), if they have full mental capacity and if they are absolutely entitled to the trust property.

Saunders v Vautier [1841] 41 E.R. 482, Ct of Chancery
Facts: A testator, by his will, bequeathed to his executors and trustees all the East India stock upon trust to accumulate the dividends until the beneficiary should attain twenty-five. Once reached this age, the trustee was required to transfer capital and accumulated income to the beneficiary. At the age of 21, Vautier

claimed the fund. **Ratio: The issue for the court was whether the trustees should transfer trust. Wherever a beneficiary with an absolute interest under a trust is *sui juris,* i.e. of full age and not a lunatic, he may call for the trust property which represents that interest, and the trustees are obliged to transfer the legal title of it to him; if he is a sole beneficiary, this will result in the complete collapse of the trust. When the beneficiary has an absolute indefeasible interest in the legacy, it is not bound to wait until the expiration of the period.** Application: The Defendant was held entitled to terminate the trust since he had the full beneficial interest.

The rule in **Saunders v Vautier** [1841] 41 E.R. 482 represents a significant limitation upon the settlor's 'freedom of trust', but it can be justified in two ways:

> There might be something of an 'anti-trust' justification, as follows: while it is fine to empower owners to created structured gifts of property where this is essentially the only means of giving the benefits of property, as for example when money is provided for minor children, this power should not be used to allow an owner to control his beneficiaries when they are fully competent to look after themselves. If you give property to someone, you naturally take the risk that they will use that property in ways which are foolish or which otherwise might defeat your hopes. But that is the price of treating people, including donees of property, as autonomous individuals. The law of trusts should not, therefore, allow settlors to treat sane adults as children, and so the principle of **Saunders v Vautier** reflects the law's desire that all individuals, once *sui juris,* should be treated as capable of running their own affairs, including their rights over property.

> The second justification is related, and concerns the idea of equitable ownership. In the eyes of equity, the beneficiaries are the owners of the trust property, not the settlor. They have the rights against the trustee, and must enforce the trust themselves. When they reach full age, in essence the trust is in their hands. They can enforce their rights against the trustee

or not, may consent to the trustees acting outside the terms of the trust, i.e. doing what would otherwise be a breach of trust, and may vary the terms of the trust as they wish. The settlor has no say in any of this. Thus they are (in theory) in full control of the property via the office of the trustee. But if that is so, why cannot they do with their property what they like, as can any other full owners, and in particular, take the property out of the trust completely if they so desire?

Doctrine of notice - 'Equity's Darling'

It is important to pinpoint that beneficiaries' rights are not absolute rights. There is one person called 'Equity's Darling' whose right may prevail over the beneficiaries' ones. The doctrine of notice is an equitable doctrine that dictates where certain conditions are fulfilled equity will regard a bona fide purchaser for value without notice as "Equity's Darling". It is a good faith party that gives money without knowledge of the trust. Equity's Darling takes the property free of any rights of the beneficiary. Therefore, if the purchaser of the property is Equity's Darling, the beneficiary will not be able to have the property itself back, but only a substitute of the property.

General Principle: The bona fide transferee of the property trust for value without notice acquires good title over the property.

MCC Proceeds Inc v Lehman Bros International (Europe), The Times, 14 January 1998
Facts: The Claimant was a company controlled by Mr Maxwell and members of his family that took over Macmillan Incorporated. Macmillan Inc placed shares in a subsidiary in the name of a nominee company controlled by Mr Maxwell, called Bishopsgate Investment Trust plc. Bishopsgate held the legal title while Macmillan retained the beneficial interest in the shares. Later on Bishopsgate pledged the shares with the Defendant, without notifying Macmillan. The Defendant subsequently sold the shares to another company. MCC sued the Defendant on the ground that they had beneficial interest in the shares so that to be entitle of recovery them. **Ratio: Whether the Defendant falls within the category of the so-called bona fide purchaser that has gotten a legal interest in a property without notice of any breach of Trust, he cannot be held liable. Application:** The Court of Appeal found in favour of the Defendant on the ground that the company acquired good title to the shares, free from any claims.

Types of Trusts

Inter vivos – Created by the settlor when he is alive.

A. **Public Trust** – Trusts created for the benefit of the public are public trusts. These include:

- **Purpose Trust** - A purpose trust is a type of <u>trust</u> that has not <u>beneficiaries</u>, but instead exists for advancing non-<u>charitable</u> purpose of some kind. Trusts for charitable purposes are also technically purpose trusts, but they are usually referred to simply as <u>charitable trusts</u>.

- **Charitable trust** - A charitable trust is a type of public trust, created exclusively for charitable purposes. The trust is established for the benefit of the public. The trust must benefit the society or a large part of the community.

B. **Private Express Trust** – Those trusts created for the benefit of people are private trusts. It is a Trust expressly created by the parties, not inferred by the law from the conduct of the parties. Under this category there are two possible types of Trust: Fixed Trust and Discretionary Trust.

- **Fixed Trust** - A fixed trust is one where the terms of the trust are determined and stipulated exhaustively at the outset by the settlor. These include who is a beneficiary, what is he or she to get, when they are to get it and on what conditions if anything. If the trust instrument stipulates all of these matters then the trustee's dispositive function becomes mechanical, in that he does not have to exercise judgment just follow what is set out in the instrument. This is the traditional type of trust. A trustee holds a property for multiple beneficiary or a single one. The important aspect of a fixed trust is that the trust fund itself dictates what the beneficiaries are going to get. It is the trust that states what each beneficiary will receive. It is not compulsory to attribute equal share to the parties. A settlor may decide to give 1 per cent to one beneficiary and 99 per cent to the second beneficiary. The trust itself stipulates what each beneficiary will receive.

Figure 3: A diagram showing equal distribution under a fixed trust.

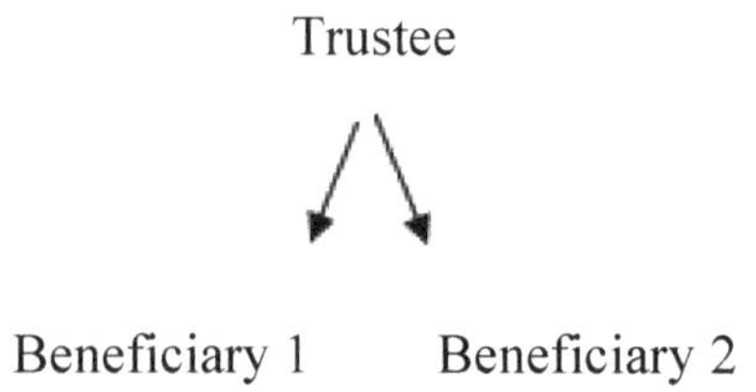

Trustee

Beneficiary 1   Beneficiary 2

½ of trust fund or an "EQUAL" share each

Two are the main problems that arise with fixed trust. First, trusts were often created as a way to be fiscally efficient in order to reduce tax liability. Whether the beneficiary's share is fixed, the interest will be easily taxable. Second, fixed trusts may be seen a bit too inflexible since they cannot be changed in the light of possible future needs of the beneficiaries. For these reasons, fixed trusts have become obsolete to a certain extent.

- **Discretionary Trust** (it can be either *inter vivos* or testamentary) – The settlor does not determine on the trust document how much property each beneficiary will get. It will be discretion of the trustee to decide. Since tax cannot be applied until the property has been received, discretionary trusts play a better role in the fiscal life of a person. How does the trustee exercise discretion? The trustee acts in the best interest of the beneficiary as a whole. He will look at all beneficiaries and at all their needs in deciding who is going to get what. However, if the trust is a discretionary one, this refers to a dispositive discretion, where the trustee will have to exercise a discretion in determining what property to pay to a beneficiary. For example, Y leaves all my money to friend X to be divided at his discretion amongst my children in such proportions that he may think appropriate.

Figure 4: A diagram showing distribution under a discretionary trust.

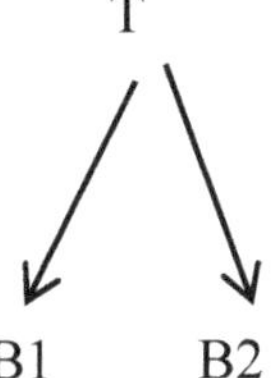

% of trust fund "as trustees think fit"

Advantages of a discretionary trust

A discretionary trust may be used in avoiding loss in Bankruptcy. For example, if X leaves all his money to his sons, A and B. If B becomes bankrupt the trustee will have to pay B his share of the property, even though this will become payable to creditors. If the trustee is given some discretion as to how to distribute the share of property between A and B, the trustee could simply not pay any money to B if the money was used to go to creditors. He would simply withhold payment until such time as bankruptcy proceeding had been concluded and free of debt.

The dispositive discretion

Where there is a discretionary trust, the trustees are subject to certain duties in relation to the exercise of discretion. First, clearly they have to stay within the terms of the discretion. If the trust instrument says *"the trustee must divide the money at their discretion amongst A, B and C"*, there is no discretion to give money to D. Secondly, the discretion must be exercised by the person who is given the discretion, you can't delegate discretion, the trustee must decide the appropriate course.

General Principle: Trustees who exercise a power of appointment, under a discretionary trust, without exercising their discretion because they did not realise that it existed, are in breach of their duty to consider the appropriateness of the appointment, and the appointment will be invalid.

Turner v Turner [1984] Ch 100
Facts: The settlor created a trust for the benefit of his wife and children. The trust contained a discretionary power to distribute capital or income out of the trust fund to all or any of the beneficiaries. The settlor appointed as trustees his father, sister-in-law and her husband. None of them had understanding of trust matters. In exercising the power of appointment the trustees divided the trust in favour of the four children. By a deed, the trustees revoked the appointment of the settlor's eldest son and appointed the remaining three children as the sole beneficiaries of the trust fund. **Ratio: it was held what might first appear to have been a decision of trustees may prove on questioning not to have been a decision. Where a power is exercised in form but not in substance then the appointment will be declared void. Application:** The purported appointments must be set aside. The trustees had not exercised their discretion in making the appointments and were in breach of that duty.

General Principle: Sometimes the trust instrument will stipulate steps to be followed by the trustee when exercising discretion. It might just state as the trustee thinks fit, in this event the trustees have to consider what appropriate criteria they must use, these criteria must be rationally exercised.

R v District Auditor ex p West Yorkshire MCC (1986) 26 RVR 24
Facts: Application by local authority for a declaration that

payment to the West Yorkshire Trust was ultra vires and was not rendered unlawful by applicant's motives and did not require consent by the secretary of state. **Ratio: A settlor stated in the trust instrument the criteria that had to be taken account off when exercising discretion. Application:** It was doubtful whether review was appropriate as the auditor had not yet determined the matter. Without creating a procedural precedent however, it was clear the trust neither could neither take effect as a valid charitable trust nor as private trust as there was no certainty as to beneficiaries.

The trustees will have to ensure they are properly acquainted with every factual fact and information which is necessary, in order to exercise discretion. First for example if there is a small family and they have to pay money amongst the three children, then the trustee's must find out about the three children. What are their circumstances? Does one have a disability, which may justify a larger proportion of the pay out? They cannot exercise discretion without facts. There is no use of criteria when there is no fact to which applies the criteria.

Second, another type of discretionary trusts is large discretionary trusts, which involve paying out employees or members within a large group such as a company or society. In this type of situation trustees cannot get the same type of information about thousands of beneficiaries as in the small family discretionary trust. Thus the trustee is expected to survey the field. This involves discovering information relevant to exercising the discretion, putting up posters, asking people to apply.

Exhaustive and non-exhaustive discretionary trusts

There are many subdivisions of discretionary trusts but the overall concept binding them all together is that the trustees must exercise discretions vested in them before any potential beneficiary becomes entitled to income of the trust. A discretionary trust may be either exhaustive or non-exhaustive in nature.

- **Exhaustive trust**

Exhaustive trusts require the distribution of all the income but grant the trustees discretion to determine how that income is applied between the beneficiaries. For example, if X leaves all his money on trust to Y (trustee) for 21 years, but he must allocate the income generated by the trust property, as they think fit among his children each year, this type of trust would be exhaustive.

- **Non-exhaustive trust**

This grants the trustee's discretion over how much of the income is distributed as well, perhaps, as over the identity of the beneficiaries who were to receive that income. A non-exhaustive discretionary trust provides the power to accumulate income vested in the trustees for the beneficiaries.

A non-exhaustive discretionary trust can be stated in two ways:

- There is a discretionary trust to distribute the income (mandatory) subject to a power to hold any part of the income and accumulation.

- There is a trust to accumulate income subject to a power to pay out to the children.

The way in which the trust is stated in practice makes no difference. However, in theory it makes a difference. In one case prima facia there is a duty to distribute and consciously exercise a power to withhold. Conversely, in another case they have prima facia obliged to accumulate the money and consciously exercise a power to distribute. It can make some difference to how they approach the question. The reason this is important is because the test for certainty (in **Re Baden's Deed Trusts** (No. 1), **McPhail v Doulton** [1971] AC 424) to be applied in ascertaining the validity of a trust would depend on whether it was a discretionary trust or a power. On the terms of trust in **McPhail v Doulton** the trust would have been invalid if it was one interpretation and valid on the other interpretation, this is why it is important to establish which formulation it was.

Trusts arising from the operation of the law

- **Resulting Trust**

Whether an express Trust fails (for instance, when the beneficiary dies or when there is a surplus of trust funds left over after the trust purpose has been achieved.), the trustee hold the property in resulting trust for the settlor. Here, for example, a settlor attempts to set up a trust but the beneficial interest either wholly or in part "results" or returns to the settlor. This may happen in various situations, such as where the property is conveyed to trustees upon certain trusts which fail or which do not exhaust the beneficial interest. The part that is undisposed of results back to the settlor. For example, if there is a gift on trust for A for life, and then on trust for X if X attains the age of 21, but X dies before the age of 21 within A's lifetime, the property will result or return on A's death to the settlor.

- **Constructive Trust**

The court creates constructive trusts whether necessary in the interests of justice and conscience. For instance, whether the trustee makes a profit derived due to his position, abusing his role, that profit is held on constructive trust for the beneficiaries. These trusts are normally imposed by the courts in order to remedy fraudulent or unconscionable conduct. A constructive trust thus is remedial in effect and might arise where the trustees in breach of trust sell the property to another who, for some reason or another, is not a bona fide purchaser for value without notice ~ he or she may have knowingly received or assisted in disposing of trust property in breach of trust. In such circumstances the courts may impose a constructive trust on the third party, who then holds the property on a constructive trust for the person from whom it was obtained. Equity says that in certain circumstances the legal owner of property must hold it on trust for others. Constructive trusts are imposed by the law irrespective of the intention of the trustee and in fact may be the very last thing the new constructive trustee wants.

There is an academic argument as to the exact status of constructive trusts in this country. Some think of it as simply another form of an institutional trust in much the same way as other trusts in that they are imposed only within the limits described by precedent. Others, particularly the late Lord Denning, favour the American idea of using the constructive trust as a remedy. In **Hussey v. Palmer** [1972] 3 All ER 744 Lord Denning said that constructive trusts can be imposed "whenever justice and good conscience require it." The views of Denning have been attacked on the basis that it would create uncertainty in the law. No one would know in what circumstances a constructive trust might be imposed and that imposing a constructive trust might be accompanied by unforeseen and unconsidered consequences. However, it could be argued that the whole controversy is really rather sterile since historically all trusts were remedies.

Another example of a constructive trust being imposed because of a breach of fiduciary duty is provided by **Crown Prosecution Service v Aquila Advisory Service Ltd [2021]** UKSC 49 where the Supreme Court considered the effects of a constructive trust imposed on company directors as a result of their receipt of a secret profit or bribe.

- **Statutory Trust**

In particular circumstances the Parliament may create statutory trust. For instance, according to Section 33 of the Trustee Act 1925 a protective trust exists as life interest in favour of the principal beneficiary coupled with a discretionary trust in favour of a specified class of objects, including the principal beneficiary, on the occurrence of the determining event.

A number of statutes impose trusts, so even where there is no express declaration of a trust, they may arise under several different statutes. Probably the most significant for our purposes here arises in the context of the 1925 property legislation. The *Law of Property Act* 1925 sections 34-36 impose a statutory trust for sale whenever land is co-owned, converted into trusts of land by the *Trustees of Land and Appointment of Trustees Act* 1996. The *Administration of Estates Act* 1925 s. 33, as amended by the *Trustees of Land and Appointment of Trustees Act* 1996, imposes a statutory trust for sale on the property of people dying intestate (without a will), which directs their personal representatives to hold their real and personal property on trust with a power to sell it and hold the purchase money on trust as directed.

Other types of trust

- **Bare Trust** – Under this type of Trust the beneficiary has absolute right to the capital and assets of the Trust while the trustee has no discretion as to its management and disposal. The trustee strictly needs to comply with the instructions given by the beneficiary.

- **Protective Trust** – It is a particular type of Trust that protects beneficiaries from bankruptcy or other kinds of misfortune. Under this type of Trust, the beneficiary receives a life interest determinable on the occurrence of a particular event. Whether the event occurs (such as bankruptcy) the life interest is forfeited and the property will fall under a discretionary Trust where the beneficiary will still be part of those that may benefit under the discretion of the trustee.

- **Pension funds Trust** – The Trust property is represented by the work and remuneration of the employee.

- **Successive Interests trust**

Where the settlor has made himself trustee for the benefit of others (children), there are two different types of beneficiary:

- o **Life Tenant** - person who receives a life interest. This person gets rights to the trust property immediately. He is not going to be entitled to all the property. He is only entitled to something called 'income', not the property itself, but the profit that derives from the trust asset (dividends in case of share; rent in case of property; interests in case of money). It lasts as long as the person with the life interest is alive. When the life tenant dies, the trust asset will go to the person called remainder man.

- o **Remainderman** – he is not entitled to anything until the life tenant dies, but he then gets everything. He will not get only the income, but the entire property, called 'capital'.

Example: Portfolio of shares, you create a trust appointing yourself as life tenant so that you will keep receiving the dividends. Once you die, you can leave it to your kids.

- o **Testamentary** – you can create a trust under your will when you are dead.

No matter what type of trust you use, beneficiaries do not only have personal rights against the trustee but also proprietary rights in trust assets themselves in Equity. This means that if, for instance, the trustee steals the property, the beneficiary can get the property itself back, even if given to somebody else.

What is a power?

If you give someone a power, you are giving him an authority. You are allowing someone to deal with your property. For example a power of appointment: *'I leave my estate to my husband with a power to appoint between our children A, B and C (called the objects of the power)'*. The power of appointment does not confer **Saunders v Vautier** rights so that A, B and C cannot end the power received by the husband, take the estate and divide it on their own. They have no proprietary right. The only thing A, B, C can do is restraining improper exercise of power (for instance, any attempt to appoint outside the class).

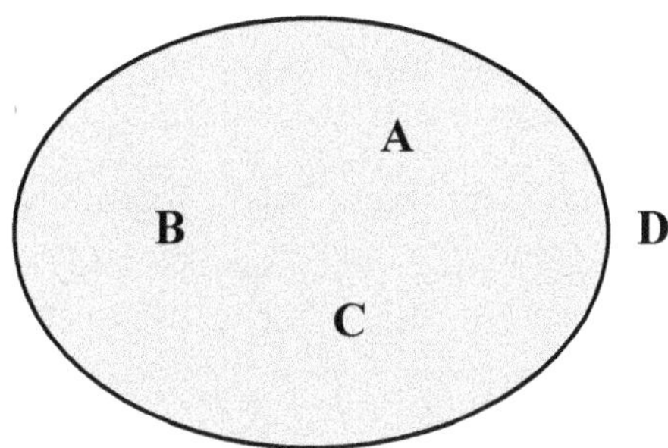

How Trusts and Powers differ?

- Fixed Trust

- Discretionary Trust + £300 to each X, Y and Z

- Power of appointment

Fixed trust - £300 to X, Y and Z in equal shares (each £100) settlor fixes who benefits and the size of each share.

Discretionary trust - £300 to such X, Y and Z as T *shall* select (£100 to X, £170 to Y and £30 to Z). The settlor defines the class and directs T to choose shares.

Power of appointment - £300 to such of X, Y and Z as D *may* select and, if no selection is made, to A.

By using *may* instead of *shall* as per discretionary trust, the purpose is to remove the obligation. Whether the settlor gives power of appointment to someone, there usually are instructions in case that person does not exercise the power. In the example, whether D does not select in the defined class, A will receive a gift over in default.

Enforcement of a trust or power

In the case of a fixed trust if a trustee fails or chose not to carry out the trust, they do not have a choice. They are legally obliged to carry out a trust in accordance with its terms and if they fail to do that the beneficiaries can go to court and the trust instrument will stipulate what should happen with the money, thus the court will simply enforce this, and order the trustee to pay. In the case of a power of appointment, if the trustee fails or chose not to carry out the power, the court cannot force the trustee to exercise the power because the trust instrument will state the trustee is not obliged to exercise a power, the court would have no reason to intervene. A difficultly that may arise, is when the object of a power complains, the trustees have not properly considered whether to use that power. This is quite a cumbersome task, because the court cannot force the trustees to use the power, they can however replace the trustees if they feel they are not properly considering using their powers. In a discretionary trust, the trustee will have to make a distribution and they have to exercise the discretion of how to make the distribution.

General Principle: If the trust has not been exercised and there has been no distribution, it will not be a breach of trust. It may well be the case the trustee is unaware of his duty to make a distribution and when prompted by the court the trustee would conform to the trust instrument.

Re Locker's ST [1977] 1 WLR 1323
Facts: Trustees of a settlement created in 1963 were given an absolute and uncontrolled discretion in applying the income of the trust fund amongst the beneficiaries. They failed to distribute such income, initially adding it to capital; but the income from 1965 to 1968 remained undistributed and was not so applied. The trustees applied for directions. **Ratio: Trustees with an "absolute and uncontrolled" discretion who fail to distribute trust income as required by the settlement may, notwithstanding their delay, still be permitted, and encouraged, by the court to distribute such accrued income amongst the beneficiaries as they see fit.**

Application: The trustees remained at liberty to distribute the arrears of income within their discretion, but should not exercise their discretion in favour of beneficiaries who became objects a reasonable time after the income to be distributed.

General Principle: Another type of discretionary trusts is the more modern type of large discretionary trusts, which involve paying out employees or members within a large group such as a company or society.

McPhail v Doulton [1971] AC 424

Facts: The settlor transferred a property to trustees to apply to net income, in their absolute discretion, to the officers, ex-officers, employees and ex-employees of a company or their relatives or dependants. The question in issue was whether the trust was valid as satisfying the test for certainty of objects. **Ratio: Lord Willberforce stated – "First the court will authorise the appointment of new trustees (new trustees would then exercise their discretion). Secondly the court would authorise representatives of the beneficiaries to prepare a scheme of distribution, for approval of the court (the representatives would be the head of department of the company whom could make appropriate suggestions as to beneficiaries). The test that must be applied to discretionary trusts is whether the trustees may say with certainty that any given postulant "is or is not a member of a class of objects", and there is no need to draw up a list of objects. Application:** The House of Lords decided that the trust was valid and changed the test for certainty in respect of discretionary trusts, making in line with the test for powers.

Powers of appointment

Power of appointment allows the trustee to dispose of the property in favour of the object of that power. For example, if X leave his friend Y all his money to be distributed among all his children and up to £5 to the RSPCA. This means the trustee has a power to leave £5 to the RSPCA, but the important thing about the power is the trustee is not obliged to do it. The trustee has discretion not only as to how to distribute the property (how much of £5), but also as to whether to distribute the property at all (whether the RSPCA should get anything at all).

Thus there are three trust arrangements:

- Fixed trust, is a mandatory trust, trustee should follow the trust instrument.

- Discretionary trust is a mandatory trust but the trustees have discretion as to how to exercise his duty.

- Powers of appointment trust, the trustee does not have to exercise his power.

The distinction between these powers is important. For example, if a case arises where the instrument stated the trustees *may* exercise discretion to divide my money among my children. The answer is not entirely clear from that wording. If they don't have to pay the children, it is a power. But it could be a discretionary trust where the money has to be paid; the trustee will have to make the distribution, although the trustees have discretion as to the division of property among the three children.

A power does not necessarily have to be exercised by a trustee. For example, X may leave all of his money to Joe on trust to be distributed equally among his 3 children, subject to the power that my wife can appoint up to £10,000 to the RSPCA. In this situation the power is not exercised by a trustee, this is a possible arrangement. In this type of circumstances, the person exercising the power is called the donee. The donee of the power is usually the trustee then he has certain responsibilities on how to exercise the power, if he is not a donee then these responsibilities are not inherent.

How to categorise powers of appointment

There are several ways to categorise powers.

1) The first distinction depends on the person that exercises the power.

- Fiduciary Power – whether the power is exercised by a trustee (solicitor; agent etc.)

- Personal Power – whether the power is exercised by someone else who is not a trustee, called donee.

The nature of the power dictates the obligations that the person with that power owes. Example of Fiduciary power:

General Principle: The obligation deriving from fiduciary powers is set out by the court in the following case.

Re Hay's Settlement Trust [1981] 3 All ER 786
Facts: In the case the trustee was directed to hold the trust fund appointing anyone except the settlor, the settlor's husband and the trustee himself. The issue was related with the validity with that power. **Ratio: The House of Lords set out the three main steps in which a fiduciary power must be exercised: (i) The trustee has a choice to exercise or not. The trustee must periodically consider whether to exercise the power received or not. (ii) Because of the responsibilities a trustee has, he has to act responsibly, properly considering the size of the class entitled to benefit, carefully analysing the range of the objects. (iii) He has to appoint appropriate individuals to benefit, deserving individuals. Application:** The court held that the power was valid. The trustee was under a duty to ensure that any appointment was within the power and to periodically consider exercising it. The power could not have been delegated.

2) The second way to categorise powers is based on the person that benefits from it.

General power – when the power is choosing from anyone in the world

Special power – power to choose from a defined class of individuals

Hybrid power – anyone, except a defined class of individuals (as in the case of Re Hay's ST)

Summary

- A trust is an equitable device created by Equity in order to transfer a property under the control of a trustee for the benefit of a beneficiary.
- The trust involves an equitable obligation, which is imperative in nature.
- Thanks to the use of Trusts the settlor may partition the asset for the benefit of several people.
- The settlor is the person that creates the Trust and set its content.
- The Trustee receives the burden of managing and administering the property under the Trust for the benefit of the beneficiaries.
- Beneficiaries have equitable rights in the property and a beneficial interest in it.
- It is important to pinpoint that beneficiaries' rights are not absolute rights. There is one person called 'Equity's Darling' whose right may prevail over the beneficiaries' ones.
- **Section 1** of the Recognition of Trusts Act 1987 states that 'For the purposes of this Convention, the term trust refers to the legal relationship created *inter vivos* or on death by a person, the settlor, when assets have been placed under the control of a trustee for the benefit of a beneficiary or for a specified purpose.'
- Creation of Trusts gives rise to a lot of advantages such as mitigation of tax pressure, protection of beneficiaries' interests etc.
- Trusts give rise to specific rights and duties attributed to settlor, trustee and beneficiary.
- Several are the types of trusts that may be created.
- It is important to distinguish a trust from a power.

Chapter 3 – The Three Certainties

Introduction

The validity of a trust is usually the main issue courts have to deal with. Generally speaking, judges will always try to uphold a trust if they can. Nevertheless, it is fundamental that all the necessary requirements are satisfied in order for a trust to be considered valid. The requirements are the following: The three certainties, formalities and constitution. This chapter will analyse in details the first category such as the three certainties: certainty of intention, certainty of subject matter and certainty of object.

The three certainties

The courts have established that three are the certainties that need to be identified in order to have a valid trust: intention to create a trust, trust property and actors involved in the trust.

The standard authority is **Knight v Knight** (1840) 3 Beav 148 in which Lord Langdale MR stated that a transfer of property subject to a stipulation will create a trust, if the words used are imperative and if the property and objects (i.e. persons intended to be benefited) are sufficiently identified. This dictum is usually reduced to the phrase that the three certainties must be present: certainty of intention, subject matter and objects.

An express private trust cannot be created unless the three certainties are present:

- Certainty of Intention;

- Certainty of Subject Matter; and

- Certainty of Objects (Beneficiaries)

These certainties are decided as a matter of construction. Therefore, the presence of certainty in any one category largely depends on the words used and the circumstances in which they arise. Since "equity looks to the intention not to the form" the courts are willing to accept any form of words provided they convey the required information or intention.

Certainty of intention

Certainty of intention refers to the settlor's intention to create a trust. The settlor must intend to make a trust. In order to determine whether the requirement is valid, the court will look at the peculiar circumstances of each case. When asking if a disposition exhibits certainty of intention, the court will examine the words and conduct of the proposed settlor to see if these conform to an intention to create a trust. Oral statements, conduct, documents, words used by the settlor etc. will be looked at in order to assess the presence of a trust relationship. For there to be a valid trust it has to be clear that the settlor intended to create a trust. It is not necessary that the settlor has a subjective intention to create a trust. It is sufficient that the settlor exhibits an intention which can be interpreted by the court, in accordance with the relevant legal principles, as an intention to create a trust. The words must impart an imperative obligation on the trustee; that is, the words must make it clear that a person holding the property is obliged to hold it for the benefit of others.

Any form of words may be used - there is no requirement to use the expression "trustee". Thus in **Re Kayford** [1975] 1 All ER 604 Megarry J stated:

"It is well settled that a trust can be created without using the word 'trust' or 'confidence' or the like: the question is whether in substance a sufficient intention to create a trust has been manifested."

General Principle: Intention to create a trust does not require the adoption of formal words such as the word "trust".

Paul v Constance [1977] 1 WLR 527, CA
Facts: The parties were the ex-wife of the deceased and his new partner before death. Mr Constance obtained a sum of money in

compensation for certain injuries and later on he and the Claimant won at the bingo. Mr Constance put all the amount in a deposit account under his name, stating the money was as much Ms Paul's as his. When Mr Constance died, Ms Paul contended that the money in the deposit account was the subject of an express trust for her benefit. The ex-wife, Mrs Constance, argued that the deposit account was part of the estate that she inherited. Ms Paul brought an action, claiming the sum deposited in the bank account. The issue for the court was whether or not there was an express declaration of trust. **Ratio: To establish that an express trust has been created there must be clear evidence from what is said or done of an intention to create a trust. No particular form of expression is necessary for the creation of a trust, if on the whole it can be gathered that a trust was intended.** Application: "The money is as much yours as mine," amounted to an express declaration of trust for the benefit of both Mr Constance and Ms Paul. The court awarded the Claimant a half share of the trust fund.

General Principle: Intention to create a trust must be assessed objectively by reference to the wording used by the settlor.

Shah v Shah [2011] 1 P. & C.R. DG19, CA
Facts: The parties were two brothers. The Claimant, Dinesh Shah, sent a letter in which he disposed 4,000 shares in favour of his brother, Mahendra Shah. The share certificate was not delivered, but Mahendra Shah was registered as new owner. Nevertheless, the Claimant tried to argue that the letter was not intended to create a trust, but it was meant to make a gift that was incomplete. **Ratio: The issue was whether the letter signed by the Claimant was sufficient to validate the intention to create a trust. The court pinpointed that the interpretation of the document should not have had regard to the subjective intention of the settlor, but to the intention manifested by the words used.** Application: The Court of Appeal confirmed the decision of the High Court. The letter showed a valid objective intention to create a trust so that the case went in favour of the Defendant.

Precatory Words

Difficulties with certainty of intention arise where a settlor or testator uses so-called "precatory" words. These are words which express a request, a hope, a desire, or a suggestion that the donee of the property will use in a particular way. The intention of the settlor must be certain otherwise the trust is not valid. The person in control of the property will be entitled to retain it beneficially.

General Principle: The use of precatory words does not create a trust. When someone leaves something in a will and says 'I hope and pray it will be used for a stated purpose', this cannot be said to be a trust.

Mugsoorie Bank v Raynor (1882) 7 App Cas 321
Facts: A man gave his widow the whole of his real and personal property, feeling confident that she would act justly to their children and divide the same whenever occasion required it of her.
Ratio: To create a trust, it should clearly create a mandatory requirement, the words must be imperative, and a hope or prayer will not suffice. Application: The court held this was not a trust due to the absence of the element of obligation.

General Principle: There has been a gradual hardening of attitude by the courts as to how precatory words are to be construed.

Lamb v Eames (1871) LR 6 Ch App 597
Facts: Mr Lambe gave his estate to his widow "to be at her disposal in any way she may think best, for the benefit of herself and her family" After he died, one of his sons had an illegitimate son, born in the lifetime of the testator, but after the date of his will. The widow died and she devised the house to trustees upon trust for one of her daughters but charged with annuity for the illegitimate son. When the latter tried to obtain payment of the

annuity, the daughter disputed on the ground that the widow had only a power of disposition amongst the family. On first instance, the judge held that the widow was entitled to devise to the illegitimate son. The daughter appealed. **Ratio: The question for the court was whether those words created any trust affecting the property. By looking at the words the court must evaluate the intention of the testator. Application:** The Court of Appeal in Chancery confirmed the decision at first instance. The widow took the property absolutely and she disposed of the power received in a legitimate way.

General Principle: Beneficiaries are not to be made trustees unless intended to be so by the testator.

Re Adams and Kensington Vestry (1884) 27 Ch D 394
Facts: The testator gave his real and personal estate "unto and to the absolute use of my dear wife, Harriet...in full confidence that she will do what is right as to the disposal thereof between my children, either in her lifetime or by will after her decease." The question that arose was whether there was a trust for the children or did the widow take absolutely. **Ratio: Under these words the widow took an absolute interest in the property, unfettered by any trust in favour of the children. Application:** The widow took absolutely. The court stated that they had to "look at the whole of the will which he will have to construe."

General Principle: The court will look at the meaning of the words, their true effect and at the intention of the testator as expressed in the will.

Comisky v Bowring-Hanbury [1905] AC 84, HL
Facts: The testator gave to his wife "the whole of my real and personal estate...in full confidence that she will make such use of it as I should have made myself and that at her death she will devise it to such one or more or my nieces as she may think fit and in default of any disposition by her thereof by her will or testament I hereby direct that all my estate and property acquired by her under this my will shall at her death by equally divided among the

surviving said nieces." **Ratio: In construing a will the word of the testator must first be construed irrespectively of rules of law, real or imaginary and the whole will must be looked at in order to find out what the testator's intention was. Application:** It was held that the testator intended to make a gift to his wife, with a gift over of the whole property at her death to such of the nieces as should survive her, shared according to the wife's will, and otherwise equally. The testator did not create a trust. He left the property to the wife absolutely.

Trust or power?

It may be unclear whether a settlor intends to impose a trust on the trustee or intends merely to give him a donee a power of appointment. Consider the following statement: "£100,000 to my trustees for distribution to my relations as my trustees shall in their absolute discretion think fit". The issue is in the meaning of the word 'distribution': 'It is an imperative and mandatory direction imposing an obligation upon them to distribute, or is it rather to be interpreted as 'available for distribution', thus creating no obligation but giving the trustees a power which they may exercise if they so choose. The distinction can become blurred depending on the words used in the will or trust instrument. Penner suggests:

'The settlor's use of the word 'power' is not determinative, but words such as 'shall' or 'to be', as in 'shall distribute' or 'to be divided amongst' seem quite clearly to be imperative and mandatory, strongly indicating the imposition of a duty, and thus a trust. Finally, where a trust is intended but fails for a reason that would not invalidate a similarly framed power, the court will not save the gift by treating it as a power'.

Failed gift

Where a gift or a declaration of trust is made, if it is not carried out as legally required, the court will not accept a declaration has been made.

General Principle: If the attempt to make a gift fails, the court will not rescue the gift.

Jones v Lock (1865) 1 Ch App 25
Facts: Mr Jones had children with a first wife and one son nine months old with the second wife. He came back from a business trip and put a cheque into the hand of his son of nine months saying 'I give this to baby for himself and put the check into the safe'. Mr Jones also got in touch with his solicitor saying 'I shall come to your office on Monday to alter my will, that I may take care of my son'. On the same day he died. The issue was whether Mr Jones intended to make a declaration that he held the cheque in trust for the child. **Ratio: Lord Cranworth, L. C. said '*I regret to say that I cannot bring myself to think that, either on principle or on authority, there has been any gift or any valid declaration of trust. The cheque was in the man's name he had made no efforts to endorse the cheque over to his son or to a trustee for the baby*'. Important transactions of this kind have to be carefully judged since the effect of declaration of trust may be very significant. The father had the intention to give something to the child but the facts had to be looked at in an objective way. Application:** The father did intent to give something but he did not intent to enable the child to bring an action of trover for the cheque. The father simply meant to say that he could make a provision for the boy.

Certainty of subject matter

Certainty of subject matter refers to the trust property. In order for a trust to be valid it is essential that the settlor has properly described it in order to identify it. The question is: What property is the property subject to the trust? The trust property has to be specified at the outset along with the beneficial interest to be taken in the trust property. If the trust property is not defined with sufficient precision, the trust will be invalid.

General Principle: There is no trust when a person failed in designing the subject of the trust properly.

Palmer v Simmonds [1854] 2 Drew 221

Facts: *A* testatrix left on trust "the bulk" of her residuary estate to her heir. She had confidence in him that, if she should have died without lawful issue, he would have left 'the bulk' to four named persons equally. **Ratio:** *"What is the meaning then of bulk? The appropriate meaning, according to its derivation, is something which bulges out… Its popular meaning, we all know. When a person is said to have given the bulk of his property, what is meant is not the whole but the greater part, and that is in fact consistent with its classical meaning. When, therefore, the testatrix uses that term, can I say that she has used a term expressing a definite, clear, certain part of her estate, or the whole of her estate? I am bound to say that she has not designated the subject as to which she expresses her confidence; and I am therefore of opinion that there is no trust created; that [the residuary legatee] took absolutely, and those claiming under him now take"*. **Application:** Since it was not possible to carve out from the residue that portion which was to be held on trust, the trust failed and the lasting beneficiary took the whole property absolutely.

General Principle: The property that is subject to the trust must be capable of satisfying the test for certainty. The main factor to look at is the description given by the settlor in order to identify the property.

Sprange v Barnard (1789) 2 Bro CC 585

Facts: The case concerned a disposition of £300 in joint stock annuities (i.e., a wasting asset) left "for my husband (…) and at his death, the remaining part of what is left, that he does not want for his own wants and use, to be divided between my children". **Ratio: The formula or mode of ascertainment of the trust property specified by the settlor must be sufficiently precise to enable the courts to identify the trust property. Application:** The court held that the husband was absolutely entitled to the £300. The subject matter for the children was not specified and the husband was entitled to the £300, because the trust for the children had become void through not defining the subject of their benefit.

General Principle: Where the trust property is certain, but the interest to be acquired by the beneficiaries is uncertain, the trust fails.

Boyce v Boyce (1849) 16 Sim 476

Facts: A testator left four houses in trust 'one for Maria, whatever she shall choose and the other three to Charlotte'. Maria predeceased the testator. The effect of this was to cause the gift to her to lapse (as it is a rule of succession law that the beneficiary must, subject to one or two exceptions, survive the testator). One of the houses thus fell into residue. **Ratio: The issue for the court was whether Charlotte was entitled to acquire one of the properties. Since Maria was supposed to select the house and she could not do it, the intended express trust failed.** Application: It was held that Charlotte's gift failed for uncertainty as to her beneficial interest as it was impossible to decide which of the three houses she was entitled to. The result was that the four properties were held on resulting trust for the testator's estate. Bear in mind that if Maria had survived the testator, even though only for a split second, then the trust would have been valid as Maria's estate could have made the choice and Charlotte would have been certain as to her beneficial entitlement. This case demonstrates that judges in 1849 were maybe excessively concern with certainty in a very doctrinal way.

General Principle: The certainties must at least be respected so as to define the basic parameters of the trust. If the settlor adopts a term that has not specific technical meaning, the trust may fail.

Re Kolb's Will Trusts [1962] Ch. 531

Facts: A testator bequeathed the residue of his estate to his trustees on trust to invest the proceeds of sale in stocks, shares and debentures "in the blue chip category". These directions were inserted in the will under clause 6. The trustees asked the court to give interpretation to the investment clause. They wanted to know whether the clause was validly created and possibly invest in other type of shares. **Ratio: The issue for the court was in the construction of the investment clause in the will. In large public company the term 'blue-chip- usually refers to safe shares, but it is not a precise term. Application:** The court held the clause void because it was not objective and precise enough to satisfy the test of certainty. The direction to invest in blue chip shares was no certain to be enforceable.

General Principle: A gift of a reasonable income for life may be valid.

Re Golay's Will Trusts [1965] 1 WLR 969
Facts: A testator directed that 'Tossy' (Mrs Florence Bridgewater) was "*to enjoy one of my flats during her lifetime and to receive a reasonable income from my other properties.*" **Ratio: The words 'reasonable income' directed an objective determinant of amount, which the court could, if necessary, apply. 'Reasonable' is a test that the court deals with on a daily basis. Courts can objectively ascertain what a reasonable income is. Application:** Ungoed-Thomas J upheld a direction to executors to let 'Tossy' (Mrs Florence Bridgewater) enjoy one of the testator's flats during her lifetime '*and to receive a reasonable income from my other properties.*' The court let the trustees decide which flat, the subject matter was uncertain although it was not so uncertain as to be unworkable.

Discussion of Re Kolb and Re Golay

In **Re Golay's Will Trust** [1965] 1 WLR 969 the court decided that the case satisfied the certainty of subject matter since it contained a degree of objectivity. Nevertheless, it could be argued whether the judgment was in line with previous cases. In the last edition of Parker and Mellows the decision has been described as inconsistent with contemporaneous decisions on the same matter. Nevertheless, the case seems to be consistent with the practice the courts were trying to introduce in order to avoid to set aside too many trusts.

Todd highlights this

"case should be contrasted with Re Kolb 's WT, where the view appears to have been taken of the term 'blue-chip' securities. In Re Golay's WT, the view appears to have been taken that the yardstick actively defined, since it was conceded that the court would have no difficulty in quantifying 'reasonable income'. No doubt Golay was close to the line because different trustees might apply the yardstick differently, so as to reach different results, but that is no different from 'residing' in Gulbenkian (below). In both Golay and Gulbenkian there was only one test, whereas in Kolb different persons might reasonably differ as to the test to be applied".

General Principle: A different approach was adopted in the modern case of Ottaway v Norman [1972] Ch 698 where the court was willing to adopt a different interpretation, under which a similar type of situation could be valid.

Ottaway v Norman [1972] Ch 698
Facts: A lived with his housekeeper, B, in a house, which he owned. A was a widower and had a son C by his former marriage, and A and B had for many years lived as man and wife. A made a will in which he left the house to B absolutely. There was clear evidence that, both before and after the will was made, A had informed B and C that his intention was that B should have the house for her life and that C should have it thereafter, and that B had always agreed. Immediately after A's death B made a will leaving the house to C. B later changed her will and left the house to D. After B's death C claimed the house from B's executor under a secret trust. **Ratio: It is perfectly possible for a secret trust to confer a life interest on the trustee with an obligation on the trustee to dispose of the property in a certain way by will. Application:** In view of the clear evidence that A had informed B of his intention that she should take the house subject to an

obligation and that B had accepted the obligation, she was bound by it. The fact that the obligation involved B's leaving the property in a certain way by will and not an *inter vivos* transfer was irrelevant. Accordingly, B's executor was bound to transfer the house to C. In this case the trust was described as a floating or suspended trust because it the trust floated until the wife died and then it came into operation.

Uncertainty of Property Cases

A problem, which may arise in this type of case, which the courts did not have a chance to address: What if B had mixed her money she received from her husband, with her own money or money of a husband she has remarried, this would make it very difficult to identify which money constituted the trust and what was hers to leave for D. It has been suggested this case illustrates that modern judges nowadays are more inclined to try and find a way to validate a trust, than the judges in some of the older cases who may be more inclined to invalidate a trust for the sake of maintaining certain rules, maybe the modern judge is more confident that they can find a way to implement a trust, even though its meaning is not certain.

General Principle: There is no trust when the property cannot be identified in a mass of similar property. The absence of proper means to identify the trust property from a mass of similar properties may render the trust invalid.

Re London Wine Co Ltd [1986] PCC 121
Facts: The Defendant was a company dealing in wines. Purchasers were provided with a document of title confirming the title as sole and beneficial owner of the wine. According to the contract for sale, once the customer had bought the wine, it would have been stored for him by the vendor in the warehouse. The company went into liquidation. Customers claimed their wines on the ground that a trust was created. **Ratio: Since there were no means of identifying the property acquired by the Claimants from the mass of similar property, the certainty of subject**

requirement failed. Application: It was not possible to work out which wine belonged to them. Oliver J – wine company, hold wines for some customers in the warehouse. The wine was never specifically separated. The general creditors wanted the wine to be sold to pay the debts, while the customers wanted the wine they paid for.

Re Goldcorp Exchange Ltd [1995] 1 AC 74
Facts: The Defendant was a company that dealt in gold and other precious metals. The company sold unascertained bullion for future delivery. Customers received an invoice or certificate verifying their ownerships. The company was supposed to maintain a separate and sufficient stick to meet the customers' purchase, but it failed to do so. The company went into liquidation. Purchasers tried to recover their gold. **Ratio: The court needs to know specifically which gold belongs to the customers. Notwithstanding that one bar of gold was worth as much as another one, you still need to have a proprietary right in a specific piece of property. Application:** – Lord Mustill explained that *"It is understandable that the claimants, having been badly let down in a transaction concerning bullion should believe that they must have rights over whatever bullion the company still happens to possess. Whilst sympathising with this notion their Lordships must reject it, for the remaining stock, having never been separated, is just another asset of the company, like its vehicles and office furniture. If the argument applies to the bullion it must apply to the latter as well, an obviously unsustainable idea."* Therefore, the court held that the purchasers had not acquired title since it was not known to what goods that title related.

General Principle: When the trust property consists of shares, the identification of them only requires the quantification of the interest on its own.

Hunter v Moss [1994] 1 WLR 452
Facts: A company, called Moss electronics, owned by Mr Moss director. Mr Hunter worked for the company. Mr Moss gave Mr

Hunter 50 of the shares to be on trust for his employee. The shares were never segregated but Mr Moss gave Mr Hunter a proportion of dividends to reflect equitable ownership of 50 shares. The company got sold to a bigger company for a large profit. The shares were sold and Mr Hunter went to court to try and get his part. **Ratio: When any 50 shares out of a total of 950 could satisfy a trust, an oral declaration was not void for uncertainty if the shares were indistinguishable from each other.** **Application:** Dillon J held that there was a valid trust that there was no uncertainty of the subject matter. His main reason for this was that if the transfer of shares had been done by will when Moss had died then it would have been valid, so it must also be valid here by declaring himself trustee of the shares

Affirmed in

Re Harvard Securities [1998] BCC 567
Facts: The Defendant was a company dealing in stockbroking activities. The company went into liquidation and the issue was whether the company or its former clients held the beneficial interest in two groups of shares held by the company. **Ratio: When the shares out of a total can satisfy a trust, it does not matter whether the shares are indistinguishable from each other. Neuberger J had to follow Hunter v Moss as binding precedent in English law. Application:** The court held that a valid trust was created and that the former clients had a beneficial interest in the shares.

Certainty of object - Who are the beneficiaries of the trust?

'Objects' are a generic term, but here the term certainty of objects is used to describe or define the beneficiaries, more precisely who the objects are, what they are to receive and when they will receive it. The concern here is that basically the beneficiaries must be certain and identifiable. The basic rule was sent out by Lord Willberforce in **McPhail v Doulton** [1970] UKHL 1:

> '*...a trust should be upheld if there is sufficient practical certainty in its definition for it to be carried out, if necessary*

*with the administrative assistance of the court, according to the
expressed intention of the settlor '.*

Lord Willberforce points out that the object of a trust does not
have to be absolutely certain, just 'sufficient' with 'practical
certainty'. Moreover, the 'administrative assistance' suggests
where certain types of cases will go to court on a constructive
summons and the court will provide constructive meaning of a
trust instrument.

The certainty test varies according to the nature of the trust, for a
fixed trust there is need for a greater degree of certainty, because
the trustees are mechanically implementing the trust. Contrast to
a discretionary trust, the trustees are exercising discretion anyway,
thus it is not so important if the beneficiaries are not so well
defined. Contrasted to powers, there is even less need for a
sufficient practical certainty needed than with discretionary trusts.

The concern here is that basically the beneficiaries must be certain
arid identifiable. This area is by no means clear. A bequest of 'my
house Blackacre and £25,000 on trust for my brother Jim' creates
no problems provided the testator has only one brother named Jim.
In such a case it is clear who the beneficiary is. However,
difficulties would arise if the testator had more than one brother
with the same name. Unless resolved by the limited ability to
admit extrinsic evidence, the gift will fail. Most of the problems
that have arisen in this area have been encountered in relation to
class gifts. Until recently it was important to distinguish into
which category a particular gift or trust fell as the certainty
requirements varied accordingly. The categories, which are
important, are:

- Fixed trust

- A discretionary trust (or trust power);

- A mere power

It should be understood at the outset that the courts have devised tests in relation to each category, which tests need to be satisfied in order to determine whether there is certainty of objects. Once the test for the particular category is satisfied, then there is certainty of objects. Otherwise the power or trust fails.

Fixed trust

In the case of fixed trusts, the trustees have no discretion at all. The shares to be taken in the trust by the beneficiaries are predetermined by the settlor or testator. It follows that a fixed trust must, for its execution, have beneficiaries, which are also known so that a complete list can be made of them (complete list test). Specifically, a complete list of all a trust's beneficiaries must be capable of being drawn up. This is the view of Jenkins LJ in **IRC v Broadway Cottages** [1955] Ch 20. If the complete list is not capable of being drawn up then the trust fails for uncertainty of objects, and a resulting trust is set up.

For instance, 'my trustees shall divide the property amongst my acquaintances of good moral character'. Such a trust would fail, as it would be a breach of trust to distribute only to those that the trustees could find if there were in fact others.

General Principle: It is possible to attribute the equal shares expected only by knowing exactly how many beneficiaries are involved. It is essential to know who the beneficiaries are.

Inland Revenue Commissioners v Broadway Cottages Trust [1955] Ch. 20 (overruled)
Facts: The settlor was Mr Timpson that created a settlement whose subject was £80,000 to be held on trust for the wife of the settlor and the other persons specified in the schedule. The issue was that the beneficiaries were not identifiable when the trust came into operation. **Ratio: Jenkins LJ *"It must, we think, follow from the appellants' concession to the effect that the class of 'beneficiaries' is incapable of ascertainment … that the trust of the capital of the settled fund for all the beneficiaries living or existing at the termination of the appointed period, and if more***

than one in equal shares, must be void for uncertainty, inasmuch as there can be no division in equal shares amongst a class of persons unless all the members of the class are known."
Application: The trusts were not such as the court could enforce. The trusts were void for uncertainty.
Mere Powers

These transfers are different from discretionary trusts. Discretionary trusts are to a certain extent imperative, while powers are entirely discretionary. For this reason, the court will never be involved in ordering or ensuring distribution. However, in the case of a 'fiduciary power in the full sense', the court may direct the donees of the power to consider the exercise of the power as in **Mettoy Pension Trustees Ltd v Evans** [1991] 2 All ER 513. Moreover, if no appointment is made the property will revert to the settlor or to the testator or to their estates or to the persons designated as taking in default of appointment.

Thus, as powers are entirely discretionary, there is no need to have a complete list. Nevertheless, some form of certainty test is required in order to ensure that the trustees or donees of the power stay within the bounds of the power. In other words, there must be some criteria to ensure that there is no appointment to a non-object (that is, someone outside the class). If it is impossible to determine between objects and non-objects, then the power fails for uncertainty. The relevant test for certainty of objects is that laid down in *Re* **Gulbenkian's Settlements** [1970] AC 508.

General Principle: The test is that a power would be valid if it could be said with certainty whether any given individual is or is not a member of the class.

Re Gulbenkian's Settlements [1970] AC 508
Facts: The trustees were given a power to apply income from the trust fund to maintain, among others, any person in whose house or in whose company or in whose care Gulbenkian may from time to time be residing and there was a gift over in default of appointment. **Ratio: per Lord Upjohn *"...with respect to mere powers, while the court cannot compel the trustees to exercise***

their powers, yet those entitled to the fund in default must clearly be entitled to restrain the trustees from exercising it save among those within the power. So the trustees or the court must be able to say with certainty who is within and who is without the power." **The power would not fail merely because the donees of the power could not come up with a complete list *('the* any individual' test). There must, therefore, be some criteria available to the donees or trustees, which enable them to decide in every case whether a person is within the class, or not. If these criteria can be satisfied, then the power is valid with regard to certainty of objects. Application:** In upholding the power the House of Lords held that the individual ascertainability test was the applicable test for powers.

Discretionary trust

A discretionary trust is a trust for a class in which the trustee is given the ability to determine the individual shares within that class. Thus the appointment 'all to one' would be possible.

Before 1971, if no appointment was made, the court considered that it had to carry into effect the trust element, but could only do so by making an equal division amongst all the members. It thus followed that if no complete list could be drawn up the discretionary trust would fail. Further, it would fail even if the trustees were perfectly willing to exercise the power given to them. This meant that the mere possibility of future intervention by the court and the impossibility of drawing up a complete list rendered the trust void from the outset. The authority for this was **IRC v Broadway Cottages Trust Ltd** [1955] Ch 20.

After 1971, the change as to the test for certainty of objects in respect of discretionary trusts came about as a result of the case of **McPhail v Doulton** [1971] AC 424 (*sub nom* **Re Baden**). In that case the House of Lords had to consider the validity of the following clause: 'the trustees shall apply the net income of the fund in making at their absolute discretion grants to or for the benefit of any of the officers and employees and ex-employees of the company or to any relatives or dependants of any such persons in such amounts...' It was accepted as a list. The House of Lords held that the distinction as to the tests for certainty of objects between mere powers and discretionary trusts was arbitrary, illogical and embarrassing. Accordingly, they overruled the complete list requirement with regard to discretionary trusts. They held that the appropriate test for this category is the Gulbenkian test for mere powers, namely the trust is valid if it can be said with certainty that any given individual is or is not a member of the class' (Per Lord Wilberforce.)

General Principle: The modern test for certainty of object for discretionary trusts is called 'individual ascertainability test'. The power to appoint the beneficiaries is valid if it can be said with certainty whether any given individual is or is not a member of the class and does not fail simply because it is impossible to ascertain every member of the class.

McPhail v Doulton [1971] AC 424
Facts: The settlor transferred by deed to trustees shares in a company for the benefit of the employees of the company, their relatives and dependants. The issue was whether the trust satisfied the test for certainty of object. **Ratio: In order to satisfy the test, the discretionary trust must say with certainty who is or is not a member of the class of objects. Application:** The House of Lords held that there was a trust and laid down the test for certainty of object.

McPhail v Doulton was then remitted back to the Chancery Division where it became known as **Re Baden Deed Trusts (No 2)** [1973] Ch 9 in order to decide whether the clause in question was valid under the Gulbenkian test. It was held that it was valid and the next of kin appealed again to the Court of Appeal: **Re Baden Deed Trusts (No 2)** [1973] Ch 9. The Court of Appeal had difficulty in applying the Gulbenkian test. The majority appeared to start from the relatives meaning all blood relatives (i.e. however remote). This meant that there were some people who might be relatives or who, alternatively, might not be, it being the case that it is impossible to find out whether or not two people might be remotely related. It was argued that this meant that the trust failed on the test propounded by the House of Lords (i.e. could it be said with certainty of any person, no matter who, that he is or is not a member of the class?). Sachs LJ said that the House of Lords test was one of linguistic, not evidential certainty, and that a person who could not prove himself to be a relative in fact was not a relative. Megaw LJ seemed to agree but added that it must be possible to say of a substantial number of people whether or not they were within the class. Stamp LJ disagreed: he considered that the trust would fail unless the word 'relatives' was construed as meaning next of kin or nearest blood relatives.

General principle: A trust, like a power, is valid if it can be said with certainty that any given individual is or is not a member of the class of beneficiaries.

Re Baden Deed Trusts (No 2) [1973] Ch 9
Facts: A settlor created a trust for the benefit of the staff of his company. According to Clause 9 of the trust, the trustees had to apply the net income of the fund in making at their absolute discretion grants to or for the benefit of any of the officers and employees or ex-officers or ex-employees of the company or to any relatives or dependants of any such persons. When the settlor died the executors alleged that the trusts were void for uncertainty. **Ratio: Once the court had made that decision the trustee's tried to implement the trust, but there was further litigation over what was actually meant, by the is or is not test. Each judge had a different opinion of what was meant by the is or is not test. The trust was upheld although each judge provided a distinct stance as to the is or is not test.**

- **Lord J Sachs** emphasised that the court was concerned only with conceptual certainty test and not evidential certainty. Sachs LJ was able to validate the trust only by adopting very wide definitions of both *'relatives'* and *'dependants'*, enabling a clear line to be drawn between those who were within and without the class. He took the view that relatives were defined as any persons who are linked by a common ancestor. The meaning of people with a common ancestor is clear although, it is clear there may also be evidential problems, Sachs LJ believed evidential certainty was not an issue here. He observed that *'dependants'* had already been defined by the courts, for example in relation to the Workmen's Compensation Act 1897, but he was also able to adopt a bright line definition by taking the view *'that any one wholly or partly dependent on the means of another is a "dependant".'*

- **Lord J Stamp** emphasised that the is or is not test was not just about conceptual certainty, a class can be conceptually certain, but it can still fail the is or is not test because of evidential uncertainty. It must be possible for the trustees to make a comprehensive survey of the range of objects, but he did not think it would be fatal if, at the end of the survey, it was impossible to draw up a list of every single beneficiary. LJ Stamp took the view that relatives defined as any persons who are linked by a common ancestor, was evidentially uncertain. He would have taken the view that the trust failed, had he not felt compelled to follow an early House of Lords authority, which had held that a discretionary trust for *'relations'* was valid, *'relations'* being defined narrowly for distribution purposes as *'next of kin'*.

- **Lord J Megaw** adopted a different solution, however, requiring that as regards a substantial number of people, it can be shown with certainty that they fall within the class. This is rather a vague test — clearly it is not enough to be able to show that *one* person is certainly within the class, as this test was rejected in **Re Gulbenkian's Settlements** [1970] AC 508. Presumably, the test requires evidential, as well as conceptual certainty. For example, relatives defined as any persons who are linked by a common ancestor, LJ Megaw took the middle line and believed with that class if you could always show a substantial number of people, then they are relatives.

Application: The court held that the trust was valid. The reasoning behind the judgment was based on the differentiation between powers and trusts. The content of clause 9 amounted to a power so that it was valid. The test of certainty did not need to be applied to the clause.

Argument in favour of Lord J Stamp's view - It would seem LJ Sachs would uphold a trust that cannot be carried out. It is very well saying all you need is conceptual certainty, but if you do not have any evidential certainty the trust will not be viable. LJ Stamp recognises the realities that a trust should not be validated if it cannot be carried out.

Argument against Lord J Stamp view - One objection is that the way LJ Stamp interpreted the is or is not test, seems to resurrect the complete list test for discretionary trusts which was rejected by the House of Lords as the incorrect test. According to Stamp's view that you have to be able to establish evidential certainty and who is in the class and who is not, this makes it unnecessarily strict on the class, which more or less amounts to resurrecting the complete list test.

Aspects of certainty

The following analysis of types of certainty is quite helpful in understanding the rules the courts:

- *Conceptual or semantic certainty*

- *Evidential certainty*

- *Ascertainability*

- *Administrative Workability or Capriciousness*

Conceptual or semantic certainty

Conceptual certainty refers to the degree of precision in the language to define the class of beneficiaries. This refers to the definition of classes of beneficiaries and if that class of beneficiaries is well defined. If the language is well defined, conceptual certainty will be established. For instance, if it was stated 'everyone born within the London metropolitan postal district', the definition of the class of people would be considered clear and precise. Alternatively, if it was stated 'everyone born in the vicinity of London', the meaning would not be precise. The first expression is conceptually certain and the second expression is conceptually uncertain.

The description of the beneficiary must be certain. A further example stems from **McPhail v Doulton** [1970] 2 All ER 228. In the case there is reference to *'my first cousins'* and to *'people under a moral obligation to me'*. If both of these classes are compared, the former statement is certain in meaning thus, conceptually precise but the second one is not conceptually certain because it is vague to say what counts as a moral obligation.

Each possible meaning might be precise. When the statement is ambiguous, it lacks conceptual certainty. With ambiguity it would be possible for the court to suggest which meaning, if there is an expression with two possible meanings both of which are precise, the court can usually say which was intended. But in the case of a vagueness there is not much the court can do, if something is too vague it is conceptually uncertain.

Sometimes, one-way of defining conceptual uncertainty, what is seen in case and literature, is to say, 'can you say of any hypothetical person, where he falls into the class'. When you say hypothetical, you can then decide what features of that person are, if the meanings are clear then you can always say whether a hypothetical person falls into that class or not.

Evidential certainty

Evidential uncertainty refers to those circumstances where a class is well defined in meaning and is accordingly conceptually certain, but it may be impossible to say that the person belongs to the class due to lack of evidence. For instance, the expression 'People born in the borough of Hillingdon between 1960 and 1962' is conceptually certain, but it may not be straight forward to establish who exactly falls within the class. It is conceptually certain, but it may fall short of being evidentially certain, if an applicant beneficiary is unable to produce a birth certificate as evidence.

Ascertainability

The notion of ascertainability refers to the question of the whereabouts or continued existence of persons who are clearly members of a class. It does not refer to the question "who are members of the class"? For instance, A class may be defined in terms of indisputable conceptual clarity, *e.g.* "the brother and sisters of X." There may in the particular case be no evidential difficulty whatever in so far as it may be possible to draw up a complete list of all those persons who have been born brothers and sisters of X. There may on the other hand be some doubt as to "the whereabouts or continued existence of some members [of the class]."

Administrative Workability or Capriciousness

Administrative workability refers to the problem of actually administering the trust, a meaning of a trust could be clear, it could be free of problems of evidential certainty and it is known who falls inside or outside the class along with their whereabouts, but nevertheless, the nature of the trust could be such, that it is practically unworkable to carry out the trust. In **Re Baden (No. 1)** [1970] UKHL 1 Lord Wilberforce said:

"There may be a third case where the meaning of the words used is clear but the definition of beneficiaries is so hopelessly wide

as not so form 'anything like a class,' so that the trust is administratively unworkable…"

General Principle: In order for a trust to be enforced, it must be administratively unworkable. A too large number of beneficiaries may result in the invalidation of the trust.

R v District Auditor, ex p West Yorks MCC (1986) 26 RVR 24, noted [1986] CLJ 391

Facts: The council wished to create a discretionary trust of £400,000 to be applied for a list of purposes 'for the benefit of any or all or some of the inhabitants of the county of <u>West Yorkshire</u>.'

Ratio: The court focused on the fact that it was administratively unworkable for the court to distribute such small amounts to all people. Even though the trust was not 'capricious', it was too difficult and costly to enforce. Per LJ Wilberforce *'The definition was hopelessly wide as to be incapable of forming anything like a class'*. **Application**: The court held that since there might be as many as two-and-a-half million beneficiaries the trust would not take effect as an express private trust. It was unworkable since the proposed class was so wide as to be unascertainable in practical terms. Furthermore, the trust was a non-charitable purpose trust, and therefore void in law.

Resolution of uncertainty

Cases that illustrate the application of the aspects of certainty:

General Principle: A settlor may validly empower his trustees to add to a class of beneficiaries of the settlement. A power is not void for uncertainty merely because wide in ambit.

Re Manisty's ST [1974] Ch 17

Facts: By a settlement made in 1971, the settlor gave the trustees discretion to pay, apply, appoint or settle the trust funds for the benefit of any of the beneficiaries within 79 years of the date of the settlement. He also gave them power by any deed or deeds revocable or irrevocable to declare that any persons, corporations or charities should be included in the class of beneficiaries. In

1972 the trustees by deed purported to exercise the power by adding to the class the settlor's mother and any person who should for the time being be his widow. Doubts having arisen as to the validity of the power, they took out an originating summons to determine its validity. **Ratio: A special power in favour of a class is valid if it can be said with certainty whether a given person is a member of the class, and an intermediate power is likewise valid. The mere width of the power does not render it uncertain. Application:** The court held that the settlor was not precluded by the doctrine of non-delegation from conferring an intermediate power on his trustees. The power in question was not invalid for uncertainty. The settlor was entitled to confer absolute discretion on his trustees and was not obliged to provide guidance on how it was to be exercised.

General Principle: If an expression is uncertain, the trust will fail.

Re Coxen [1948] Ch 747
Facts: In the case there was a gift subject to a condition. According to the condition the person would receive the gift if in the opinion of the trustees he has ceased to reside in at a certain place. The first issue was whether this expression was conceptually certain. **Ratio: Evidential uncertainty is where there is a question of fact it is impossible to answer, such as when a Claimant cannot prove he is a beneficiary. This does not necessarily invalidate the trust. Application:** The court said this was a conceptually certain expression, it is not completely certain but it has sufficient practical certainty. The court also considered if the expression had not been certain, the trust would have been valid because the trustees had a power to decide.

General Principle: Where a trust gives rise to a power coupled with a duty and it is not possible to predict that the donee knows all persons who might be objects of the power (since such objects include any person whom the donee considers to have a moral claim) the trust will be void for uncertainty.

Re Leek [1969] 1 Ch 563

Facts: The deceased involved in the case was the managing director of a company. The company arranged for the taking out of an approved pension scheme insurance policy by the company as trustee for the deceased. The trust was subject to certain further trusts and provisions which included a statement that in the event of the death of the deceased before retirement age all benefits *"shall be held by the company upon trust for the benefit of such ...other persons as the company may consider to have a moral claim upon you."* **Ratio: The trustees can always take a view on who have a moral claim on the testator. Application:** The court held that the first part of the trust was void for uncertainty of objects by virtue of the inclusion of "*persons the company may consider to have a moral claim upon*" the deceased. Nevertheless, the court explained that the uncertainty could be resolved because of the trustees' opinion.

General Principle: An ambiguous condition precedent may be valid by way of a benevolent construction of the condition.

Re Tuck's Settlement Trust [1978] Ch 49

Facts: Mr Truck set up trusts in 1912 providing that an income should be paid to the successors to his baronetcy providing that each was of the Jewish faith and married and living with an "approved wife". If separated, the successors had to be certified by one of two designated chief rabbis as being so through no fault of his. **Ratio: "Jewish blood" meant "some" Jewish blood and there was no uncertainty in the bequest. Normally a third party cannot resolve conceptual uncertainty, but in this particular case, a chief rabbi, who in the nature of his office has to take view of who counts as a Jewish person, can be taken into consideration in removing the uncertainty. Application:** A settlement providing for payment of an income to a beneficiary so long as he is of the Jewish faith and married and living with an "approved wife " of Jewish blood from at least one parent brought up in and not having departed from the Jewish faith, any doubt to be resolved by one of two designated rabbis, was held not void for uncertainty.

General Principle: When the words used by the settlor are contained in a condition of defeasance, the court may hear extrinsic evidence of the surrounding circumstances to show the meaning attributed by the testator.

Re Tepper's WT [1987] Ch 358
Facts: Mr Tepper was a testator that left certain bequests to beneficiaries provided that "they shall not marry outside the Jewish faith." **Ratio: The words "the Jewish faith" are not necessarily void for uncertainty when contained in a condition of defeasance, and the court may hear extrinsic evidence of the surrounding circumstances to show the meaning attributed by the testator. Application:** Whether the beneficiaries' interests were vested but liable to be divested, or were contingent interests, the proviso was a condition of defeasance. However, the words were not necessarily void for uncertainty, and the court would adjourn the question for the parties to file extrinsic evidence of the surrounding circumstances to show the meaning attributed to the words by the testator.

Summary

- The validity of a trust is usually the main issue courts have to deal with.

- Three are the certainties that need to be identified in order to have a valid trust: intention to create a trust, trust property and actors involved in the trust.

- Certainty of intention refers to the settlor's intention to create a trust. The settlor must intend to make a trust.

- Difficulties with certainty of intention arise where a settlor or testator uses so-called "precatory" words.

- Certainty of subject matter refers to the trust property. In order for a trust to be valid it is essential that the settlor has properly described it in order to identify it.
- Certainty of objects refers to the beneficiaries, more precisely who the objects of the trust are. The beneficiaries must be certain and identifiable.

- The test for certainty of object depends on the type of trust.

- Fixed trust refers to the so-called 'list test'. The settlor must have clearly listed the beneficiaries of the trust.

- The test for certainty of object in the presence of discretionary trusts is the 'any given postulant test' or the 'is or is not' test or 'individual ascertainability test'.

- Four are the main aspects of certainty of objects: Conceptual or semantic certainty, Evidential certainty, Ascertainability, Administrative Workability or Capriciousness.

Chapter 4 – Formalities

Introduction

Equity has been created with the purpose to light the complexity of Common law. For this reason, Equity has never been strongly based on the fulfilment of specific requirements. Only occasionally Parliament has imposed the adoption of formal requirements that vary in accordance with the subject-matter of the trust, the nature of the interest involved and the mode of creation: *inter vivos* (during one's lifetime) or by will (must comply with the Wills Act 1837). Most of these formalities were originally introduced by the Statute of frauds 1677.

No formalities are required to create a lifetime trust of *pure personalty* (i.e. of money or shares). On the contrary, lifetime trusts of land and of will trusts of both land and personalty require compliance with the following conditions.

Creation of an express trust

In order to create an express trust, the following criteria have to be met:

- Has the trust (or the disposition of an interest under a trust) been declared properly? (formalities)

- Is there clear intention to create a trust, is the trust property and are the beneficiaries of the trust sufficiently certain? (certainty)

- Is there a possibility that a power has been created? (trusts and powers)

- Has the trust property been transferred in the proper manner? (constitution)

An express private trust can be created *inter vivos* or by will. An *inter vivos* trust is created by a settlor and takes effect during his (or her) lifetime. A trust created by will is created by a testator (or testatrix, if female) in the presence of two independent witnesses and takes effect on the death of the testator.

There are several requirements for the valid creation of an express private trust, but the underlying objectives of the requirements are that the settlor or testator should have acted in such a way as to enable the courts, if necessary, to intervene to enforce the settlor's or testator's wishes.

General requirements to create an express trust

The essential requirements are:

- Capacity,

- Formality,

- Certainty, and

- Constitution of trusts.

The settlor or testator must be legally capable of declaring a trust and the intended beneficiaries must be capable of being beneficiaries. The settlor or testator must demonstrate that he intends to create a trust, following whatever form may be necessary in the circumstances. The settlor or testator must make it clear who is to benefit under the trust, and identify the property that is to be subject to the trust.

- **Capacity**

Any person of full age, such as over the age of 18 as stated in **Section 1(1)** of the Family Law Reform Act 1969, may create an express trust of any property which is capable of disposition, provided he (or she) is of sound mind.

By **Section 1(6)** of the Law of Property Act 1925, a minor cannot hold a legal estate in land, although he can hold an equitable interest in land. It follows, then, that a minor cannot create a trust of a legal estate in land since this can never vested in him in the first place. A minor can create a trust of other property – that is, property other than a legal estate in land, and that will include any equitable interest in land the minor possesses. Furthermore, a minor cannot make a valid will unless he is a soldier or sailor on active service, as stated in the Wills (Soldiers & Sailors) Act 1917. A trust created by a minor is voidable until a short time after his attaining 18th birthday. If the minor does not repudiate the trust within a reasonable time of this date, then the trust will be valid and binding. Although even to create a voidable trust, the minor must be old enough to appreciate the nature of his act. If he does not, then a resulting trust arises.

- **Statutory formalities to create an express trust**

While the general rule of Equity is that "Equity looks to the substance and not to the form", some statutory provisions have overlaid this area. The statutory provisions applicable depend on:

1. if the property subject to the trust relates to land or other property

2. if the trust is created *inter vivos* or by will

3. if whether the subject matter of the trust (the trust property) is a legal or an equitable interest. The subject matter of the trust will be a legal interest where the settlor owned the property absolutely. The subject matter of the trust will be an equitable interest where it is the interest of the settlor under and existing trust.

To illustrate the difference between a legal interest and an equitable interest, the following example may be useful: Your uncle created a trust by declaring that he would hold his legal interest in 10,000 shares in ABC plc on trust for you for your life. You then declared that you would hold your interest under that trust on trust for me. The subject matter of the trust created by your uncle is a legal interest. The subject matter of the trust you have created is an equitable interest.

- **Certainty**

The courts have established that three are the certainties that need to be identified in order to have a valid trust: intention to create a trust (the so-called certainty of intention), trust property (the so-called certainty of subject matter), and actors involved in the trust (the so-called certainty of objects). These three certainties are discussed in details in Chapter 3.

- **Constitution** (Chapter 5)

A settlor wishing to declare an express trust is required to do it through either a self-declaration of trust or a transfer of property to the trustees, subject to a direction to hold upon trust for beneficiaries. Chapter 5 is entirely devoted to the constitution of express trusts.

The formalities for the creation of a trust depend of the nature of the interest (legal or equitable), the mode of creation (inter vivos or by will) and on the subject matter of the trust.

<u>**Legal interests**</u>

At first, we will focus on the formalities of the transfer of legal interests. A legal interest reflects the *indicia* of ownership; the owner of a legal interest on a property has a right to have a title of property and may enforce it through litigation. Generally the legal title is held by the settlor.

3. **Inter vivos**

There are two methods of creating an *inter vivos* trust:

a) A settlor can declare himself to be the trustee of property he owns so that he will thereafter hold it for the benefit of others (Method 1).

b) A settlor can transfer the property to trustees and declare that those trustees will hold the property on trust for the benefit of others (Method 2).

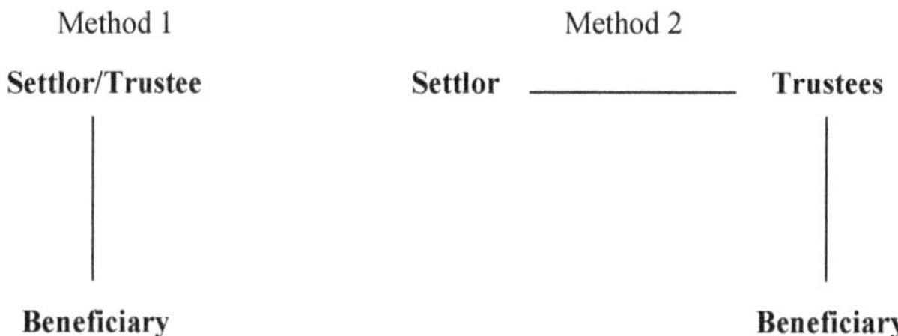

Figure 1: The two methods available to create an inter vivos trust.

Both methods require a valid declaration of trust, but only Method 2 requires a transfer of the trust property.

Declaration

The rules regulating formalities required to declare *inter vivos* trusts depend on their nature. Trusts of personalty are any forms of trusts which do not relate with land or interest in land. Conversely, the notion of trusts of land designates all trusts that relate with land or interest in land.

- **Declarations of trust of personalty**

Any declaration that relates to something that is not land or an interest in land can be made orally. No statute or rule of law requires a declaration of trust concerning any form of property other than land or interests in land to comply with any particular formality, and declarations of trusts concerning any other property can therefore validly be made orally.

General Principle: Declaration of trust of a chattel does not need to be in writing.

Rowe v Prance [1999] 2 FLR 787

Facts: The parties were a couple that shared fourteen years together. Mr Prance promised to marry and live with the Miss Rowe. Mr Prance bought a boat declaring it was for the couple to live on and belonged to them both. The boat was bought by using Mr Prance's money and registered in his name. Miss Rowe terminated the rent of her accommodation to live on the boat. After two years from the purchase, the couple split up and Miss Rowe sought a declaration of express trust in relation to the boat. **Ratio: The regular use of words that indicate the joint possession of a property may be considered sufficient to create an express trust. Application:** The court held in favour of Miss Rowe. By looking at the frequent use of the word 'ours' in relation to the boat, Mr Prance intended to be understood by the Claimant as she had a beneficial interest in the boat.

- **Declaration of trust of land**

This is governed by **Section 53(1)(b)** of the Law of Property Act 1925. The declaration needs only to be evidenced in writing. The declaration of trust itself may be oral provided there is some evidence in writing that the declaration has been made. The writing must show that the trust is intended to exist and the nature of the beneficial interests. The writing does not need to create all the terms of the trust, though these must sufficiently appear.

It may arise that the settlor executes a deed transferring his land to a trustee with the intention, known to the trustee, that the settlor intends that the trustee will hold the property on trust for the beneficiary. If there is no evidence in writing of the declaration of trust, the trustee may then attempt to claim that the settlor intended him to have the property absolutely because the requirement of writing found in **Section 53(1)(b)**: "*A declaration of trust respecting land or any interest therein must be evidenced in writing signed by some person who is able to declare such trust or by his will*" has not been complied with. In such a circumstance, "*Equity will not allow a statute to be used as an instrument of fraud*" and will impose a constructive or resulting trust on the trustee, thereby by-passing **Section 53(1)(b).** The courts may do this since **Section 53(2)** specifically states that: *"This section does not affect the creation or operation of resulting, implied or constructive trusts"*.

General Principle: The equitable principle on which a constructive trust is raised against a person who insists on the absolute character of a conveyance to himself for defeating a beneficial interest, which, according to the true bargain, was to belong to another, is not confined to cases in which the conveyance itself was fraudulently obtained.

Bannister v Bannister [1948] 2 All ER 133

Facts: The settlor was a woman who owned two cottages in Essex. She made an oral contract for the sale of the properties to the trustee (her brother-in-law), subject to her being allowed to live rent free for as long as she wished in one of them. The conveyance documents made no mention of this arrangement. Later her brother-in-law (the trustee) claimed possession of the cottage which she was living in, and said that Section 53(1)(b) prevented her from claiming that the property was held on trust for her (*"A declaration of trust respecting land or any interest therein must be manifested and proved by some writing signed by some person who is able to declare such trust or by his will."*).
Ratio: It is not required that the conveyance is based on specific technical formalities in order for the trust to be valid.
Application: The court held that the trustee brother-in-law held the property as constructive trustee for the settlor. Mrs bannister was given a proprietary right under constructive trust.

General Principle: Section 53(2) of the Law of Property Act 1925 provides that the requirements of Section 53(1) do not affect the creation or operation of implied, resulting and constructive trusts.

Hodgson v Marks [1971] 2 All ER 684 (CA)

Facts: Mrs Hodgson, an elderly widow, voluntarily transferred her house to Evans, her lodger. They orally agreed that the house would be held in Evans' name, but that it would remain Mrs. Hodgson's. Evans then sold the house to Marks, who was unaware of the oral agreement between Evans and Mrs. Hodgson. **Ratio: The question was whether Mrs Hodgson was entitled to protection against Marks as the owner of an overriding interest on the ground that she was a person in actual occupation of the land. The Court of Appeal prevented the same section from being an instrument of fraud by finding that a resulting trust had come into existence. Application:** The Court of Appeal held that, although her agreement with Evans was not evidenced in writing as required by **Section 53(1)(b),** Evans held the house on a resulting trust for Mrs. Hodgson, who was, therefore, equitable owner of the house. Her right to the house constituted an overriding interest under the Land Registration Act 1925, **Section 70(1)(g).**

Transfer to the trustees

Do remember that this requirement only applies to *inter vivos* trusts created by Method 2. The question here is: Which formalities are required for the valid transfer of property from the settlor to the trustees?

The answer is that the transfer to the trustees must comply with the rules applicable to the particular property concerned. Legal estates in land must be transferred by deed, equitable interests and copyrights by writing, chattels by a voluntary deed or by an intention to give coupled with a delivery of possession, and shares by the appropriate form of transfer followed by registration. Since 1996 it has been possible to transfer shares in certain quoted companies electronically, thereby avoiding the need for transfer forms and share certificates, but this doesn't detract from the principle that legal title only passes on registration.

The settlor must do all in his power to divest himself of the property to be made subject to the trust. He must comply with the formalities relevant to the type of property in order to affect the transfer.

- **Transfer of Land**

The transfer of a legal fee simple or lease to the trustees must be made by way of a deed. No other form of transfer will be effective. The transfer is governed by **Section 52(1)** Law of Property Act 1925 that states:

"All conveyances of land or any interest therein are void for the purpose of conveying or creating a legal estate unless made by deed."

- **Transfer of Shares**

The transfer of shares from the settlor to the trustee is governed by the Companies Act 1985 **Section 183**. As an example of a 'chose in action', shares are intangible items of property such as a debt, the title to which can be asserted only by taking legal action in the courts. These require special formality in order to be transferred. The settlor must execute a share transfer form and lodge it, with the share certificates, with the company, which will then register the trustees as legal owners of the shares in accordance with the requirements laid down by the articles of association of the company.

General Principle: If the transfer of an equitable interest depends on the performance of a third party and the transferor has done everything required, the transfer will be held effective in equity as constructive trust.

Re Rose [1952] 1 All ER 1217
Facts: On 30 March 1943 the settlor completed the share transfer forms and these was sent to the company. The company did not register the change in ownership until 30 June 1943 – three months later. The settlor died more than five years after the execution of the transfers, but within 5 years of their registration by the company. No estate duty (the equivalent of Inheritance Tax today) would have been payable if the gift had been made 5 years or more before his death. The question that arose was whether or not the gift had been effective at the date of the execution of the

transfer or the date of registration by the company. **Ratio: The settlor had done everything he could to divest himself of his shares in favour of the trustees (by completing the share transfer form and sending it with the company). Application:** The Court of Appeal held that the transfer did not have to be charged with tax since the transfer of the shares was held to have started from the fulfilment of the form by the transferor.

General Principle: The court set out the modes of creating an express trust. The transferor must do everything expected in order to transfer the property. The requirements will depend on the type of property.

Milroy v Lord (1862) 4 De GF & J 264

Facts: The settlor had executed a voluntary deed purporting to transfer shares to a trustee on trust for the Claimant. In order for the transfer to be completed, the transferor had to fulfil a form and register the shares in the name of the transferee in the company's book. The settlor did not complete the transfer. **Ratio: Equity does not perfect an imperfect gift. If the transfer is ineffective, the trust will become unenforceable. The mere fact that there was an intention to transfer the shares to the trustees will not give rise to a valid trust. Application:** The court held that no trust had been constituted. The voluntary gift was incapable of transferring legal title since that could only be achieved by the completion of a share transfer form and registering the name of the transferee in the books of the bank.

- **Transfer of Debts** (choses in action)

Debts are choses in action, governed by **Section 136** Law of Property Act 1925. In order for a settlor to transfer a debt of a chose in action to the trustees, the transfer must be in writing signed by the settlor.

Transfer of other Property

All those properties that fall within the category of 'choses in possession' are governed by the common law. 'Choses in possession' are those corporeal things, moveable, tangible and visible, always in someone's possession.

In order to affect a valid transfer of this type of property to the trustees, the settlor must either:

- physically transfer the property to the trustees with the intention of transferring the legal title to them, and not merely lending it to them, or

- execute a voluntary deed transferring the legal title to the trustees.

2. By will

Where a trust is created by will, then the declaration of trust is contained in the will must comply with the formalities set out in **Section 9** of the Wills Act 1837 (as amended by **Section 17** of the Administration of Justice Act 1982:

"No will shall be valid unless:

it is in writing, and signed by the testator, or by some other person in his presence and by his direction; and

it appears that the testator intended by his signature to give effect to the will [usually by signing at the end]; and

the signature is made or acknowledged by the testator in the presence of two or more witnesses present at the same time; and

each witness either –

attests and signs the will; or

acknowledges his signature in the presence of the testator (but not necessarily in the presence of any other witnesses) in the presence of the testator (but not necessarily in the presence of the other witnesses).

The transfer of the trust property to the trustees occurs on the testator's death when the trust property vests in his executors, who hold it in a fiduciary capacity pending transfer to the trustees, who may be and often are also the executors.

When the property is land the transfer must be made by way of written assent (Administration of Estate Act 1925 Section 1). This process is the same for both legal and equitable interests.

Equitable interests

Secondly, certain formalities are proper to the transfer of equitable interests. Since the Judiciature Acts (1873 and 1875) equitable principles can be applied to common law courts. The equitable title is the beneficial interest in property. It includes the right to enjoy property. In a trust, the equitable interest is generally held by the beneficiary.

1. *Inter vivos*

Again, a settlor can make a declaration of trust and transfer the equitable interest to the trustees or he may simply declare himself to be the trustee of the trust property.

Declaration

- **Declaration of Personalty**

No specific formality is required for a declaration of trust where the subject matter of the trust is personalty.

- **Declaration of Land**

A declaration of trust of an equitable interest in land must comply with **Section 53(1)(b):**

"A declaration of trust respecting land or any interest therein must be manifested and proved by some writing signed by some person who is able to declare such trust or by his will."

Transfer to the trustees

The transfer of an equitable interest to a trustee (Method 2) is regulated by **Section 53(1)(c)** LPA1925 that states:

"A disposition of an equitable interest or trust subsisting at the time of the disposition, must be in writing, signed by the person disposing of the same, or by his agent thereunto lawfully authorised in writing or by will".

Thus any disposition of any equitable interest in any form of property must be in writing (not evidenced in writing as with **Section 53(1)(b)**) and signed by the settlor or his lawfully authorised agent.

General Principle: An appointment of benefits under a pension scheme after death by a member to a nominee does not as such amount to an equitable assignment, or to a testamentary paper, nor, probably, a disposition of a subsisting interest.

Re Danish Bacon Co. Ltd Staff Pension Fund Trusts [1971] 1 WLR 248

Facts: An employee, in approved form, signed and witnessed, nominated his wife under a pension fund. He then by letter changed his nomination. **Ratio: The written declaration may arise from two or more documents which, when read together, dispose of the equitable interest. Application:** These documents, when read together, supplied the necessary writing.

Disposition

Although so far there has been a lot of detail, it is straightforward. Unfortunately, the question of what is meant by the term 'disposition' used in **Section 53(1)(c),** does complicate the issue.

It has been correctly stated above that there are no formalities that have to be complied with in order to make a declaration of trust in respect of an equitable interest in personalty. However, in some circumstances the courts have decided that what appears to be a declaration of trust in fact amounts to a disposition. Where this happens, the settlor must comply with **Section 53(1)(c)** and, to be valid, the 'declaration' must be in writing, signed by the settlor or his lawfully authorised agent.

When does a declaration amount to a disposition?

In **Grey v IRC** [1960] AC 1 it was argued that the expression "disposition" was confined to "grants and assignments", that is transfers. However, this argument was rejected by the House of Lords who applied a very wide meaning to the term 'disposition. The court said that the requirements of **Section 53(1)(c)** will have to be complied with in any situation where a beneficiary who, having a beneficial (equitable) interest at the beginning of a transaction, ceases to have that interest at the end of it.

General Principle: Where there is no writing there is no disposition. Stamp duty is payable when one disposes of an equitable interest in writing but if the trustee attempts to evade stamp duty by disposing of an interest under a trust without the use of a written instrument, the trust will fail.

Grey v IRC [1960] AC 1
Facts: The settlor, Hunter, made 6 settlements of nominal sums in favour of his grandchildren. He subsequently transferred substantial blocks of those shares to the trustees which they held on trust for him. He then orally instructed the trustees to hold the shares on trust for his grandchildren and later executed documents confirming his oral declaration. These transactions amounted to an attempt to avoid the payment of stamp duty. The question that arose was whether the trusts of the shares in favour of the grandchildren were created when Hunter orally instructed the trustees to hold them for the grandchildren or when the documents were executed. On this question rested the liability to pay stamp duty, which was payable where an instrument is used. The point being that if no instrument was used, no stamp duty would be payable. **Ratio: If Hunter had validly transferred his interest in the shares orally, he would avoid the duty, which of course**

he wanted to do. Of course the Inland Revenue did not want the court to decide that it had to be done in writing so that duty would be payable. The whole transaction, therefore, consisted of three stages:

1. a transfer by the settlor of the shares to the trustees to hold as nominees on his behalf (no change in beneficial interest here, therefore only the equivalent of 50p duty payable then (it is now £5, but still a nominal sum);

2. oral direction to the trustees that they were to hold the shares on trust (no duty); and

3. subsequent written declaration of a trust.

Without Section 53(1)(c) the oral direction to the trustees that they were to hold the shares on trust would have been sufficient to pass the equitable interest and so no duty would have been payable. Application: The court decided in favour of the Revenue. The court said that before the direction to the trustees Hunter had an equitable interest in the shares but afterwards did not. Hunter had therefore made a 'disposition' of his equitable interest that required compliance with Section 53(1)(c). By Section 53(1)(c) the disposition had to be in writing and since the disposition was not effective until the written declarations of trust were signed, stamp duty was payable on that document.

General Principle: A specifically enforceable contract may avoid the need for compliance with Section 53 (1)(c) because it gives rise to a constructive trust, which are exempt (LPA 1925 Section 53 (2)).

Oughtred v IRC [1959] 3 All ER 623, HL
Facts: Mrs. Oughtred owned 200,000 shares for life, remainder to her son, Peter. She also held 72,700 shares absolutely. On her death her estate would have had to pay duty on both the settled shares and those she held absolutely. To reduce the liability, she orally agreed to transfer her 72,700 shares to Peter, and in return

he agreed to release his remainder in the 200,000 shares to her. Later documents were executed confirming the transaction. The IRC claimed stamp duty on the transfer of Peter's interest in the 200,000 shares. Mrs. Oughtred argued that the transaction had been oral and therefore did not attract stamp duty and that the documents were merely nominal. In response the IRC argued that the oral transfer was ineffective because of s. 53(1)(c). Mrs. Oughtred's argument went like this: When she made the oral agreement with Peter she obtained an equitable interest in the remainder. Peter was therefore merely a constructive trustee for her interest – the beneficial interest had already passed to her. Because there was a constructive trust, s. 53(2) applied and so the transaction was not void under s. 53(1)(c). Thus the documents merely confirmed/declared what had already taken place and had transferred nothing of value. **Ratio: Ownership is not complete because by the contract the purchaser only acquires rights against the vendor. In order to have rights against the whole world a document of transfer is required. A specifically enforceable contract may avoid the need for compliance with Section 53 (1)(c) because it gives rise to a constructive trust, which are exempt (LPA 1925 Section 53 (2)). Application:** The majority of the House of Lords rejected the argument on the basis that whatever the purchaser acquired under the contract, full ownership could only be acquired by the completion of the appropriate documents of transfer.

Special circumstances where declaration is not a disposition

There are however some situations where declarations on the basis of the above would appear to be 'dispositions' within **Section 53(1)(c),** but where the courts have said that they are not.

Consider a trust created by Method 1 or 2. In **Grey v IRC** [1960] AC 1 the court defined a disposition as having an interest at the beginning and having nothing at the end. Could it not be argued that in creating a trust a settlor is 'disposing' of his beneficial interest requiring compliance with **Section 53(1)(c)**? What is the position when the equitable interest and the legal interest are 'reunited'? Will this be a 'disposition' requiring compliance with **Section 53(1)(c)**?

In **Vandervell v IRC** [1967] 2 AC 291 the House of Lords decided that **Section 53(1)(c)** has no application where the disposition was intended to dispose of both the legal and equitable interests in the property. **Section 53(1)(c)** only applies to dealings where the equitable interest is divorced from the legal interest.

First you should note that where trustees hold property on a bare trust for the beneficiary, then under the rule in **Saunders v Vautier** (1841) 4 Beav 115, the beneficiary can instruct the trustees to transfer the legal title to anyone the beneficiary nominates (including himself), e.g. X. This is logical, since otherwise, the beneficiary would have to transfer his equitable interest to X who would then have to instruct the trustees to transfer the legal title to him. In transferring the legal title to X, the trustees would have to comply with **Section 52(1)** formalities, i.e. execute a deed. When the beneficiary transfers his equitable interest to X, you would think that **Section 53 (1)(c)** would have to be complied with.

General Principle: Where the legal and the equitable interest are intended to be transferred together there is no need for a separate written disposition of the equitable interest.

Vandervell v Inland Revenue Commissioners [1967] 2 AC 291
Facts: Vandervell wished to give the Royal College of Surgeons (RCS) £150,000 in order to endow a chair in Pharmacology. He planned to give this sum to the RCS by allowing the RCS to receive dividends on 100,000 shares in a company that Vandervell controlled, until the sum of £150,000 had been raised. The shares were held by a bank as nominee on trust for Vandervell. In 1958, at Vandervell's direction the bank transferred the shares to the RCS. Part of the arrangement was that the College granted to the trustees of a trust set up in 1949 for Vandervell's children (VT Ltd) an option to acquire the shares for £5000 – far less than the market value of the shares – at any time within 5 years. The arrangement did not make it clear for whom, in the event of VT Ltd exercising the option and acquiring the shares, it was to hold the shares on trust. Eventually dividends worth £150,000 were paid to the College and in 1961 VT Ltd exercised the option and bought the shares for £5000. The Inland Revenue claimed surtax from Vandervell on the dividends paid to the College on the basis that because of the option Vandervell had not fully divested himself of the shares and that therefore the dividends fell to be treated as his income.   The IRC argued that when Vandervell (who held an equitable interest in the shares under a bare trust) directed the bank to transfer the shares to the College, Section 53(1)(c) required the disposition of an equitable interest to be in writing signed by the person disposing of the interest or his lawfully authorised agent, and since there had been no such written disposition by Vandervell of the equitable interest, it therefore remained with him, and he had not absolutely divested himself of the shares. **Ratio: As long as there is no evidence that show the transferor had no intention to transfer the beneficial interest, there is no need for written evidence of the transfer of an owner's equitable interest in property if he transfers the legal estate in it. If the legal and equitable title is being transferred together to the same person, there is no need for a separate written disposition of the equitable interest.**

Application: Just to complicate matters, on the facts of the case the House of Lords upheld the assessment, because it decided that the option was held by VT Ltd on a resulting trust for Vandervell. However, on the point about Section 53(1)(c), the court rejected the argument that where the beneficial owner intended to transfer both the legal and equitable interests to another, the transfer of the equitable interests had to independently comply with s. 53(1)(c). Thus had the option not been retained, Vandervell would not have had any interest in the shares and his legal transfer by the bank to the College would have divested Vandervell of all interest.

Disposition of a sub-trust

In the context of 'disposition' it should be considered now the question of the sub-trust. Earlier you were given an example of a sub-trust. For instance, your uncle created a trust by declaring that he would hold his legal interest in 10,000 shares in ABC plc on trust for you for your life. You then declared that you would hold your interest under that trust on trust for me. What you have created is a sub-trust – a trust of your interest under a trust.

The question is in relation to the declaration of sub-trust. Is there no need to comply with any formalities or is it a disposition of an equitable interest requiring compliance with Section 53(1)(c)? The answer here is, it depends! It depends on whether, in the example, you retain active duties in respect of the trust or whether you 'drop out of the picture'.

General Principle: In the case of a sub trust, the person who exercises the active duties holds for the new beneficiary.

Grainge v Wilberforce (1889) 5 TLR 436
Facts: A father, the settlor, held a trust for life for his son, the applicant, under a written contract. The land was actively carried out by the settlor. The applicant, declared a new trust for his own son under another written agreement. The applicant tried to challenge the first trust in order to hold the trust for the new beneficiary
Ratio: It may be necessary to give oneself active duties to

perform if declaring a trust of ones' equitable interest. If there are active duties then it can be argued that a whole new trust has been declared and that if it is not land it can be oral and effective. If there are not active duties, there will be a disposition of an equitable interest and therefore ineffective if not in writing. If no active duties but there is writing, then the effect is that the settlor drops out the picture and the trustee holds for the new beneficiary (i.e. it is a disposition within Section 53(1)(c). Application: The court decided that if the beneficiary under the original trust retains active duties in respect of the sub-trust then this will not be a 'disposition' requiring compliance with Section 53(1)(c). By retaining those active duties in respect of the sub-trust the beneficiary has created a new equitable interest under the sub-trust. If, however, the beneficiary does not have any duties, so that in fact he has dropped out of the picture, the original trustee is holding on trust directly. The disposition will therefore require compliance with **Section 53(1)(c)**.

2. By will

Wills must comply with the **Section 9** of the Wills Act 1837 that requires wills to be:

In writing and signed by the testator, or by some other person in his presence and at his direction

It appears that the testator intended by his signature to give effect to the will

The signature is made or acknowledged by the testator in the presence of two or more witnesses present at the same time.

<u>Summary</u>

- Since Equity has been created with the purpose to light the complexity of Common law, Equity has never strongly required the fulfilment of specific requirements in order to create a valid trust.

- The reasoning behind the requirement of some formalities is mainly based on the avoidance of fraud.

- *Inter vivos* trusts may be created informally such as orally.
- In order to create a transfer of land, the settlor must comply with **Section 52(1)(c)** of the Law of Property Act 1925.

- In order to create a trust on death, the settlor must comply with Section 9 of the Wills Act 1837.

- **Section 53(1)(c)** establishes the requirements necessary to dispose of a subsisting equitable interest.

- Wills must comply with the **Section 9** of the Wills Act 1837.

- A settlor can make a declaration of trust and transfer the equitable interest to the trustees or he may simply declare himself to be the trustee of the trust property.

- No formality is required for a declaration of a trust where the subject matter of the trust is personalty.

- A declaration of trust of an equitable interest in land must comply with **Section 53(1)(b).**

- A disposition of an equitable interest, must be in writing, signed by the person disposing of the same, or by his agent thereunto lawfully authorised in writing or by will.

Chapter 5 - Constitution

Introduction

Where trust property is vested in the trustees, the trust is said to be "completely constituted". It is then binding on the settlor, who cannot change his mind and revoke the trust (unless the trust specifically authorises revocation - which is rare). The beneficiaries have enforceable rights even though they may have given no consideration for the trust.

If the trust property is not vested in the trustees, the trust is incompletely constituted. As Riddall has put it: "a trust is completely constituted when the settlor has done all in his power (according to the nature of the property concerned) to vest the trust property in the person(s) who are to hold it as trustee or trustees. Until this time is reached, the trust is incompletely constituted".
A trust is constituted by either:

i) The settlor declaring that certain property vested in him is to be held henceforth by him on certain trusts (a self-declaration of trust); or

ii) By the settlor effectively transferring certain property to trustees and declaring the trusts upon which the trustees are to hold such property.

Modes of creating express trusts under the rule in Milroy

The principle laid down by Turner LJ in **Milroy** identifies the various modes of creating an express trust.

General principle: In order to create an express trust or to transfer property (legal title), the settlor or transferor is required to do everything excepted of him in order to vest the property in the name of the intended transferee.

Milroy v Lord (1862) 31 LJ Ch 798

Facts: The settlor executed a voluntary deed purporting to transfer shares in the Bank of Louisiana to Lord to be held for the plaintiffs. The shares could only be legally transferred by the appropriate transfer form (not by a deed) followed by registration of the new owner in the company's books, which was never done. The settlor handed the share certificates to Lord, who had a general power of attorney to act on behalf of the settlor which would have enabled him to register the shares in his name. Dividends were subsequently received by Lord and distributed to the plaintiffs until the settlor's death, three years later.

Ratio: The Court of Appeal in Chancery decided that, as the shares had not vested in Lord, there was no trust, despite the settlor's clear intention to create one. As Turner LJ explained in this case: "Under the circumstances of this case, it would be difficult not to feel a strong disposition to give effect to this settlement to the fullest extent and certainly I have spared no pains to find the means of doing so, consistently with what I apprehend to be the law of the court; but, after full and anxious consideration I find myself unable to do so. I take the law of this court to be well settled, that [1] in order to render a voluntary settlement valid and effectual, the settlor must have done everything which, according to the nature of the property comprised in the settlement, was necessary to be done in order to transfer the property and render the settlement binding upon him. [2(i)] He may, of course, do this by actually transferring the property to the persons for whom he intends to provide, and the provision will then be effectual, and [ii] it will be equally effectual if he transfers the property to a trustee for the purposes of the settlement, or [iii] declares that he himself holds it in trust for those purposes; and if the property be personal, the trust may, as I apprehend, be declared either in writing or by parole; [3] but, in order to render the settlement binding, one or other of these modes must, as I understand the law of this court, be resorted to, for there is no equity in this court to perfect an imperfect gift. The cases, I think, go further, to this extent, that if the settlement

is intended to be effectuated by one of the modes to which I have referred, the court will not give effect to it by applying another of those modes. If it is intended to take effect by transfer, the court will not hold the intended transfer to operate as a declaration of trust, for then every instrument would be made effectual by being converted into a perfect trust."

Application: Generally, there are two modes of constituting an express trust and the onus is on the settlor to execute one (or in exceptional circumstances both) of these modes for carrying out his intention.

The transfer of shares in a private company

In general, with shares of a public limited company, the directors may not refuse to register the transfer of shares. However, with a private limited company, there is frequently some provision in the company's articles of association (part of its constitution) restricting the transfer of the company's shares. Depending on the terms of the articles of association, the directors of a private limited company may refuse to register the transfer.

General principle: Once the legal owner of shares delivers to his donee the share certificate and properly executed share transfer form relating to those shares, he will have done all within his own power to transfer the shares to the donee.

Re Rose [1952] 1 All ER 1217
Facts: Eric Rose executed two transfers of shares in a company called Leweston Estates. The first transfer was expressed to be in favour of his wife- in consideration of love and affection. Second transfer also in her favour and another individual on certain trusts. Two transfers presented for stamping on April 12 1943 and then presented to the Co. for registration on June 30 1943. Rose died a few years afterwards, and the question arose as to whether a sufficient length of time in accordance with various finance statutes had elapsed before his death so that these shares need not be taken into account for assessing death duty on his estate.

Ratio: The deceased had done all in his power to divest himself of the shares and to vest them in the transferees, and the transfers were effective as between the deceased and the transferees to divest the deceased of beneficial ownership and to constitute the transferees the beneficial owners of the shares; the circumstances that the transferees must, to perfect their legal title, apply for and obtain registration, did not prevent the transfers from so operating, and pending registration the deceased was the trustee for the transferees of the legal estate in the shares which still remained in him; and therefore, the gift of the beneficial interest in the shares had been made and completed prior to April 10 1943, and no estate duty was exigible. While giving his judgment Evershed MR said: "…The settlor did everything which, according to the nature of the property comprised in the settlement, was necessary to be done by him in order to transfer the property-the result necessarily negatives the conclusion that, pending registration, the settlor was a trustee of the legal interest for the transferee".

Application: Generally, transferring shares in a private company requires the use of the proper instrument of transfer and the registration in the company's books. The Companies Act 2006 outlines the procedure that is required to be followed in order to transfer shares in a private company.

The Stock Transfer Act 1963 requires shares to be transferred by the transferor signing a stock transfer form in favour of the transferee. (Electronic transfers are also now possible.) The transfer must be registered in the share register of the company (in respect of which the shares are being transferred). To do this, the existing share certificate together with the stock transfer form must be sent to the company's registrar. Title only passes on registration of the transferee as the new shareholder.

The company usually has an absolute discretion to decide whether to register the new applicant without giving reasons for its decisions. In addition to this, the company deals only with the registered legal owner of the shares.

General principle: Where a donor had manifested an immediate and irrevocable intention to donate shares to another, signed a transfer form to this effect and instructed an agent to complete the transfer of the legal title to shares in a private company, the donor can no longer deny the interest acquired by the donee.

Pennington v Waine [2002] EWCA Civ 227

Facts: Ada Crampton wanted to transfer 400 of her shares in a company to the second defendant- her nephew Harold Crampton- and to make him a director thereof which, under the articles of association, required the second defendant to hold at least one share in the company. Ada signed a share transfer form and the company's auditors wrote to the second defendant to inform him of the share transfer and asking that he complete the prescribed form of consent to act as a director. The second defendant signed the form and it was countersigned by Ada. The signed share transfer form was retained by the auditors and was not sent to the second defendant. Ada died having executed a will in which she made specific gifts of the balance of her shareholding but made no mention of the 400 shares. In an action brought by the executors of Ada's estate the fifth and sixth defendants, who were residuary beneficiaries under the will, sought a determination of whether there had been a valid equitable transfer of the shares.

Ratio: The Court held that since the gift of 400 shares became effective when Ada signed the transfer form there was no requirement for the form to be delivered to either the second defendant or the company in order to make the gift complete, and the shares did not form part of C's residuary estate. As Arden LJ has put it in this case: "Thus explained, the principle that equity will not assist a volunteer at first sight looks like a hard-edged rule of law not permitting much argument or exception. Historically the emergence of the principle may have been due to the need for equity to follow the law rather than an intuitive development of equity. The principle against imperfectly constituted gifts led to harsh and seemingly paradoxical results. Before long, equity had tempered the wind to the shorn lamb. It did so on more than one occasion and in more than one way.""

Application: Where the donor has done everything he could to express his intention of transfer to the donee; he is no more permitted to deny the interest acquired by the donee. In **Khan v Mahmood [2021]** EWHC 597 (Ch), the Pennington logic is used without criticism to improve the flawed gift. Marcus Smith J seems to view Pennington as a broad modification of the rule in Milroy v Lord that allows the establishment of a trust in unsuccessful transfer instances if there is unconscionability. This is contentious.

Self-declaration of trust

An alternative way of creating an express trust is by way of a self-declaration. A settlor declares that he presently holds specific property on trust, indicating the interest, for a beneficiary. The settlor is the creator of the trust and the trustee. He simply retains the property as trustee for the relevant beneficiaries.
General principle: A failed gift will not generally be construed as an intention to declare oneself trustee.

Jones v Lock (1865) LR 1 Ch App 25
Facts: The case concerned an unendorsed cheque. MR Jones, returning from a trip he was scolded for not bringing a present for the baby. He gave the baby a cheque he had been paid. Mr Jones said "I give this to baby; it is for himself". The wife was worried the cheque would get torn and so it was taken from the baby's clutches and put in a safe. Nothing else happened to it and six days later Mr Jones died and in his will his property was left to his children from the first marriage.
Ratio: It was held that the settlor had not endorsed the cheque to his son, the property in it had not been transferred and the court rejected the argument that he had declared himself a trustee of the cheque.
He had intended an absolute gift, which entails giving away all benefit to, control of and obligation for the property.
Application: An intention of absolute gift is distinct from the intention to declare oneself a trustee, where the settlor/trustee retains control of the property and assumes the onerous obligation of a trustee.

No self-declaration of trust following imperfect transfer

The Court will not automatically imply the self-declaration mode of creating a trust if there has been an imperfect gift or transfer of the property to the intended recipient. The intention to give is fundamentally different from the intention to create or declare a trust. Accordingly, an imperfect transfer will not be construed as a valid declaration of trust.

General principle: If the donor intended to create a gift but fails to transfer the relevant property to the donee, the Court will not assist the intended donee to order that the intended gift be perfected.

Richards v Delbridge (1874) LR 18 Eq 11
Facts: Mr Delbridge led a life as a bone manure merchant and his very young grandson helped him. Mr Delbridge knowing he was dying wrote a deed saying "This deed and all thereto belonging I give to Edward from this time forth with all stock in trade". The deed was given to Edward's Mother and Mr Delbridge died. No mention of the lease was made in his will. **Ratio: The Court held that there was no intention to create or declare a trust, despite the fact that it was undisputed that the deceased intended a gift. In that case Sir George Jessel MR said: "For a man to make himself a trustee there must be an expression of intention to become a trustee, whereas words of present gifts shows an intention to give over property to another, and not retain in the donor's own hands for any purpose, fiduciary or otherwise".**
Application: Despite the transferor's intention to benefit to another by means of a transfer (whether on trust or not), the transferor ought not to be treated as a trustee if this does not accord with his intention.

The settlor may expressly adopt both methods of creation

The settlor may expressly manifest an intention to transfer the relevant property to third party trustees (transfer and declaration mode) and, prior to completing the transfer, to declare himself a trustee for the beneficiaries (self-declaration mode). In this event, the trust will be perfect, provided that the third party trustee acquires the property during the settlor's lifetime. In other words, the self-declaration of trust is regarded as conditional of an effective transfer of the property to the third party trustee.

General principle: The self-declaration of trust is perfect since the effective transfer of the property occurs during the lifetime

of the settlor, regardless how the third party trustee acquires the property.

Re Ralli's Will Trusts [1964] Ch 288
Facts: A testator left property on trust for his wife for life, remainder to his daughters. His daughter, Helen, covenanted in her marriage settlement to settle property including after-acquired property on certain trusts. She died while her interest under her father's will was still in remainder. On her mother's death, Helen's interest fell into possession.

X was then the sole surviving trustee of the father's will trusts and, as such, the legal title to the property subject to the will trusts was vested in him. X was also the sole surviving trustee of Helen's marriage settlement, and he asked the court whether Helen's interest under her father's will trusts formed part of her estate or should be held on the trusts of Helen's settlement, for beneficiaries who were volunteers. **Ratio: The Court held that X held the property on the trusts of Helen's settlement. When he acquired the title to the property, the settlement became completely constituted. As Buckley J puts it in this case: "He is at law the owner of the fund and the means by which he became so have no effect on the quality of his legal ownership".**
Application: Since the third party trustee acquires the property during the settlor's lifetime, the trust is perfect.

No trust of future property

General principle: It is not possible to create an express trust of property that does not exist or property that may or may not be acquired by the settlor.

Re Ellenborough (1903) 1 Ch 697, HC
Facts: Emily Towry Law executed a voluntary settlement that she would transfer property she expected to inherit under wills of her siblings but she did not transfer the property she inherited from her brother into the trust. **Ratio: The Court held that it will not enforce a voluntary covenant and this involved 'expectancies' (future property) under wills. In this case, Buckley J stated**

that "The question is whether a volunteer can enforce a contract made by deed to dispose of n expectancy. It cannot be and is not disputed that if the deed had been for value of trustees could have enforced it ... Future property, possibilities, expectancies are all assignable in equity for value. But when the assurance is not for value, a court of equity will not assist a volunteer".

Application: The following terms "future", "after acquired", "*spes*" property cannot be used to designate the object of valid express trust.

For example, it is not possible to create an express trust of lottery winnings in the future. It should be noted that it is however possible to create a contract in such terms.

Incompletely constituted trusts

If the trust property is not vested in the trustees, the trust is incompletely constituted. If no consideration has been given for the incompletely constituted trust, it is void, subject to certain exceptions. Equity will not compel the settlor to make the trust completely constituted (i.e. to perfect an imperfect gift). The equitable maxim "Equity will not assist a volunteer" will generally be applied. In addition to this, "Equity will not perfect an imperfect gift". As was the case in **Milroy**, equity will not assist a volunteer. This means that if a settlor fails to transfer property to a trustee then equity will not intervene to save the trust by treating the settlor as a trustee who holds the property on trust. However it is not true to say that equity will never assist volunteers. There are a number of cases where equity has done so.

General principle: The non-volunteer who has furnished valuable consideration will derive from the agreement to create a trust all the benefits accorded to a beneficiary under a perfect trust.

Pullan v Koe [1913] 1 Ch 9

Facts: The parties to the marriage and the issue of it are within the marriage consideration, that is to say, equity treats them as though they had given consideration; so they are not volunteers. **Ratio: The Court held that the covenant was enforceable on behalf of the children of the marriage. The trustees, as representatives of non-volunteers, were entitled to trace the intended trust's assets on behalf of the non-volunteers. The claim was treated as equivalent to an action brought in respect of a perfectly created trust.**

Application: The non-volunteer will be entitled to bring a claim directly against the reluctant settlor for an equitable remedy in order to have the agreement enforced and the limitation period will not operate.

Covenants to create trusts before the contract

It is important to distinguish between the creation of a trust or settlement and a covenant or contract to create one. Once a settlement is created, the beneficiaries become owners in equity of their share of the settled property. But if the settlor has covenanted to create a settlement or to add property to an existing settlement, the rights of the intended beneficiaries depend on whether or not they can compel the settlor to complete the settlement. Traditionally, they could not do so if they were volunteers; for equity does not assist a volunteer. If, however, a person had provided consideration, including marriage consideration, they could enforce the covenant. This doctrine has been qualified by the Contracts (Rights of Third Parties) Act 1999, the effect of which is that in certain circumstances a third party who has not provided consideration will nevertheless be able to enforce the covenant in his own right.

General principle: The party to a covenant to create trusts before the contracts is entitled to sue the reluctant settlor for damages if he refuses to settle the property.

Cannon v Hartley [1949] Ch 213
Facts: Under a deed of separation made between H, W and their daughter, H covenanted to settle after-acquired property on certain

trusts benefiting W and the daughter. When H later acquired the covenanted property, he refused to settle it. His daughter sued for damages. **Ratio: The Court ordered damages for breach of covenant. Romer J stated that "In the present case the plaintiff [the daughter], although a volunteer, is not only a party to the deed of separation but is also a direct covenantee under the very covenant upon which she is suing ... She is not asking for equitable relief but for damages at common law for breach of covenant."**

Application: In such circumstances, the covenantee will be entitled to claim damages in his own rights but of course will not be entitled to an equitable remedy because of his status of volunteer.

Effects of the contracts (Rights of Third Parties) Act 1999

In some circumstances it changes the position of volunteer beneficiaries but never to the disadvantage of the beneficiaries. This rule applies to contracts entered into after 11 May 2000. S1 of the Rights of Third Parties Act 1999 states that where a term in a contract expressly provides that a third party may enforce in his own right or where a term purports to confer a benefit on a third party, the third party may enforce the contractual term unless, on a proper construction of the contract, it appears that the contracting parties did not intend the term to be enforceable by the third party. The third party must be expressly identified by name; as a member of a class or answer a particular description. S1 therefore enables the third party to sue for damages.

S1 (5) further states: "…there shall be available to the third party any remedy that would have been available in an action for breach of contract if he had been a party to the contract (and the rules relating to damages, injunctions, specific performance and other relief shall apply accordingly)"

The rule in Strong v Bird

General principle: Where a donor intends to make a gift during his lifetime but fails to vest the legal estate in the donee,

the gift may still be perfected if legal title vests in the donee because he becomes the executor of the donor's real estate, provided the donor had a continuing intention to make the gift up until death.

Strong v Bird (1874) LR 18 Eq 315
Facts: Bird borrowed £1,100 from his stepmother who was living with him, paying £212 rent per quarter. The loan was to be repaid, over 11 quarters, by the stepmother deducting £100 per quarter from the rent paid to Bird. She made the deductions for two quarters but then expressly forgave the debt and insisted on paying the full rent per quarter till her death. Bird was appointed her executor and proved her will. The stepmother's residuary legatees sought an account of Bird for the £900 balance on the basis that the oral release of the debt was ineffective. **Ratio: Jessel MR held that the debt was released at common law by Bird's appointment as executor. Although in equity Bird would normally have been liable to account, this was displaced by proof of the stepmother's unchanged intention to forgive the debt followed by Bird becoming her executor.**
Application: It should be noted that this rule will only be applied when the donor intended to release the debt or make an *inter vivos* gift, the intention must continue until date of death and the donee must have been appointed and executor or administrator.

Doniatio mortis causa (DMC)

Also called deathbed gifts, this is halfway between a lifetime gift and a gift by will, but does not comply with the rules for either type of gift. It is a gift made *inter vivos* in contemplation of and conditional on the death of the donor. If following conditions are met, the donee can insist for the imperfect trust to be perfected (**Cain v Moon** [1896] 2 QB 283):

1. The gift is made in contemplation of death, which the donor believes to be imminent;

2. The gift is conditional on death (i.e. it is not intended to be fully effective until then and can be revoked before death);

3. There is delivery of the property; the donor must part with 'dominion' (control) of the property by handing it, or something which represents title to the donee.

For example, in the case of a chattel, delivery (coupled with the requisite intention) is sufficient to perfect the donee' s title on the donor's death.

General principle: Slipping keys into the bag of the donee on a deathbed is considered to be a valid delivery of the property.

Sen v Headley [1991] Ch 425
Facts: A man who was terminally ill told a woman friend that his house was hers and that the deeds were in a steel box. He slipped the keys to the box into her bag. **Ratio: The Court of Appeal held that there was a valid dmc of the house, by constructive delivery of the title deeds. The personal representatives should perfect the gift.**
Application: The three conditions here are satisfied, the gift is donated in contemplation of death and the property is consequently delivered before the settlor actually dies.

General principle: In the case of a *chose* in action which cannot be transferred by delivery, the donor is required to transfer the legal title to the donee by complying with the relevant formalities.

Birch v Treasury Solicitor [1951] CH 298
Facts: A, a donor, in contemplation of death, delivered to the donee, B, her Post office Savings Bank book and her Barclays Bank deposit passbook intending that the money in these accounts should belong to B on A's death. **Ratio: There was sufficient delivery of documents to establish valid DMCs of the funds in each of the bank accounts. Expert evidence was tendered on**

behalf of the passbook was essential evidence of title to the funds in the account. As Evershed MR has put it in this case "We believe that the real test is whether the instrument amounts to a transfer as being the essential *indicia* or evidence of title, possession or production of which entitles the possessor to the money or property purported to be given".
Application: In order to prove the delivery of *choses* in action, the essential evidence of title will generally be sufficient, regardless any other formal requirement.

The most notable exception is the donor's own cheque payable to the donee, as it is not "property" but a revocable mandate to the donor's bank, which ends on death (**Re Beaumont [1902]** 1 Ch 886).

Proprietary estoppel

Proprietary estoppel is a right given to a volunteer whenever a landowner stands by and allows the volunteer to improve his property by incurring expenditure on the property on the assumption that there will be a transfer to him. It arises where there is an assurance, reliance and detriment, so that it would be unconscionable to go back on the assurance. The award is based on the "minimum equity required to do justice", so the claimant does not necessarily receive what he had been led to expect.

General principle: Proprietary estoppel may be used defensively as a defense but also offensively as a cause of action in order to perfect the imperfect gift or complete an incompletely constituted trust.

Dillwyn v Llewellyn [1862] 4 De GF & J 517
Facts: a father, wishing his son to live nearby, offered him a farm so that he could build a house on the land. The son accepted the offer, expended a sum of money and built a house on the land, to the knowledge and approval of the father. The father died before a conveyance of the legal estate was ever made to the son. The son claimed to have the land conveyed to him.

Ratio: The Court noted that the father's action gave the son the impression that the land was conveyed to him. Thus, it would have been unconscionable to deny the son an interest in the property. Likewise, the father's personal representatives were estopped from denying the interest acquired in the property. They were obliged to convey the fee simple to the claimant, the son. As Lord Westbury has put it in this case: "If A puts B in possession of a piece of land and tells him I give it to you that you may build a house on it, and B, on the strength of that promise, with the knowledge of A expends a large sum of money in building a house, I cannot doubt that the donee acquires the right from the subsequent transaction to call on the donor to perform that contract and complete the imperfect donation which was made."

Application: Where it is unconscionable to deny an interest to a donee, proprietary estoppel provides him with a cause of action to perfect or complete the gift.

The modern approach to proprietary estoppel, laid down in **Taylors Fashions Ltd v Liverpool Victoria Friendly Society (1981)** 1 All ER 897, is to broaden its scope and to focus on the defendant's unconscionability, As Oliver J stated: *"The more recent cases indicate that proprietary estoppel requires a very much broader approach which is directed rather as ascertaining whether it would be unconscionable for a party to be permitted to deny that which, knowingly or unknowingly, he has allowed or encouraged another to assume to his detriment than to inquiring whether the circumstances can be fitted within the confines of some preconceived formula serving as a universal yardstick for every unconscionable behavior."*

The claimant is thus required to establish that:

- There is an assurance by the owner of land or an interest therein.
- There is a reliance on that assurance by the person to whom it was addressed (usually the claimant).
- There is some unconscionable detriment by the person to whom the assurance was made.

- There is a remedy designed to satisfy the minimum equity necessary to do justice or prevent unconscionable conduct.

General principle: Proprietary estoppel requires detrimental reliance on the assurance made by the defendant to such an extent that it would amount to unconscionable conduct on his part if the assurance is not enforced.

Gillett v Holt [2000] 2 All ER 289
Facts: The claimant spent his working life as farm manager for and as a friend of the first defendant, a landowner of substantial means. The first defendant made repeated promises and assurances over many years that the claimant would succeed for to his farming business, including the farmhouse in which the claimant and his family had lived for over 25 years. After 1992 relations between the claimant and the first defendant deteriorated rapidly. The claimant was then dismissed and the first defendant made lifetime dispositions to the second defendant and altered his will, making no provision for the claimant. The claimant brought a claim based on proprietary estoppel. **Ratio: The Court of Appeal allowed the claim and decided that the defendant's conduct had given rise to an estoppel, and the minimum equity to do justice to the claimant was for the first defendant to convey to him the freehold of the farmhouse together with a sufficient sum of money to compensate for his exclusion for the rest of the farming business. The defendant's repudiation n the assurance was unconscionable in all the circumstances.**
Application: Frequently the detriment may involve expenditure on the part of the claimant, which enhances the defendant's property, but in the domestic context may involve making a personal sacrifice based on an assurance by the defendant.
<u>Summary</u>

- Where trust property is vested in the trustees, the trust is said to be "completely constituted". If the trust property is not vested in the trustees, the trust is incompletely constituted.

- A trust is constituted by either:
  i) The settlor declaring that certain property vested in him is to be held henceforth by him on certain trusts (a self-declaration of trust) or
  ii) By the settlor effectively transferring certain property to trustees and declaring the trusts upon which the trustees are to hold such property.

- In order to create an express trust or to transfer property (legal title), the settlor or transferor is required to do everything excepted of him in order to vest the property in the name of the intended transferee.

- In general, with shares of a public limited company, the directors may not refuse to register the transfer of shares. Depending on the terms of the articles of association, the directors of a private limited company may refuse to register the transfer.

- Where a donor had manifested an immediate and irrevocable intention to donate shares to another, signed a transfer form to this effect and instructed an agent to complete the transfer of the legal title to shares in a private company, the donor can no longer deny the interest acquired by the donee.

- An alternative way of creating an express trust is by way of a self-declaration. A settlor declares that he presently holds specific property on trust, indicating the interest, for a beneficiary.

- If the donor intended to create a gift but fails to transfer the relevant property to the donee, the Court will not assist the intended donee to order that the intended gift be perfected.

- It is not possible to create an express trust of property that does not exist or property that may or may not be acquired by the settlor.

- It is important to distinguish between the creation of a trust or settlement and a covenant or contract to create one. Once a settlement is created, the beneficiaries become owners in equity of their share of the settled property. But if the settlor has covenanted to create a settlement or to add property to an existing settlement, the rights of the intended beneficiaries depend on whether or not they can compel the settlor to complete the settlement.

- Where a donor intends to make a gift during his lifetime but fails to vest the legal estate in the donee, the gift may still be perfected if legal title vests in the donee because he becomes the executor of the donor's real estate, provided the donor had a continuing intention to make the gift up until death.

- *Doniatio mortis causa* is a gift made *inter vivos* in contemplation of and conditional on the death of the donor. In the case of a *chose* in action which cannot be transferred by delivery, the donor is required to transfer the legal title to the donee by complying with the relevant formalities.

- Proprietary estoppel is a right given to a volunteer whenever a landowner stands by and allows the volunteer to improve his property by incurring expenditure on the property on the assumption that there will be a transfer to him. It requires detrimental reliance on the assurance made by the defendant to such an extent that it would amount to unconscionable conduct on his part if the assurance is not enforced.

Chapter 6 – Purpose Trusts

<u>Introduction</u>

A purpose trust is a trust created for a specific purpose. Generally, courts do not allow purpose trusts because by nature they do not comply with the so-called beneficiary principle. A trust will be seen as invalid unless there is a beneficiary, except in some types of purpose/charitable trusts. The rationale behind this is that there must be a beneficiary in whose favour the trust can be implemented by the court, there must be beneficiaries with proprietary rights in the trust fund.

Purpose trusts are void unless the trust is for the benefit of persons that are capable of enforcing the trust itself. It is accepted wisdom that the absence of a beneficiary would have the effect of leaving the trustees entirely at liberty to use the trust fund in relation to the purpose of the trust entirely as they saw fit, without the checks and balances of the beneficiary ensuring that the trustees carried out their fiduciary duties properly. Moreover, if there is no beneficiary then there will be no means by which it may be brought before the court, and this will bring the law into disrepute.

The beneficiary principle

According to the beneficiary principle, in order to have a valid trust, beneficiaries must be ascertainable. The trust must have certainty in relation to who are the beneficiaries. Beneficiaries must be ascertainable people. It is essential that the beneficiaries are legal persons. It is accepted wisdom that the absence of a beneficiary would have the effect of leaving the trustees entirely at liberty to use the trust fund in relation to the purpose of the trust entirely as they saw fit, without the checks and balances of the beneficiary ensuring that the trustees carried out their fiduciary duties properly. Moreover, if there is no beneficiary then there will be no means by which it may be brought before the court, and this will bring the law into disrepute. The root of this principle is found in the old case of **Morice v Bishop of Durham** (1804) 9 Ves Jr 399.

General Principle: The court must be able to execute a trust. In order for the court to execute a trust, beneficiaries must be ascertainable.

Morice v Bishop of Durham 34 ER 1046
Facts: A bequest was made to Bishop of Durham on trust for 'such objects of benevolence and liberality as the Bishop of Durham in his own discretion shall most approve of'. The court was asked whether a gift of residue to be applied to be valid as being confined to purposes that were charitable.
Ratio: For a trust to exist, there must be someone able to bring the trustees to court to enforce the trust obligations. Per Lord Grant MR *"There can be no trust, over the exercise of which this court will not assume control (...) If there be a clear trust, but for uncertain objects, the property (...) is indisposed of (...) Every (...) [non-charitable trust must have a definite object. There must be somebody in whose favour the court can decree performance."*
Application: The court held that the trust was not valid on the following grounds: the trust was not a gift to Bishop; the words used for its construction were too wide to consider it as a charitable trust; the beneficiaries were not ascertainable so that the trust could not be enforced for lack of certainty.

The Principle and Charitable Trusts

According to the general rule, you should not have a trust where the trustee's duties are not owed to a particular beneficiary, who are in a position to enforce it and so you should not have purpose trusts. However, this is subject to a qualification because there is an important category of purpose trusts that are valid and these are charitable trusts. These trusts are also referred to as public purpose trusts.

This rule does not apply to charitable trusts in general. Charities undertake activities, which are considered by the law to be commonly in the public interest, thus, statute creates an exceptional category for them. If certain conditions are satisfied, then a trust can be valid as a charitable trust even though it's a trust for a purpose.

The purpose must be within the range purposes that are recognised as charitable. Question arises to how charitable trusts are enforced because they would seem undermine the beneficiary principle, in that charitable trusts are purpose trusts. The answer is that there is a special procedure established, for the enforcement of charitable trusts. They are enforced through the Attorney General; the Attorney General sues in place of the beneficiary. In practice the conduct of charitable trusts is monitored by the Charities commission, the charity commissioners refer arguable breaches of duty by trustees of charitable trusts to the Attorney General and he can act against them. This mechanism is in place to enforce charitable trust, the next question that one may ask is why not extended this system to deal with all-purpose trusts.

Then we could validate all-purpose trusts and have a procedure for enforcing them. The answer is then that this procedure for enforcement of charitable trusts is at some cost to the public and the tax payer. Charity commissioners must be supported and funded along with Attorney General's actions. That cost is considered justifiable, because it is a way of promoting the use of money for charitable purposes, it encourages people to leave their money for charitable purposes and the way to do that is to provide the mechanism at the publics expense to enforce trust of that sort. There is no reason why the public should fund some mechanism to allow anyone to create a purpose trusts when the purpose is not charitable. Thus, in other cases the beneficiary principle applies and invalidates the purpose trust.

Testamentary trusts of imperfect obligation

Testamentary trusts of imperfect obligation are defined as trusts which have no defined human beneficiary and which, at first, appear to infringe the beneficiary principle in that these trust are clearly for a purpose.

In order for a purpose trust to be held valid despite the general rule of the beneficiary principle, some requirements have to be satisfied:

- The trust must fit one anomalous/exceptional cases

- There must be certainty of purpose

- The trust must comply with the rule against inalienability

In this chapter, we will successively analyse these three requirements for testamentary trusts of imperfect obligations. The study of gifts to unincorporated associations will be presented separately in Chapter 7.

Anomalous/exceptional cases

There are some so called anomalous cases, they are called trusts of imperfect obligation and these are anomalous case where the courts have permitted a trust for a purpose contrary to the beneficiary principle. There are limited types of exceptions to the beneficiary principle, aside from the case of charities, which is itself already an exception to the beneficiary principle.

- **Trusts for saying private masses**

An anomalous case is where money is left for the saying of mass for the soul of the testator. Religious activities are usually charitable. The question for the court was whether private masses were charitable events or not. If the religious activity is private but takes place in the church, people that participate can still receive a benefit that is considered public. Private masses are considered valid private purpose trust as long as they do not happen inside close private walls.

General Principle: Saying of private masses amounts to a valid private purpose trust.

Gilmour v Coats [1949] AC 426
Facts: A group of cloistered nuns received a gift by will. The question for the court was if the trust had a public benefit so that to satisfy the necessary requirement to be enforceable. **Ratio: For a trust to be enforceable it must be charitable and show evidence of public benefit. Application:** Since the nuns were strictly cloistered so that they had no contact with the outside world, the court did not find any public benefit behind the trust.

- **Trusts for monuments and graves**

A testator leaving money on trust for the maintenance of his own grave creates a valid trust even if there is no beneficiary in it.
The leading case for this was **Re Hooper** [1932] 1 Ch 3.
Monuments and graves not physically attached to church are not considered charitable.

General Principle: The construction and maintenance of tombs and monuments is a valid trust.

Mussett v Bingle [1876] WN 170
Facts: A testator created a trust composed by two amounts of money. £300 had to be used for the erection of a memorial. £200 was left for the maintenance of the monument.
Ratio: In order for a non-charitable trust to be valid, it must fall within one of the exceptions the law allows. One of the exceptions is represented by the construction of monuments and graves.
Application: The court stated that the trust could be considered a valid gift. Nevertheless, it was held that the 200 pounds did not respect the rule of perpetuity because the settlor did not specify the duration of the maintenance of the memorial.

Re Hooper [1932] 1 Ch 3
Facts: The testator gave a sum of money for the upkeep of a tablet and a window in a church and for maintaining certain family graves and monuments outside the church. The trust for the tablet and the window was upheld as a charitable trust, since it was part of the fabric of the church. The trust for the family graves and monuments outside the church was also upheld, but as a private purpose trust rather than a charitable trust.

Ratio: In order for a trust to maintain a monument to be valid, the settlor must specifically state the duration of the maintenance. Application: The court held that the disposition for the maintenance of the monument was valid since the trust clearly stated they should maintain the monuments as long as they were authorised by the law. Twenty-one years is the duration the law allows money to be held for the maintenance of a monument.

- **Trusts for the maintenance of animals**

Another exception is represented by those trusts created in order to leave money for the care of the testator's animals and pets.

General Principle: Gifts done for the benefit of specific animals such as pets are treated as private purpose trusts and they can be valid.

Pettingall v Pettingall (1842) 11 LJ Ch 176
Facts: The testator left a fund that was supposed to be administrated by the executor by spending £50 per annum for the benefit of a black mare. After the death of the mare, the surplus funds were to be given to the executor.
Ratio: Trusts to maintain animals may be valid.
Application: The court considered the wishes of the testator the content of a valid trust. The testator left funds in trust to provide for maintenance of his horses and dogs for as long as they should live. The gift was valid.

No more exceptions

The connection among these categories is historical. Those are the categories that had been taken to court after the case of **Morice v Bishop of Durham** (1804) 9 Ves Jr 399. The court has clearly stated that there will be no more exception to the beneficiary principle.

General Principle: Non-charitable trusts must be for beneficiaries and not abstract purposes.

Re Astor's Settlement Trusts [1952] Ch 53

Facts: A settlor established a discretionary trust for a variety of purposes including " . . . the maintenance of good understanding, sympathy and co-operation between nations, the preservation of the independence and integrity of newspapers; the protection of newspapers from being absorbed by combines or being tied by finance or otherwise to special . . . views". **Ratio: The rights that the trust creates require ascertainability of those to whom the rights themselves belong such as the beneficiaries.**

Application: In holding that these trusts failed for the lack of an ascertainable beneficiary, Roxburgh J acknowledged that great difficulties arise with private purpose trusts. As a matter of practice one could not happily contemplate large funds of money being used for purposes over which the court has no control.

General Principle: A trust that is not charitable must have ascertainable beneficiaries in order to be effective.

Re Endacott [1960] Ch 232

Facts: A testator transferred his residuary estate to the Devon Parish Council 'for the purpose of providing some useful memorial to myself'.

Ratio: A trust that is not charitable must have ascertained or ascertainable beneficiaries in order to be effective.

Application: The court held that no out-and-out gift to the Council was created, but the testator intended to impose an obligation in the nature of a trust on the Council, which failed for uncertainty of objects.

Certainty of purpose

Certainty of purpose refers to the 'ascertainability' concept. The purpose which the money is going to be used must to be sufficiently clear and certain. It is obvious that the rights of the beneficiaries will be illusory unless the court is capable of ascertaining to whom those rights belong. As Roxburgh J underlined it: "If an enumeration of purposes outside the realm of charities can take the place of an enumeration of beneficiaries, the purposes must be stated in phrases which embody definite concepts and the means by which the trustees are to try to attain them must be prescribed with a sufficient degree of certainty".

General Principle: Trusts are valid only when made for purposes that are charitable.

Re Endacott [1960] Ch 232
Facts: A testator transferred his residuary estate to the Devon Parish Council 'for the purpose of providing some useful memorial to myself'.
Ratio: A trust that is not charitable must have ascertained or ascertainable beneficiaries in order to be effective.
Application: The court held that no out-and-out gift to the Council was created, but the testator intended to impose an obligation in the nature of a trust on the Council, which failed for uncertainty of objects. The exceptions are historical accidents, they are Troublesome, anomalous and aberrant ... will not be extended. No extension to the existing categories.

General Principle: When means by which trustees must carry out the trust are unspecified and the beneficiary is unnamed, the trust is void.

Re Astor's Settlement Trusts [1952] Ch 53
Facts: A settlor established a discretionary trust for a variety of purposes including "(…) the maintenance of good understanding, sympathy and co-operation between nations, the preservation of the independence and integrity of newspapers; the protection of newspapers from being absorbed by combines or being tied by finance or otherwise to special (…) views". **Ratio: A trustee would not be expected to be subject to an equitable obligation unless there was somebody who could enforce a correlative equitable right, and the nature and extent of that obligation would be worked out in proceedings for enforcement.**
Application: The trust failed because of lack of beneficiaries.

Perpetuity Rule

The perpetuity rule exists in order to limit the extent to which a testator can control what happens to his money after his death. The basic idea of Perpetuity Rule is that if you have built up money during your lifetime, you should be able to determine, what happens to it after your death, but only for a limited period, possibly for the next couple of generations up to your grandchildren. After this period, control of the money goes and this principle is given effect by the Perpetuity Rule. The perpetuity period is a period defined by law it is typically defined as to be the testator's lifetime plus twenty-one years. Charities are exempt from the perpetuity rule.

The connection of perpetuity rule and purpose trusts, involves a simpler rule of perpetuity trust. If a trust was set-up for a purpose, where it could be said that the capital could never be touched and the income would be used for a purpose. Thus, if the capital is kept intact, then in theory the purpose could go on forever, the income being used from year to year for the same purpose, this would be a perpetual trust. The perpetual trust or any trust, which will go to continue longer than the perpetuity period, is going to be invalid. Even where a purpose trust is allowed, as in the anomalous cases, it will only be allowed for the duration of the perpetuity period and not longer than that. Charities are exempt from the perpetuity rule as they are in the beneficiary rules.

Endowments

Sum of capital must be kept intact and cannot be spent. What happens if the capital is invested and it generates an income that becomes available for the trust? You cannot tie up the income indefinitely, in perpetuity. There must be a max period where the trust comes to an end. The principle behind this is dead people cannot instruct living people indefinitely.

<u>Rule against inalienability</u>

You cannot transfer or sell a property to someone else. You cannot tie up money or properties indefinitely. Up to 21 years from the death of the testator you can apply the property for the purpose. The person setting up the trust must relinquish control during the perpetuity period. When the 21-year period is reached, the trust fails. The trust needs express wording to limit duration. You must be sure from the start that the trust will end after 21 years. However, the 21-year period represents the basic one. This can be extended to about 80-100 years.

General Principle: The law does not allow trusts that purport to be eternal. They will fail.

Re Hooper [1932] 1 Ch 38
Facts: The testator gave a sum of money for the upkeep of a tablet and a window in a church and for maintaining certain family graves and monuments outside the church. The trust for the tablet and the window was upheld as a charitable trust, since it was part of the fabric of the church. The trust for the family graves and monuments outside the church was also upheld, but as a private purpose trust rather than a charitable trust. **Ratio: In order for a trust to maintain a monument to be valid, the settlor must specifically state the duration of the maintenance. ´So long as the law allows´ is one of those statements that allows the trust to be valid. Application:** The court held that the disposition for the maintenance of the monument was valid since the trust clearly stated they should maintain the monuments as long as they were authorised by the law. Twenty-one years is the duration the law allows money to be held for the maintenance of a monument.

Selecting a longer perpetuity period

Fixed period of 125 years under Perpetuities and Accumulations Act 2009 does not apply. According to **Section 18** this period does not apply to purpose trusts, but only to people trusts. For purpose trusts, we must use the common law.

Comparative perpetuity periods

Twenty-one years is the standard period for the trust to run from the death of the settlor. If you nominate a life in being the perpetuity period will be calculated: LIB outlives testator + 21 years. For this reason, when selecting the Life in Being it should be better to choose a baby.

The Denley approach

The settlor may create what appears to be at first a purpose trust but this trust may be considered to be valid because actually benefiting human beneficiaries. On this issue, the courts had to consider whether the trust or gift was merely for the promotion of a purpose *simpliciter* as the **Astor** case declares it void, or whether the trust is capable of being enforced and is therefore valid.

The Denley Purpose Trust is a special formal purpose trust. It does not fit into the traditional exceptions. The position taken by the court in the case appears to be that the beneficiary principle will be struck down for abstract or impersonal purposes, purposes that do not directly or tangibility benefit an identifiable group of people. But if the purpose is sufficiently narrow and concrete, with identifiable group of people, then those people can enforce the trust.

The court, in a very old case **(Re Bowes),** devised a framework for the **Re Denley** approach.

Re Bowes (1896) 1 Ch 507

Facts: A testator let a fund for the planning on trees on a land for the benefits of his sons. The express purpose of planting trees was not mentioned as imperative but merely mentioned by the testator. The sons did not want the money to be used for the planting and directly claimed the fund. **Ratio: Purpose trusts might be enforceable if the settlor makes it clear that the motive relative to the benefit of ascertainable individuals is greater than the motive of the purpose itself.**
Application: The main testator's motive for the trust was the benefit of his sons; therefore the mere mention of the purpose of trust, if it is not imperative, is not taken into account.

The three conditions that must be satisfied for **Re Denley's Trust Deed** [1969] 1 Ch. 373 to work is:

- Ascertainable individuals (group of people)

- Non-abstract purposes (purpose cannot be too vague, something that is clear and specific). For instance, sports ground was not too abstract.

- Comply with perpetuity rules (the trust in the case expressly limited the trust).

General Principle: It is possible to enforce a purpose trust when it directly benefits a particular person.

Re Denley's Trust Deed [1969] 1 Ch. 373
Facts: The settlor of a trust deed inserted in the disposition a clause in relation of how the trustees should have dealt with the transferred land. Clause 2 stated that the land had 'to be maintained and used as and for the purpose of a recreation or sports ground primarily for the benefit of the employees of the company and secondarily for the benefit of such other person or persons as the trustees may allow to use the same'. If the number of employees had dropped below 75 per cent or the company had gone into liquidation, the land would have gone to the General Hospital. The question for the court was whether clause 2 constituted a valid trust or whether it was void as non-charitable purpose trust with uncertain beneficiaries.
Ratio: Non-charitable purpose trust does not comply with the beneficiary principle. Nevertheless, the rule against enforceability of non-charitable purpose trusts is confined to those cases where beneficiaries are abstract or impersonal.
Application: Since the employees that benefitted from the trust were ascertainable, the trust was not void for uncertainty. Employees represented an ascertainable class.

General Principle: In the case of Gibbons v. Smith [2020] EWHC 1727 (Ch), the concept was used to legitimise a trust of property owned by an unincorporated organisation. However, the court did not explore the foundation upon which the rule is based.

Gibbons v. Smith (2020) EWHC 1727 (Ch)
Facts: The circumstances surrounding the second judgement, Gibbons v. Smith, were significantly different from the first. In that instance, the claimants consisted of the personal representative of the last living trustee of land that was held on trusts that may have been charitable, as well as a member of the club or charity (depending on whether or not the trusts were really charitable). The requested information included, among other things, a determination was sought of the court of whether or not the trusts associated with the property were charitable. **Ratio: The**

court applied the **Re Denley** principle to property that had been handed to an unincorporated organisation. The court came to the conclusion that the land had been held on trust from its inception and hence fell within the purview of that rule. When the association ceased to exist, it was instructed that the property be sold, and the revenues were to be shared among the members who were still a part of the group in March 2013, which was the last day on which it was obvious that the association existed.

Application: The Denley principle was applied in Gibbons v Smith [2020] EWHC 1727 (Ch) to validate a trust of land held by an unincorporated association without discussion of the doctrine.

Summary

- A purpose trust is a trust created for a non-charitable purpose.

- Generally, courts do not allow purpose trusts because by nature they do not comply with the so-called beneficiary principle.

- According to the beneficiary principle, in order to have a valid trust, beneficiaries must be ascertainable.

- This rule does not apply to charitable trusts in general.

- Four are the categories that represent an exception to the general rule that purpose trusts are void: saying of mass; monuments and graves; bequest of money to look after specific animals; miscellaneous.

- The court has decided that private masses are considered valid private purpose trust as long as they do not happen inside close private walls.

- A trust created for the erection of monuments or graves is considered a valid purpose trust if there is an express desire by the trustee to perform the task required.

- The court has clearly stated that there will be no more exception to the beneficiary principle.

- According to the perpetuity rule, lands etc. should not be subjected for too long to a trust.

- It is not possible to tie up money or properties indefinitely.

- According to the rule of inalienability a property must be transferable at some point in time.

Chapter 7 – Unincorporated Associations

<u>Introduction</u>

What is an Unincorporated Association?

An unincorporated association is a body of two or more people who come together to pursuit a common purpose, which is not a business purpose. They are bound by mutual rights and obligations established by a contract between them. Which will govern among other things the questions of how you join and leave the association and how the association's properties will be dealt with.

There is an important distinction between an Unincorporated Association and an incorporated body like a company. There are many bodies, such as sports clubs and societies and other types of voluntary bodies such as Amnesty International. Such bodies may be incorporated, like larger sports clubs, this would make the company, and thus giving it a separate legal personality, which means the company can make a contract or own property. An unincorporated association does not have a separate legal personality; at law an unincorporated association does not exist as an entity. It's merely a form of contract between members with no distinct status.

Theoretical problems with unincorporated associations holding money

The problem for our purposes with unincorporated associations is: how does an unincorporated association hold its money or property? Unlike a company an unincorporated association cannot itself hold money because it is not a legal person. The question is: how does it hold its money? In practice an unincorporated association would typically have a treasurer and the money would be held by him (in a bank account or in his wallet for a smaller association) on trust. The treasurer will have legal title to hold and control the money. It then has to be asked: what is the nature of this trust?

One possibility is that the treasurer holds the property on trust for the benefit of all the members of the unincorporated association, in equal shares. This explanation does not really fit the bill, because in an unincorporated association the idea is that money is held for the association, and if it is said the treasurer holds it on trust in equal shares, the implication of this is that each member owns part of the funds and can choose to spend it as he wants or wishes, this is not what is intended and this does not reflect the reality. A further problem that can be imagined is people leaving and joining the association, for example does someone who joins immediately acquire a share in the trust or the money that comes into the association after he has joined, what about if someone leaves the association implication is he is allowed to take his share with him, thus this justification of a trust for members is problematic.

An alternative hypothesise is that the money is held on trust for all present and future members. An objection to this type framing is that it is contrary to the perpetuity rule, if there is a possibility that there is a interest under the trust might nest long into the future outside the perpetuity period then the trust will fail, and the trust would be invalid under the perpetuity rule.

Another possibility is that the treasurer holds the money for the unincorporated association on trust for the purposes of the association. This would appear correspond to be more realistic of the nature of the basis of the trust. However, this is also objectionable because there is no beneficiary in this trust and that it is a purpose trust, thus failing under the beneficiary principle.

The definition of an unincorporated association

A definition of the association is given in **Conservative and Unionist Central Office v Burrell [1982] 2 All ER 1**. In this case, the Court held that the conservative party was no an unincorporated association, because association was not formally understood as carrying this nature. Lawton LJ proposed a definition for the notion of association: "(An unincorporated association means) ... two or more persons bound together for one or more common purposes, not being business purposes, by mutual undertakings each having mutual duties and obligations, in an organisation which has rules which identify in whom control of it and its funds rests and on what terms and which can be joined or left at will".

General Principle: An unincorporated association is an "artificial and anomalous conception". It is regarded as a continuing entity and as something other than "An aggregate of its members".

Leahy v A-G for New South Wales [1959] AC 457, PC
Facts: A gift was left to an association of nuns, and it was held these nuns formed an unincorporated association. The property that was left to them was a large grazing farm. **Ratio: The court said there was two ways of interpreting this gift, either it was a gift to the nuns individually, i.e. for the treasurer to hold for the nuns in equal shares. Application:** The court held however this was not plausible as an explanation of a gift, it was not intended as a gift to each nun separately. The alternative was that the property was left on trust to promote or pursuit the purposes of the association the court said that this would be void under the beneficiary principle. In addition, the court said if the money was held on a permanent endowment then it would fall foul of the rule on perpetual trusts. A permanent endowment will always be perpetuations and will offend against the perpetuity rule because it is implicit that permanent endowment will carry on forever.

It seems the decision of the court is very doctrinaire and rather rigid. Its implication appears to be that unincorporated associations cannot hold money, this case appears to leave no explanation to how unincorporated association hold money, which is a very curious position, because there are many unincorporated associations and they do in practice all hold money and use it, according to **Leahy v A-G for New South Wales** [1959] AC 457 there appears to be no sound legal basis for it. However, since this case the courts have found other plausible explanations for the legal basis for unincorporated associations to hold money.

If the money belongs to the members it is an implausible account in reality, or it is held on a purpose trust which makes it invalid, thus how does find an alternative plausible explanation.

General Principle: A purpose trust could be valid if it appears to be that the performance of that purpose will directly or tangibly benefit a particular identifiable people.

Re Denley's TD [1969] 1 Ch 373
Facts: This concerned a trust for a piece of land to be maintained and used as and for the purpose for a recreational sports ground. Trustees of land were directed by the trust deed to maintain land for use as a sports ground "primarily for the benefit of the employees of the company and secondarily for the benefit of such other person or persons (if any) as the trustees may allow to use the same." **Ratio: Particular identifiable people can be recognised by the law as having the standing to enforce the trust, so by this means overcoming the mischief of the behind the beneficiary principle and the problem of no one being in a position to enforce the trust. Application:** The funds of an unincorporated association are held on a **Re Denley's TD** [1969] 1 Ch 373 purpose trust. On the basis that members of the association will benefit directly and tangibly from the purpose of the trust, which is to carry out the purposes of the association.

Inward and outward looking unincorporated associations

The case of **Re Denley's TD** [1969] 1 Ch 373 seems to offer basis for property holding in an unincorporated association, but it appears to explain only certain types of unincorporated association. For this reason, a distinction has been drawn with inward looking and outward looking associations. An inward looking association is an association, which is designed to benefit its own members, like a sport club, people all join a sports club for the benefit they derive from it.

On the other hand, there are outward looking associations where people get together to provide some benefit to other people, an example might be a voluntary group to help people in the third world, or an environmental group. This has never been decided but it would appear that a **Re Denley's TD** [1969] 1 Ch 373 purpose trust could *only* really explain what is involved in an inward looking association, because only in an inward looking association does the performance of a purpose directly and tangibly affect the members themselves. This is one problem with the **Re Denley's TD** [1969] 1 Ch 373analysis of property holding, it appears not to explain property holding in general, for unincorporated associations.

Gifts to subsisting members as an accretion to the funds

The Contract Holding Theory

The other analysis the courts have developed in recent years, for property holding in unincorporated associations, comes from the case of **Neville Estates v Madden** [1963] Ch 832, and this is the so called contract holding theory.

General Principle: Unincorporated associations are a form of charitable trust. For this reason, once the charitable nature of the trust created for the benefit of the public has been established, the unincorporated association is allowed to hold the property.

Neville Estates v Madden [1963] Ch 832
Facts: The case concerned a gift to the Catford synagogue, which was an unincorporated association. The question for the court was what form of gift was intended. The judge had to decide how the synagogue would take receipt of the gift. The judge had to consider different possible options of property holding in the association. **Ratio: If the gift was to the association for its purposes, it would be invalid under the beneficiary principle.** **Application:** The court said the gift could be upheld as a gift to the association or to the members of the association subject to their

respective rights and duties to one another, as members of the association, this is what is called the contract holding theory.

There has been some controversy since then about exactly what contract holding theory means. What the case said was that the gift takes effect to the members, subject to the terms of the contract between them. There is a suggestion that there is no trust involved, it is just a contractual arrangement. That cannot be correct because there still is a trust, when the money goes to the treasurer and he holds it on some form of trust. The question is what is the nature of this trust? The answer is the trustee holds the money on trust and the terms of the trust that bind the money are whatever terms of the contract between the members, that relate to the terms of use and control of the money. The association in its rules will particularly have provisions dealing with how the money if the associations should be spent and those rules actually form a contract between members those are the terms on the trust that governs the associations funds. This is not the same thing as a purpose trust in the normal sense, because these rules of association are contractual rules that can be altered at any time by the members.

This is a compromise position it is not a purpose trust, there is no binding purpose, but neither is it a trust for members absolutely in the sense they can claim their share, it is a trust whose terms consist of the rules of the association, which means at any one time, money must be applied in the accordance with the association's purposes, but those purposes can be altered by the members and in fact money can be distributed among the members. So ultimately the money does belong to the members but in a rather attenuated way.

There have been a number of recent cases concerned with contract holding in unincorporated associations and the courts have used either **Re Denley's TD** [1969] 1 Ch 373 or contract holding theory or some obscure combination in an attempt to validated gifts.

General Principle: The court looks at the wording and subject matter of the gift in order to interpret trusts to unincorporated associations.

Re Recher's WT [1972] Ch 526
Facts: The case concerned a legacy in a will to a non-charitable unincorporated association called the London and Provincial Anti-Vivisection Society. Society was an outward looking association campaigning against animal vivisection and there was a provision which said if the association was wound up then any remaining surplus funds should be given to a similar body. The rule actually implied that the money should not go to the members, but this rule could be changed by the members and the association. Under the contract holding theory the members always collectively own the money in that indirect sense, so there would never be a problem under the beneficiary principle.
Ratio: The gift takes effect as an accretion to the ordinary funds of an association, which they meant subject to the contract holding theory. The legacy goes into the association's ordinary funds and is held subject to the terms of the association's rules and these being subject to change by the members.
Application: The judge said that the money is not subject to a trust imposed from the outside of the association. The only trust governing the money is the trust in accordance with the terms of the association's own rules. The gift takes effect as an accretion to the ordinary funds of the organisation, (held subject to the contract holding theory) different from that which the testatrix had had in mind, to be held on the terms of a contract different from that contemplated by her, so the gift failed.

General Principle: As long as the perpetuity rules are complied with, private purpose trusts which confer a benefit on ascertainable individuals are valid, even in the presence of a gift to an unincorporated association.

Re Lipinski's Will Trust [1977] 1 All ER 33
Facts: The testator, Mr Lipinski, bequeathed half of his residuary estate to the Hull Judeans (Maccabi) Association, which was non-

charitable and unincorporated, "in memory of his wife, to be used solely in the work of constructing new buildings for the association and/or improvements in the said buildings." The money was left for a particular purpose.

Ratio: The purpose specified was one that would directly and tangibly benefit the members of the association. The construction of new building was one that would directly and tangibly benefit the members of the association.

Application: The court held that the trust was valid. The beneficiaries were ascertainable individuals such as the members of the association.

Advantage of Re Denley's Trust Deed [1969] 1 Ch 373 purpose trusts

The advantage of **Re Denley's TD** [1969] 1 Ch 373 is that you can interpret the purpose as being binding, a binding purpose trust, but it will only be valid with certain types of purpose, and an abstract or impersonal purpose would invalidate a trust under **Re Denley's TD** [1969] 1 Ch 373. Then you have to either say that the purpose was a motive under contract holding theory or the gift would be invalid. The other thing to remember if a trust takes place under **Re Denley's TD** [1969] 1 Ch 373 then the money is not subject to the same money as the associations ordinary funds, it is subject to a separate trust imposed by the under the terms of the gift, in theory the treasurer of an associations would have to keep the money separate, they would have to be a separate trustee created by the donor. Trust money can never be mixed, it has to be kept distinctly separate for the purpose of accountability and to make sure that the trust is properly used.

One of the major problems with this case is that, the judge cannot say that this gift will take place under one of these two basis. Sometimes judges do give alternative grounds for a decision; either is sufficient for my decision. In this case it does not really make sense, because it makes a big difference to the association which ground is the right one, on one basis the association are bound to fulfil the purpose and on the other basis they are not. On one basis, they must keep the money separate and on the other they can mix it with the association fund.

The issue the court had to consider was there another way upholding the gift, in an informal or lose collection of people that do not amount to an unincorporated association. If they do not amount to unincorporated association you cannot use the contract holding theory, because if you're not an association then you won't have contracts between members governing the application of funding. Moreover, if the gift is to abstract or impersonal then it cannot be interpreted as a **Re Denley's TD** [1969] 1 Ch 373 purpose gift, then the court is faced have allowed gifts to be interpreted under mandate theory.

General Principle: If a gift to an association is challenged, the court will look at the facts in order to understand if it is possible to adopt the contractual approach.

Re Grant's WT [1979] 3 All ER 359
Facts: This case concerned a gift to a constituency labour party for the benefit of the headquarters in Chertsey, then to the national labour party in default. If the headquarters ceased to be in the Chertsy district. Essentially this was a gift for the benefit of the constituency party headquarters in Chertsy, but if the headquarters moved then there would be a default gift over to the Labour Party absolutely. The issue was whether this was a valid gift.
Ratio: (1) The gift infringed the perpetuity rule. The way the gift was drafted implied that there was to be a permanent endowment and capital was keep intact while the income used. Upon the proviso and gift over in default suggests that T anticipated constituency party headquarters would eventually become unnecessary the implication of this was the capital had to be kept intact and the income used, in the event of the condition failing. (2) The gift would fail because it could not take place under the contract holding theory.
Application: The gift was held to be invalid.

<u>**Special gifts to unincorporated associations**</u>

Mandate Theory for lifetime gifts

The mandate theory is a means of contractual theory and the idea is that the money goes as an outright gift to the treasurer and then the treasurer is under a contractual obligation to the donor to spend the same amount of money he received for the specified purposes, if he fails to do this then he has a contractual obligation to pay back the gift to the donor. The apparent problem with this is a donation of this type cannot be made through a will because there can be no contract with a deceased person. Second, to understand an important objection we need to draw a distinction between a personal claim and a propriety claim. If you have a personal claim against someone then it is just a claiming for an amount of money not for an asset, which has a propriety claim. With mandate theory, if a gift is made to the treasurer and he does not make the payment and he goes bust, then the donor will not get the money back. However, if the money was held on trust then the donor will get back his money.

General Principle: The mandate theory only applies to lifetime gifts. The reason why it cannot work with gifts by will is that the donor's death would revoke the mandate.

Conservative and Unionist Central Office v Burrell [1982] 2 All ER 1

Facts: The Central Office of the Conservative Party was assessed to corporation tax on its income for the five years ended March 31, 1976, on the ground that it was an unincorporated association, therefore a company within Income and Corporation Taxes Act 1970 Section 526(5).

Ratio: The judge was not prepared to accept the conservative party was unincorporated association, because he said the association was not formally understood as carrying this nature.

Application: The court dismissed the Crown's appeal, that the Central Office was not an unincorporated association, since there was no mutual understanding among all members of the party, no mutual rights and obligations, and no rules governing control.

Useless and capricious purposes

Trusts that carry purposes considered capricious or useless are void as a matter of public policy.

General Principle: Valuable properties that are part of trusts and are used for purposes that are completely capricious cannot be considered valid.

Brown v Burdett (1882) 21 Ch D 667
Facts: Testatrix devised a freehold house, yard, garden, and outbuildings, to trustees and their heirs, upon trust to block up all the rooms of the house (except four rooms in which she directed that a housekeeper and his wife should be placed in occupation), and the coach-house, for twenty years; and subject thereto upon trust for a devisee in fee. She directed her trustees to visit the house and premises once in every three months to see that the trusts were effectually carried out, and declared that if any trustee should neglect or refuse to carry out the trusts aforesaid, any real or personal estate given or intended to be given to him by the will should go to the persons therein named, absolutely.
Ratio: Bacon V-C held that 'I think I must "unseal" this useless, undisposed of property' and gave a declaration that the house was 'undisposed of by the will, for the term of twenty years from the testatrix's death.'
Application: There was intestacy as to the twenty years' term in the house, yard, garden, and outbuildings.

Dissolution of unincorporated associations

What happens to the funds of an unincorporated association when the association is dissolved? Assuming there is an unincorporated association, and that the money is held under a contract holding theory, then if the association is wound up, what happens to the funds depends on the contract which binds the members. Sometimes an unincorporated association will not make any explicit provision stating what should happen to the fund in the event of dissolution. Then some terms must be implied into the contract by the court.

Distribution of surplus funds

The distribution of the surplus fund depends on the way the money is held:

- Under a contract holding theory or

- On a **Re Denley's TD** [1969] 1 Ch 373 purpose trust

Money held under the contract holding theory will go to the members. Money held under the **Re Denley's TD** [1969] 1 Ch 373 purpose trust will go back to the person who contributed the money. Sometimes it will not make a difference; sometimes the money has been raised or contributed by the members. Under the contract holding theory the current members at the time of dissolution will get the money. But if it is a resulting trust, it will go back to the people who contributed. In this case past members and present members may not get anything. Also under the contract holding theory the assumption is that members are equal, unless the rules say otherwise. If it is under **Re Denley's TD** [1969] 1 Ch 373 purpose trusts, then the money will go to the contributors in the amounts that they contributed. The logic behind this is that money goes where it came from, in proportion to the contribution.

Who will get the money?

The two leading cases on this question of dissolution, they were similar cases both concerned with pension funds. These constabulary pension funds were set-up through unincorporated associations and all the members contributed to this pension fund. They contributed money through subscriptions and by raising money in other ways. The money was held by a treasurer who would use the money to pay pensions either to retired contributors or to dependants of killed officers. The associations had their rules stipulating as to how money would be applied.

Bona vacantia

General Principle: Surplus assets that are *bona vacantia* should go to the Crown.

Re West Sussex Constabulary's Benevolent (1920) Fund Trusts [1971] Ch 1

Facts: Various donations and contributions from donors became part of a fund that was supposed to provide benefits to widows and dependants of the West Sussex police force.

Ratio: Money from identifiable donors should be returned on a resulting trust analysis. All other money, including member contributions, did not belong to members but passed to the Crown as *bona vacantia*.

Application: Once members had received their contractual benefits and had no further entitlement to the fund, the rest of the fund went to the Crown as ownerless property.

The problem with **Re West Sussex Constabulary Fund** [1971] Ch 1 is that the judge did not give any consideration to how the money was held. It was assumed that the money was held on a trust, the terms being stipulated within the gifts and contributions made. Thus it is equivalent of saying it was a **Re Denley's TD** [1969] 1 Ch 373 purpose trust, although the case of **Re Denley's TD** [1969] 1 Ch 373 was not referred too.

The judge said if the unincorporated association was wound up then it was a case where the trust would fail and there would be a resulting trust, for the people that contributed. Members of the association would get some money back only in proportions of their own contributions. Some of the money had come from outside contribution like lotteries and discos and some money had been made by way of donation and also through collection boxes. The judges here said the basic principle here was the money should back to the contributors in the proportions contributed. He qualified this in certain ways, first he said where there had been small contributions via the collecting box, there was no resulting trust because it they could not be understood that contributors had a retaining interest. Thus this money was ownerless and *bona vacantia* to the crown. The judge also considered the money, which had been paid through a lottery or disco ticket and he stated that these people must be effectively considered to have relinquished any interesting the money because they had received a contractual benefit in exchange for their money.

General Principle: First, it must be found out where the money came from and return it in proportion to the contributors. If those contributors have relinquished all interest, then the money goes to the crown instead.

Re Bucks Constabulary Fund [1978] 2 All ER 571
Facts: In this case there were four categories of giving donations and legacies contributions from members' entertainment such as raffles and Sweepstakes, and collecting boxes. Where the makers of the donations were identifiable, the donations could be returned. Contributions from members could be distributed in accordance with the rules of the association. The proceeds of the entertainment were not capable of being returned to the people who participated on the basis that people who had contributed that money had received the entertainment they paid for and therefore had no right to the return of their property — their interaction had been based on contract and not on trust.

Ratio: Past members have no rights in the asset of an unincorporated association as the words used by Walton J clearly stated. *'I can see no reason for thinking that this analysis is any different whether the purpose for which the members of the association associate are a social club, a sporting club, to establish a widows' and orphans' fund, to obtain a separate parliament for Cornwall, or to further the advance of alchemy'.* **Application:** It was held that it is impossible to return the property to the subscribers on the basis that their transfers of property were both outright gifts and made anonymously.

General Principle: The trustee of the pension fund has to make a judgment of their future liability and they have to work out whether they have enough funds to fulfil the trust.

Davis v Richards & Wallington Industries Ltd [1990] 1 WLR 1511

Facts: The trust involved the occupational pension scheme of a company, applied to the court to discover how to treat a surplus on termination of the scheme following the liquidation of the group. R&W was comprised of a group of companies. The interim trust deed provided that associated companies were to execute a definitive trust deed and rules were to be made with R&W's approval. The group got into financial difficulties in 1981 and on 1 August 1982 the pension scheme was terminated. However, the definitive trust deed was not executed until 6 August 1982. **Ratio: A surplus cannot be held on resulting trust where it is not possible to impute an intention that it should be so held. Application:** The court held that the employers' contributions could be regarded as resulting trusts. Therefore, employers were in equity entitled to the surplus derived from their contributions. However, no such resulting trust was created vis a vis the employees' contributions and transferred funds. Thus, if any surplus was derived from those sources, it devolved *bona vacantia*.

Summary

- An unincorporated association is a body of two or more people who come together to pursuit a common purpose, which is not a business purpose.

- The problem for our purposes with unincorporated associations is how an unincorporated association holds its money or property. Unlike a company an unincorporated association cannot actually itself hold money because it is not a legal person.

- An inward looking association is an association, which is designed to benefit its own members, like a sport club, people all join a sports club for the benefit they derive from it.

- Outward looking associations are those where people get together to provide some benefit to other people.

- When dealing with cases related to property holding in unincorporated associations, the court applies the so-called contract holding theory.

- If there is not an unincorporated association, the contract holding theory cannot be used, since there will not be a contract between members governing the application of funding.

- Valuable properties that are part of trusts and are used for purposes that are completely capricious cannot be considered valid.

- If the association is wound up, what happens to the funds depends on the contract, which binds the members.

- On this question of dissolution, the associations had their rules stipulating as to how money would be applied.

Chapter 8 – Secret Trusts

<u>**Introduction**</u>

A testator is a person who dies having made a valid will. The legatee is a person who inherits personal property under a valid will, as opposed to a "devisee" who takes real property under a will. Normally a testator creates a testamentary trust in order to transfer his properties after death, in accordance with the requirements established in Section 9 of the Wills Act 1837. A will is a public document so that its details are revealed to the public. Nevertheless, the testator sometimes may prefer not to reveal the details of his will. The reasons may be several: the existence of specific beneficiaries such as a lover or an illegitimate child may compromise the testator or the testator may be undecided as to who is to benefit. For these reasons, the testator may opt for a secret testamentary trust. Secret equitable obligations are testamentary trusts that represent the content of the will of the testator that does not want to reveal all/part of the content of the will. During his lifetime, the testator communicates to a trustee his intentions to create a valid secret gift/trust that has effect after the death of the testator. The details of the trust will not be inserted in the testator's will.

Two types of secret trusts

There are two types of secret trusts:

- The fully secret trust is fully concealed on the face of the will. The will transfers the property to the legatee without mention to the existence or the terms of a trust.

- The half secret trust is partially concealed on the face of the will. The will acknowledges the existence of a trust but does not give further details about its terms.

General Principle: In the absence of fraud or other special circumstances, the standard of proof applied in order to assess whether a trust carries a secret nature is the ordinary civil standard of proof. The burden is on the person that claims the trust to exist.

Re Snowden (Deceased) [1979] Ch 528
Facts: The testatrix was a childless widow that lived with the brother during the last six months of her life. By will, she gave the residue of her estate to her two executors and trustees to hold for her brother absolutely. According to her solicitor and executor, the testatrix was not sure how best to deal with the properties so that she decided to leave legacies to nephews and nieces 'leaving it to the brother to split up the remainder as he thought best'. The brother died few days after. By will he left his estate to the son, nominated executor and sole residuary beneficiary. The question was whether the estate was held on trust for the brother's son absolutely or for the nephews and nieces on the basis that the gift of residue to the brother might have been a secret trust. **Ratio: The standard of proof to look at is the ordinary balance of probabilities test. The test had to establish whether the brother was bound by a secret trust or was just subject to a moral obligation to look after the division of the estate.** Application: The court held that the brother was sole beneficiary so that the estate could go to the son. The reasoning behind this decision was that the terms of the obligation were too uncertain to be enforceable as a trust. They could only be a moral obligation. Furthermore, the standard of proof applied to secret trust was held not to be exceptionally high. Nevertheless, the ordinary balance of probabilities test did not satisfy the assessment of a valid secret trust.

Justification for enforcing Secret Trusts

One of the questions that may arise by looking at secret trusts is why the court recognises testamentary trusts that do not comply with the Wills Act? Two are the main reasons behind this:

- **Avoidance of fraud**

Since the trustee is the only person aware of the existence of a secret trust, he may keep the property for himself. Prevention of fraud is the main reason why courts have opted for a wider interpretation of what is valid and what is not.

As Lord Buckmaster has put it : "*A testator having been induced to make a gift on trust in his will in favour of certain named persons, the trustee is not as liberty to suppress the evidence of the trust and thus destroy the whole object of its creation, in fraud of the beneficiaries*".

- **'Dehors the will'**

The dehors the will theory is based on the consideration that secret trusts are inter vivos trusts and they operate outside the will. This theory circumvents the argument that secret trusts do not comply with the usual requirements to wills. This approach was advocated by Lord Summer in Blackwell v Blackwell (1929) AC 318:

"The court of equity finds a man in the position of an absolute legal owner of a sum of money, which has been bequeathed to him under a valid will and it declares that, on proof of certain facts relating to the motives of the testator, it will not allow the legal owner to exercise his legal right to do what he wishes with the property. In other words it lets him take what the will gives him and then makes him apply it as the Court of Conscience directs, and it does so in order to give effect to the wishes of the testator, which would not otherwise be effectual".

Fully secret trusts

According to the general rule, wills must comply with the formalities set up in Section 9 of the Wills Act 1837 such as: the will must be in writing and must be signed in the presence of two witnesses. When the testator does not want to reveal existence and terms of a trust, there will not be witnesses during the creation of the will. Therefore, it seems that secret trusts contravene the requirements of the Wills Act 1837. This is only apparent. The court has set specific formalities applied to secret trusts that stem from the case of **Kasperbauer v Griffith** [2000] WTLR 333.

- Intention to create the trust

- Communication of the trust to the intended trustee

- Acceptance of the trust by the trustee

Intention

General Principle: It must be clear that the testator intends to impose a binding legal obligation on the trustee.

Kasperbauer v Griffith [2000] WTLR 333
Facts: When writing the will, the testator used the following words 'my wife knows what she has to do' in relation to the family house. The question for the house was whether the words showed a clear intention to set up the trust.
Ratio: It must be clear that the testator intends to impose a binding legal obligation on the trustee.
Application: The court held the words too vague to consider the trust validly created on the ground that it was not clear whether the testator intended to create a binding legal obligation or just a moral domestic obligation.

When the trust is outright concealed on the face of the will, the trust is called fully secret trusts. In the will, there is no mention of the trust and its terms. It appears as an absolute gift to the person that receives it. Its existence and terms do not appear on the will. The testator communicates to the trustee that a specific property will pass to him for the benefit of an intended beneficiary after his death even if the trust is not mentioned in the will. The trustee will therefore be the only one aware of the existence of the trust, the terms of it and the property subject to the trust.

Communication

It is essential that the communication of a fully secret trust takes place before death. There must be communication of both existence and terms of the trust. The donor must communicate, orally or in writing, the subject-matter of the trust before dying. If the testator communicates existence and terms of the trust only to one of the trustees, only the one that has received communication will be bound, unless the gift relates to a joint tenancy. In fact, all tenants are bound to a joint tenancy as long as the communication has taken place before the execution of the will. Nevertheless, the general rule requires all the trustees to be aware of the existence and terms of the secret trust. Their acceptance represents an essential element for the validity of the secret trust.

General Principle: The testator must, during his lifetime, notify the beneficiaries of his selection.

Wallgrave v Tebbs (1855) 69 ER 800
Facts: The testator pointed the two Defendants administrators and executors as joint-tenants of £12,000 free from legacy duty. He gave directions that the legacy should have been used for charitable purposes. The Defendants stated that they had not communication with the testator about the will or wishes with respect to the disposition of the property.
Ratio: The communication between testator and Defendants should have taken place any time before the death, before or after the signing of the will.
Application: The court held that testator and Defendants missed the communication of the construction of a trust. The Defendants received the legacy free from the trust.

General Principle: The method of communication is valid if the trustee is aware of the content of the existence and terms of the secret trust.

Re Keen's Estate [1937] Ch 236
Facts: By will a testator gave to his trustees 10,000l to hold on trust for the benefit of some persons and charities. He then

provided his trustees of a sealed envelope in which he declared to have written the name and address of a secret beneficiary. The trustees were informed of the content.

Ratio: Providing that the trustee is aware that the envelope contains the terms of a secret trust and he accepts it on that basis, the method of sealed envelope is acceptable.

Application: In relation to the validity of the sealed envelope, the court held that a sealed envelope might amount to a valid method of communication. Nevertheless, the trust was held invalid on the ground of inconsistency. In fact, the will referred to a future communication that was inconsistent with a communication already made with the envelope.

Where a testator leaves a property for two or more legatees, but do not inform all of them of the terms of the trust, the question arises as to whether the uninformed legatees are bound by the communication to the informed legatees. If the communication was made to the legatees before or at the time of the execution of the will and they take as joint tenants, the uninformed are bound to hold for the purposes communicated to the informed legatees. However, if these two conditions are not satisfied, the uninformed legatees are entitled to take the property beneficially.

Acceptance

The testator must reasonably believe that the trust has been accepted to consider it validly created.

General Principle: The trustee may show or infer his acceptance even by silence.

Ottaway v Norman [1972] Ch 928
Facts: By will a testator left his bungalow to the housekeeper and £1,500 as legacy. Evidence showed that between testator and housekeeper there was an oral agreement that after her death the estate would have gone to the testator's son and daughter-in-law. Instead by will the housekeeper left everything to another person.
Ratio: To create a valid secret trust it is essential to show that the testator has communicated his intention to the donee. The

donee must accept expressly or by acquiescence the obligation. Once accepted, the means of carrying out the obligation was immaterial.

Application: The court held that the testator created a valid secret trust that bound the housekeeper in leaving the estate to the son and daughter-in-law.

The court reaffirms in **Titcombe v. Ison [2021]** 1 WLUK 624 that, aside from the formality criteria, a secret trust must satisfy with the other important elements for the foundation of a trust. These conditions include maintaining secrecy and maintaining financial independence. Consequently, in this instance, there existed a claimed entirely hidden trust; nonetheless, the most important issue was whether the dead had any purpose to form a trust at all or rather to impose a simple moral or familial responsibility on the receiver of the property (using the test in **Kasperbauer v. Griffiths**). According to the evidence, this was nothing more than a moral or familial responsibility; as a result, there was no hidden trust.

<u>**Half Secret Trusts**</u>

Half secret trusts are those arrangements between the testator and the trustee where it is clear from the will that the property is left on trust for the benefit of someone, but the terms of the trust are not specified, they are kept secret. The half secret trust will be valid if there is consistency with the will and the communication takes place before or contemporaneously with the execution of the will.

General Principle: If intention, communication and acquiescence are provided, there is no reason to doubt on the validity of the trust.

Blackwell v Blackwell [1929] AC 318

Facts: A testator left £12,000 by codicil to five people that should have invested the money "for the purposes indicated by me to them". Few hours later the trustees created a memorandum with the instructions of the testator in relation of the investment of the money. The residuary legatees claimed that the trust was invalid since the instructions were made after the codicil.

Ratio: If the details of a will are laid out around the same time as the execution of a codicil to the will, the half secret trust can be considered valid.

Application: The House of Lords held the trust validly created since the three elements of intention of the testator, communication of the trust and acquiescence by the trustees were clearly present by looking at documents and facts.

Consistency with the will is essential

General Principle: The secret trust must relate to the testator's will.

Re Keen's Estate [1937] Ch 236

Facts: By will a testator devised a legacy to two legatees, to be held upon trust for the benefit of persons and charities whose names would have been notified during his lifetime. One of the legatee received a sealed envelope on which it was written 'not to open before my death'. Later, the testator revoked the first will with a new one with the same bequest. After the testator's it was found out that the envelope contained the name of the beneficiary of the trust. The question for the court was whether the secret trust was valid.

Ratio: If the trust is inconsistent with the express terms of the will, it cannot be valid.

Application: The Court of Appeal held that the secret trust was inconsistent with the testator's will, therefore not enforceable. The reasoning was that the envelope was anterior to the new will and hence not within the language of the will.

Communication

Communication will have to take place before a will is executed or at the time of the execution of the will.

General Principle: Communication must take place before or at the time of the execution of the will.

Blackwell v Blackwell [1929] AC 318
Facts: By a codicil to his will, the testator left 12,000l to five trustees that had to hold the money upon trust for the benefit of the testator's mistress and son. Widow and legitimate son of the testator brought an action for a declaration of no valid trust of the legacy. **Ratio: The terms of the trust must be communicated before or at the time of the execution of the will to the trustees who must accept the obligation to hold the property on trust for the benefit before or at the time of the execution of the will. Application:** The House of Lords held that the trust created by codicil was valid and consistent.

Secret trustee as witness to will

According to Section 15 of the Wills Act 1837 a witness to a will cannot benefit from it. This rule applies also to half-secret trustee. Therefore, any benefit derived from the trust to a half-secret trustee will be void. The position of the law is less certain in relation to fully secret trust.

Death of, or disclaimer by, a secret trustee

The law is not clear in relation to what would happen, if the trustee died or disclaimed the trust. The court has shown its general position in few cases and it seems that the outcome changes based on the type of secret trust. However, the current position is only obiter so that the law is still uncertain.

General Principle: If the fully-secret trustee dies before the testator or disclaims the trust, the trust will fail.

Re Maddock [1902] 2 Ch 220
Facts: A testatrix left the residue of her personal estate to the trustee that was one of the executors of the will. In a written memorandum the testatrix communicated that part of the residue should have gone to a named third party. The residuary personal

estate of the testatrix eventually was not sufficient to pay her debts. The question for the court was whether the entire residue could have been used to pay the debts or if the part left the third party was preserved. **Ratio: Cozens-Hardy MR stated '***If (the trustee) renounces and disclaims, or dies in the lifetime of the testator, the persons claiming under the memorandum can take nothing against the heir-at-law or next of kin or residuary devisee or legatee.***' Therefore, if the trustee dies before the testator or disclaims the trust, the property will simply revert to the testator's estate. Application:** The court held the memorandum part of the will so that all the residue should have been used to pay the testatrix's expenses.

Death of, or disclaimer by, a secret beneficiary

If an intended secret beneficiary dies during the lifetime of the testator without a variation of the agreement, in principle his interest under the intended trust ought to lapse. However, in **Re Garnder (no 2) (1923)** Romer J came to the absurd conclusion that the secret beneficiary's interest did not lapse and his heirs were entitled to the property. It is generally recognized that this position cannot be supported in trust law. In principle, the trust will fail and a resulting trust for the testator's estate may arise.

<u>**Secret Trusts in a modern context**</u>

Despite the appearance, secret trusts are relevant nowadays as much as at the time of the case law illustrated above. A good example stems from the case of **Davies v Reveue and Customs Commissioners** [2009] UKFTT 138 (TC) that relates to Inheritance Tax.

General Principle: Secret trusts represent a relevant type of trust in the modern world.

Davies v Revenue and Customs Commissioners [2009] UKFTT 138 (TC)

Facts: The deceased was wife of a man that after dying left his estate to the wife. Estate duty was paid on his death. When the wife died, the daughters received the mother's estate that partly corresponded to what she received from the husband. HMRC tried to charge the estate to inheritance tax. The daughters claimed that between father and mother there was a secret trust for the benefit of the daughters and that the estate duty had already been paid in respect of that property when the father died. The question for the court was whether or not the property should have been left out of account for inheritance tax purposes. **Ratio: In order for a secret trust to be validly created, the trustee must be bound by the trust to hold the property for the benefit of the beneficiaries. Application:** The court held that there was no secret trust on the ground that the mother was absolute owner of the properties and not merely a trustee for the benefit of the daughters. The estate had to be taken into account for inheritance tax purposes.

<u>**Summary**</u>

- Secret equitable obligations are testamentary trusts that the testator wants to keep entirely or partially secret.

- This type of trust can be fully or half secret.

- Since this type of trusts is kept secret, it appears that secret trusts do not comply with the usual requirements for wills.

- The court has set specific requirements for secret trusts: intention, communication and acquiescence.

- When the trust is outright concealed on the face of the will, the trust is called fully secret trusts.

- It is essential that the communication of a fully secret trust takes place before death.

- Half secret trusts are those arrangements between the testator and the trustee where it is clear from the will that the property is left on trust for the benefit of someone, but the terms of the trust are kept secret.

- In order for the half secret trust to be considered validly executed, it must show consistency with the will of the testator.

- Communication must take place before or at the time of the execution of the will.

- A witness to a will cannot benefit from it.

- If the fully-secret trustee dies before the testator or disclaims the trust, the trust will fail.

- Prevention of fraud is the main reason why courts have opted for a wider interpretation of what is valid and what is not when dealing with testamentary obligations.

- The 'dehors the will' theory is based on the consideration that secret trusts are *inter vivos* trusts and they operate outside the will.

Chapter 9 - Charitable Trusts

Introduction

Charitable trusts are trusts created for a charitable purpose that benefits the society or a significant portion of it. The primary scope of adopting this type of trust was to enable property to be given for charitable purposes. Due to their public nature, they are enforced by the Attorney General.

Charitable trusts benefit of important advantages. Therefore, compliance with specific formalities is essential for validate the charitable nature of the trust:

- The purpose of the trust must be charitable.

- The charitable purpose must benefit the society or a sufficient portion of it.

- The purpose must be entirely and exclusively charitable.

Private purpose trusts created to benefit only defined individuals are by law void. On the contrary, charitable trusts are valid thanks to their public nature.

There are two Acts that discipline this type of trusts: The Charitable Act 2006 and the Charities Act 2011.

Certainty of Objects

Section 1(1) of the Charities Act 2011 defines the concept of charity.

(1) For the purposes of the law of England and Wales, "charity" means an institution which—

(a)is established for charitable purposes only, and

(b) falls to be subject to the control of the High Court in the exercise of its jurisdiction with respect to charities.

Charities are institutions exclusively created for charitable reasons and subjected to the jurisdiction of the English Law, even if the charitable purpose must be fulfilled abroad. The meaning given by Section 1(1) applies to the test of certainty of charitable purposes. In order for the test to be satisfied, the trust fund must solely be used for the charitable purpose. The charitable purpose does not need to be specified by settlor or testator. As long as the purpose is capable of being only charitable, the trust is valid. It is sufficient that the settlor or testator intends to apply the property for the charitable purpose. The purpose must be wholly and exclusively charitable.

General Principle: When a trust fails as charitable trust, the court may allow it as resulting trust.

Marice v Bishop of Durham [1804] 9 Ves 399
Facts: A fund was given upon trust for such objects of benevolence and liberality as the Bishop of Durham should approve. The question was whether the fund was charitable.
Ratio: If the object of a gift is not only charitable, the gift will fail as charitable trust. As Grant MR puts it in this case: *"It is now settled, upon authority, which is too late to controvert, that, where a charitable purpose is expressed, however general, the bequest shall not fail on account of the uncertainty of the object: but the particular mode of application will be directed by the King in some cases, in others by this court. I am not aware of any case, in which the bequest has been held charitable, where the testator has not either used that word, to denote its general purpose or specified some particular purpose, which this court has determined to be charitable in its nature"*.
Application: The court allowed the trust as resulting trust.

General Principle: If the trusts funds are capable of being devoted to both charitable and non-charitable purposes the gift will be invalid as a charity for uncertainty of objects.

IRC v City of Glasgow Police Athletic Association [1953] 1 All ER 747

Facts: In this case, an association had both charitable purposes (efficiency the police force) and non-charitable purposes (promotion of sports). **Ratio: The Court decided that the association could not be classified as charitable since it had some purposes that were not charitable. As Lord Nordman puts it:** *"The private advantage of member is a purpose for which the association is established and it therefore cannot be said that this is an association established for a public charitable purpose only. In principle, therefore, if an association has two purposes, one charitable and the other not, and if the two purposes are such and so related that the non-charitable purpose cannot be regarded as incidental to the other, the association is not a body established for charitable purposes only".*

Application: Where an association is both charitable and non-charitable, it will be declared non-charitable for uncertainty of objects.

General Principle: On construction, the court may consider benevolent purposes as having a much wider than charitable purposes.

Chichester Diocesan Fund v Simpson [1944] 2 All ER 60

Facts: A testator directed his executors to apply the residue of his estate "for such charitable or benevolent objects" as they might select. The executors assumed that the clause created a valid charitable gift and distributed most of the funds to charitable bodies. The question was to know whether or not the gifts were valid. **Ratio: The gifts failed as charity and a resulting trust was set up for the testator's estate. For Viscount Simon LC :** *"It appears to me that it inevitably follows that the phrase charitable or benevolent in a will must, in its ordinary context, be regarded as too vague to give the certainty necessary before such a provision can be supported or enforced."* **Application:**

The courts may construe the terms of a will when vague terms such as charitable purposes or benevolent objects are used.

Perpetuity

Private purpose trusts are subjected to the so-called perpetuity rule so that they can last only for a specific period. The rule of excessive duration does not apply to charities. Charitable trusts can exist perpetually. For instance, the life of universities can indefinitely be based on donations. Nevertheless, the rule applies to charitable gifts. In order for the rule to be satisfied the subject-matter of the gift must vest in the charity within the perpetuity period.

Charities

Section 1(1) of the Act states: For the purposes of the law of England and Wales, "charity" means an institution which –

(a) is established for charitable purposes only, and

(b) falls to be subject to the control of the High Court in the exercise of its jurisdiction with respect to charities.

Accordingly, a charity is an incorporated organisation or unincorporated association that has a charitable object for the public benefit.

- **Charitable incorporated organisations**

The Charities Act 2011 has introduced a specific form of organisation applied to charities, called the 'charitable incorporated organisation'. The CIO has been created with the purpose to facilitate the foundation of charities that want to benefit of the incorporation element without the creation of a company. The settlor or donor will simply need to apply to the Charity Commission for a CIO to be registered as charity. If accepted, the estate will become vested in the Charity Incorporated Organisation.

- **Unincorporated associations**

Unincorporated associations are formed by a group of people that join together in order to pursue a charitable purpose. The association is said to be unincorporated because the persons involved and the association itself are to legally separated. Usually there is a committee inside the association that is responsible in the management of the asset.

- **Fiscal advantages**

Charities and donors for charitable purposes enjoy several tax advantages such as relief from income and capital gains tax.

The *cy-pres* doctrine

The expression "cy-pres" comes from the Norman French. It literally means "near this" but has been progressively interpreted as meaning "as near as possible".

When the charitable purpose of the trust has been reached and there are residual of funds available, the remaining asset will go back to the settlor or testator by means of a resulting trust. The question is: What happens in those circumstances where the charitable trust has failed and part of the fund is still available? The *cy-pres* doctrine applies. The surplus funds will be used for another charitable purpose. In this way the charitable aspect of the trust will be preserved. Schemes may be approved by the Charity Commission and the courts for the application of the funds as nearly as possible to the original purposes as stated by the settlor.

There are two conditions to be satisfied for a *cy-pres* application: impossibility of carrying out the original charitable purpose or the existence of a surplus of funds after fulfilment and a general charitable intention by the donor as opposed to a specific intention.

- **Impossibility**

General Principle: The *cy-près* doctrine requires the impossibility or impracticability of carrying out the original charitable purpose.

Re dominion Students' hall Trust 1947 1 Ch 183
Facts: An association declared, a while ago, its object as being to maintain a hostel for "European students". A limited company was created for charitable purposes with a scheme: achieving the object of the organization by providing a hostel to every student regardless of the race. **Ratio: The test of impossibility was construed broadly and satisfied where a limited company was formed for charitable purposes. As Evershed put it: *"It is true that the word impossible should be given a wide significance. It is not necessary to go to the length of saying that the original scheme is absolutely impracticable ... It is said that to retain the condition, so far from furthering the charity's main object might defeat and it would be liable to antagonise those students, both white and coloured, whose support and good will it is the purpose of the charity to sustain. The case, therefore, can be said to fall within the broad description of impossibility."***
Application: The impossibility test lies on a broad conception of impossibility that may encompass many situations.

The impossibility criterion will also be satisfied when the existence of a surplus of funds after the charitable purpose has been fulfilled to apply. This possibility has been enshrined by the Charities act 2011.

- **General charitable intention**

The general intention of the donor is considered by the courts as being opposed to specific intentions. Here, the question for the courts was to determine whether the donor intended to benefit a general purpose or a specific charitable and identifiable body.

General Principle: A general charitable intention underlines the paramount element of charity as prevailing over the methods to fulfil the purpose.

Re Lysaght 1966 Ch 191
Facts: A testatrix bequeathed £5,000 to a College for scholarships allocated to students with disqualification for Jews and Roman Catholics. The College declined the gift but said that if the religious conditions was excised it would accept it. **Ratio: The court recalled the paramount intention of general charitable intention in order to supress a religious conditions that was undermining the noble cause of allocating funds to a college for studentships. Buckley J insisted on the distinction between general and specific charitable intention:** *"A general charitable intention may be said to be a paramount intention on the part of the donor to effect some charitable purpose which the court can find a method of putting into operation, notwithstanding that it is impracticable to give effect to some direction by the donor which is not an essential part of his true intention – not, that is to say part of his paramount intention. In contrast, a particular charitable intention exists where the donor means his charitable disposition to take effect if, but only if, it can be carried into effect in a particular specific way".*
Application: A broad margin of appreciation is left when it comes to construction of general charitable intention.

General Principle: Where there is an initial failure of the charitable institution, it is essential to prove a general charitable intention before the funds are applied *cy-près.*

Kings v Bultitude 2010 EWHC 1795 HC
Facts: In this case, the claimant is the executor and trustee of the will of the deceased. The gift in the will was in favour of a specific charitable purpose that ceased to exist after the death. However, the residuary estate of the deceased was transferred to another charitable institution, without proof of intention of the testatrix. The question was whether the situation involved a subsequent or initial failure of the charitable purposes.

Ratio: The gift stemming from the deceased's will was valid, and it has been correctly interpreted as relating to an initial failure.

Application: In order to apply a will *cy-près* it has to be proven before that there was a general charitable intention.

Nevertheless, there is one type of event where the courts have dispensed with the need to prove a general charitable intention. These are the cases that involve a subsequent failure of charitable purposes, when for example the charitable bodies exist at the appropriate date of vesting but cease to exist subsequently. The courts applied this exception to several situations:

- When the charity existed at the testator's death but was liquidated before the gift took effect (see **Re slevin 1891 2 Ch 236**).

- Where a charitable association ceased trading three years before the testatrix's death but was dissolved shortly after her death (see **Phillips v Royal Society for the Prtoection of birds 2012 EWHC 618**).

The public benefit element

Section 2(1) of the Charities Act 2011 defines charitable purposes as a purpose that presents a public benefit. In order to qualify for charitable status the entity is required to promote a benefit to the society in general or a community.

In 2008 the Charity Commission published some guidelines on the public benefit requirement that was modified few years later. It insisted on the distinction between the two aspects of the public benefit requirement.

On the one hand, the benefit aspect is identifiable an capable of being proved. It has to comply with one of the 13 charitable purposes laid down by the Charities act without any detriment or harm outweighing the benefit.

On the other hand, the public aspect refers to those who may benefit from the funds of the trust. It is required to be the public in general or a sufficient part of the public. However, there is no minimum standard of persons for this condition to be satisfied, this will be determined by the courts on a case by case approach taking into account the charitable purpose and impact on the public targeted. Here, family relationship, employment by an employer or other *inter se* link between people groups of individual will not satisfy the public aspect of the public benefit requirement.

Nevertheless, where trusts are introduced for the relief of poverty, they do not need to satisfy the public benefit test. This is the major exception of this requirement. The practice of the courts, since a long time before the adoption of the Charities act, has always been to exempt such trusts from the public benefit test. The justification of this exception lies on the fact that such trusts are prompted by motives of altruism from which stems inherent public benefit. This idea is illustrated by Lord Greene's Judgement in **Re Compton 1945 Ch 123**: *"There may perhaps be some special quality in gifts for the relief of poverty which places them in a class by themselves. It may, for instance, be that the relief of poverty is to be regarded as in itself so beneficial to the community that the fact that the gift is confined to a special family can be disregarded"*.

Charitable purposes

The only aspect specifically required in order for a charitable trust to be valid is the presence of a charitable purpose. The settlor or donor does not have to specify the purpose. The only essential element is the nature of the purpose that must be charitable. Prior to the introduction of the Charities Acts 2006 and 2011, jurisprudence has tried to classify the meaning of charitable purpose on the basis of the cases that reached the court. Few major categories have been recognised. Now there are 13 categories that have been enshrined by section 3 of the Charities Act. They will be presented successively. Even if the purpose of the trust seems to fall within one the categories, the public benefit element must still be ascertained.

It is important to note that, trusts having political purposes will not be considered as being charitable. This might cause trouble to charities trying to change the law.

- **The prevention or relief of poverty**

This category stems from the case of Pemsel's there the relief of aged, impotent and a poor person has been recognised as a valid charitable purpose. According to the Charities Act 2006 the categories that belong to this classification are the relief of the poor and the relief of those in need that encompasses relief of poverty and prevention of poverty. There is not a specific definition of poverty. The term can encompass those that do not have access to the usual things that belong to the everyday life on an individual or those that suffer for a temporary loss of finances.

General Principle: A person that suffers for a temporary financial difficulty may still fall into the category of those suffering of poverty.

Re Coulthurst [1951] Ch 661
Facts: This case concerned a bequest of £20,000 to trustees subject to the payment to widows and orphans of a sum depending of the decision of the trustees having regards to their financial circumstances. **Ratio: The court decided that, on construction of the terms of the gift, the gift was charitable for the relief of poverty. As Evershed MR stated in this case** *"Poverty does not mean destitution; it is a word of wide and somewhat indefinite import, it may not unfairly be paraphrased for present purposes as meaning persons who have to go short in the ordinary acceptation of that term, due regard being had to their status in life and so forth".*
Application: Trusts for persons suffering poverty may be considered as being intentioned for the prevention or relief of poverty, regardless to the fact that the financial difficulty is temporary or permanent.

In order for a trust for relief of poverty to be considered a charitable trust, it has to be proved case by case that the trust aims at benefiting the public. It is not enough to declare that the trust has been declared for the relief of poverty. The public benefit test must be satisfied. The reasoning behind this measure of control over charities created for relief of poverty is due to the fiscal advantages charities benefit.

General Principle: Before a charitable trust for the relief of poverty a specific interpretation must be given in order to assess the public benefit requirement.

Dingle v Turner [1972] AC 601
Facts: The testator decided to leave part of his estate on charitable trust for the relief of the poverty of the 'poor employees' of a company. The company had 600 employees and a significant number of ex-employees. The question for the court was whether the relief of poor employees amounted to a valid charitable purpose that could justify the benefit of the public requirement.
Ratio: In order for the trust to be considered a valid charitable one, it is essential that the trust benefits the public. As long as the beneficiaries are not specific individuals, but they represent a section of the public the public benefit test will be considered satisfied.
Application: The House of Lords held that the relief from a state of poverty for employees is a valid charitable purpose for the benefit of the public as much as charitable trusts for the benefit of relatives.

- **The advancement of education**

Education is a wide term that generally includes improving and disseminating knowledge, teaching, instruction, training and practice containing spiritual, moral, mental and physical elements.

General Principle: Education is not restricted to the classroom mode of disseminating knowledge, but requires some element of instruction or supervision.

Re Hopkins' Will Trust [1965] Ch 669

Facts: The Francis Bacon society received a gift on trust to carry out research on some Shakespeare's plays in order to identify the authorship of them. The assumption was that the plays had been wrongly attributed to Shakespeare and that their real author was Mr Bacon. **Ratio: It does not matter whether the assumption is right or wrong. It is essential that the purpose carries some kind of benefit for the public such as the attribution of some plays to Shakespeare or another author. As long as the purpose is not manifestly futile, the trust is valid.**

Application: The notion of education includes research and may encompass research of higher education.

The tax relief that stems from the charitable nature of the trust is important, mainly in relation to educational institutions. The test will be considered satisfied by looking at the beneficiaries of the trust. If the beneficiaries validly represent a portion of the public, the public element will be considered satisfied.

- **The advancement of religion**

The Charity Act 2011 refers to the broad sense of religion including monotheistic, polytheistic and religions that do not involve believing in God. The Goodman report insisted in 1976 on the fact that this should to be recognized only to monotheistic religions. Nevertheless there are not, in practice, a great number of cases recognizing non-Christian religions as being charitable. Although, Judaism has been considered being charitable in the case **Strauss v Goodsmith 1837** 8 Sim 614. In **Re South Place Ethical Society 1980** 1 WLR 1565, the court avoided the question where Buddhism was involved by underlining the advancement of education. However, the Supreme Court recently recognized the Scientology as a proper religion, in its judgement **R v Registrar general of births, deaths and marriages 2014** AC 610.

General Principle: The courts do not evaluate the merit of one religion as opposed to another, provided that the gift is not subversive of all morality, the gift will be charitable.

Thornton v Howe (1862) 31 Beav 14

Facts: A trust was created for the publication of the writings of Joanna Southcote who believed that she would miraculously conceive and give birth, at an advanced age, to the second Messiah. **Ratio: Although the judge thought that this belief or religion was completely foolish, deluded and confused, he held the gift as charitable.**

Application: Unlike trusts for the advancement of education, the courts do not evaluate the benefit to the public of religious instruction.

Considering the public benefit requirement, its benefit aspect is generally satisfied where the trust contributes to the traditional tenets of the religion when they are in line with the values of worship, tolerance, respect and peace. The public aspect is interpreted as to which extent the faith is embraced within the community.

- **The advancement of health or the saving of lives**

Section 3 (1) (d) of the Charities Act 2011 provides that *"advancement of health includes prevention or relief of sickness, disease or human suffering"*. The Charity Commission, in 2009 declared that it included *"Conventional methods as well as complementary, alternative or holistic methods which are concerned with healing the mind, body and spirit in the alleviation of symptoms and the cure of illness"*. The promotion of health has always been treated as a charitable purpose. It includes the establishment and maintenance of hospitals, the supply of contraceptives, the provision of a "home of rest" for nurses in a hospital and the provision of emergency services.

- **The advancement of citizenship**

This category includes any progress in citizenship participation to governance or community development. The Charity Commission considered that it encompasses charities promoting civic responsibility, empowerment of disadvantage communities because of social or economic disadvantages. Thus, voluntary organisations that are responsible for giving free or discounted legal advice or advice on business or employment opportunities may also satisfy this test.

- **The advancement of arts, culture, heritage etc.**

Such purposes have always been considered as charitable, event before the Charities act. Accordingly, the National Trust, the provision of museums, art galleries, craft fairs, the preservation of historic monuments will be classified as charitable under this head.

General Principle: In determining whether a collection of artefacts or assets ought to be available for public viewing, the courts consider the usefulness of the gift to society and for this purposes may take into account the opinions of experts.

Re Pinion (1964) 1 Ch 85, CA
Facts: Gifts of a studio and contents; to be maintained as a collection, were made to the National Trust. The national Trust refused the donation as a collection, although it was willing to accept selected items as valuable for display. The question for the Court was to determine whether the gifts were valuable a s a collection. The Court took into account expert reports. **Ratio: The Court, basing its decision on expert evidence, decided that the donation failed as a charity. The collection as a whole lacked any artistic merit. According to Harman LJ: "There is a strong body of evidence here that as a means of education this collection is worthless. I can conceive of no useful object to be served in foisting upon the public this mass of junk".**
Application: The courts, in order to determine if artistic donations can be declared charitable, will determine the usefulness of the gift to society. For this type of charitable purposes, the courts will look at the merit of the artwork donated.

- **The advancement of amateur sport**

According to Section 3 (2) (d) of the Charities act, *"sport"* refers to games promoting health by involving physical or mental skill or exertion. Conversely, sporting actives such as tiddlywinks, which clearly not promote health, will not be considered charitable.

General Principle: The promotion of football within schools and universities may be considered to be charitable for the advancement of education.

IRC v McMullen (1981) AC 1
Facts: The Football Association Youth Trust was established to promote football and other sports in schools and universities. The object was to provide physical education and develop the minds of the pupils. **Ratio: The House of Lords decided that the trust was charitable for the advancement of education. In this case, Lord Hailsham stated "I regard the limitation to the pupils of schools and universities in the instant case as a sufficient association with the provision of formal education to prevent any danger of vagueness in the object of the trust".**
Application: The promotion of sports may, in appropriate cases, be included under the heading "advancement of education".

General Principle: The provision of recreational facilities can be considered as charitable when it improves the conditions of life of the beneficiaries, irrespective of whether the participating members of society are disadvantaged or not

Guild v IRC (1992) 2 All ER 10, HL
Facts: A testator by his will disposed of the residue of his estate to the Town Council of North Beckwick "for the use in connection to sports". **Ratio: The Court held that the gift, namely the provision of recreational facilities, was charitable. As stated by Bridge LJ : "Hyde Park improves the conditions of life of residents in Mayfair and Belgravia as much as those in Pimlico or the Portobello Road, and the village hall may**

improve the conditions of life for residents for the squire and his family as well as the cottagers".

Application: Once again, in order to determine the charitable nature of the provisions of recreational facilities by a trust, the courts will evaluate its usefulness to society.

- ## The advancement of human rights

Section 3 (1) (d) enacts that "the advancement of human rights, conflict resolution or reconciliation or the promotion of religious or racial harmony or equality and diversity" are charitable. These values might be promoted by various ways such as empowering vulnerable groups by promoting education or provide assistance human rights violations' victims. As it was stated earlier, trusts having political purposes, such as an attempt to change the law for example will not be considered as being charitable. This concerns charities practicing lobbyism to official representatives to change de law in favour of human rights. For instance, in **McGovern v Attorney General 1981** 3 All ER 493, the High Court decided that the objects clause of Amnesty International was primarily political and therefore failed to be charitable.

General Principle: A charitable organisation must be exclusively charitable and should not seek any political purpose.

McGovern v AG (1981) 3 All ER 493, HC
Facts: Amnesty international, an unincorporated, non-profit making association, established a trust and sought registration with the Charity Commissioners. **Ratio: The organisation was not declared charitable because some of its purpose were political (for example the abolition of death penalty) and therefore did not comply with the definition of charitable purposes. Even though the organisation had mainly charitable purposes (such as the promotion of research into the maintenance and observance of human rights, they were not exclusively charitable.**

Application: The line between political purposes and the advancement of human rights might be very thin in some cases. For example, intentions to amend current law will may determine political purposes.

- **The advancement of environmental protection**

This fundamental principle of conservation of the environment includes areas of natural beauty, as well as particular species of flora and fauna. Little needs to be said as to the obvious benefit to society in promoting the protection of our planet. For example, the National Trust is charitable: **Re Verrall** [1916] 1 Ch 100, and in 2002, the Charity Commission decided that a company whose aim was to 'protect and safeguard the environment particularly through the promotion of re-use and recycling and the provision of recycling facilities' was charitable.

- **The relief of those in need because of youth, age etc.**

This category includes people in need because of youth, age, ill-health, disability, financial hardship or other disadvantages. There is an overlap with the relief of poverty here. Therefore section 3 (2) (e) has specified that this concerned the provision of accommodation or care to the groups mentioned above. According to the case law, this may also include the provision of medical care, meals or simply guidance and assistance for vulnerable groups. At first sight this would appear to preclude trusts which would benefit the rich. However there are disadvantages, such as loneliness, which cannot be relieved by wealth.

- **The advancement of animal welfare**

A trust promoting animal welfare in general or a particular species of animals will be classified as charitable. The justification for this recognition lies on the fact that these purposes seek to promote public morality by checking an inborn tendency in humans toward cruelty. In **Re Grove-Grady** [1929] 1 Ch 557, the purpose of the trust was 'to provide a refuge for the preservation of all animals, birds or other creatures not human so that they shall be safe from molestation or destruction by man'. This was held not to be charitable. The purpose did not give advantage to animals which are beneficial to mankind, protect animals generally from cruelty or denote any elevating lesson to mankind.

- **The promotion of the efficiency of the armed forces.**

Section 3 (1) (l) of the Charities act provides that "*the promotion of the efficiency of the armed forces of the Crown or of the efficiency of the police, fire and rescue services or ambulances services*" are charitable purposes. These purposes were charitable at common law. In **Re Gray** [1924] Ch 362 a gift to promote sport in a regiment was calculated to improve the physical efficiency of the army and was charitable.

- **Any other purposes**

Section 3 (1) (m) opens up a broad category of charitable purposes similar to the miscellaneous charitable purposes that were recognized by the case law before the adoption of the charities act. This is a sort of clause of flexibility that permits the court to recognize new charitable purposes as the need arises. It has been referred by the doctrine as a residual category of charitable purposes. Illustrations include:

- The general improvement of agriculture (see **IRC v Yorkshire Agricultural Society 1928** 1 KB 611)

- A gift to benefit black community (see **Re Harding 2007 EWHC 3**)

- A gift for the relief of national debt (see **Newland v AG 1809** 3 MER 684)

Summary

- The privileges enjoyed by charities are in respect of taxation, certainty of objects, the rule against perpetuities and the *cy-près* doctrine.

- Charitable trusts are trusts created for a charitable purpose that benefits the society or a significant portion of it. Their purpose must be entirely and exclusively charitable.

- Charitable trusts must the public benefit requirement. On the one hand, the benefit aspect is identifiable an capable of being proved. On the other hand, the public aspect refers to those who may benefit from the funds of the trust. It is required to be the public in general or a sufficient part of the public.

- As an exception, the public benefit test is not required when trusts for the relief of poverty are involved.

- The *cy-près* doctrine is unique to charitable trusts. In order to be applied to a trust, it requires two conditions to be satisfied: the impossibility or impracticability of carrying out the original charitable purpose and a general charitable intention.

- Where there is an initial failure of the charitable institution, it is essential to prove a general charitable intention before the funds are applied *cy-près.*

- Proof of a general charitable intention is unnecessary in cases of subsequent failure of charitable purposes.

- The Charities Act 2011 lists 12 traditional categories of charitable purposes that were already recognized by common law. An additional residual category permits to recognize new charitable purpose.

- In order for a trust to be classified charitable, it has to be covered by one of the 13 categories laid down in the Charities Act 2011.

Chapter 10 –

Resulting and Constructive Trusts

Introduction

Express trusts are trusts which are set-up by the deliberate act of a settlor. Resulting and constructive trusts arise by the operation of the law rather than directly through the intention of the settlor. In some circumstances the court may imply the existence of a trust.

<u>Resulting Trusts</u>

The expression resulting trust comes from a Latin expression *'reasalire'* which means to *'jump back'* and a resulting trust if interoperated literally from it ethnological origin the expression means that it is a trust which arises in favour of the settlor. There is a distinction that is made between automatic resulting trusts and presumed resulting trust. The creation of a resulting trust does not require an express declaration of the trust, so that the usual rules of formalities do not apply. The absence of compliance to the usual rules of formalities allows resulting trusts to be created in miscellaneous sets of circumstances, such as:

(a) When the transferor has not parted with the whole of the beneficial interest;
(b) When there is voluntary conveyance into another's name; and
(c) When a buyer has, property conveyed into the name of another and the person that puts up the money obtains a beneficial interest under resulting trust.

Courts have identified few categories of resulting trusts. Nevertheless, they do not represent a conclusive classification since new circumstances may lead to the identification of future categories.

<u>Automatic resulting trusts</u>

An automatic resulting trust is a trust that arises when an express trust has been established and the express trust fails in whole or in part. When the property of an express trust has been transferred but the trust itself fails, it becomes an automatic resulting trust. The consequence is that the trust property is held on trust for the settlor in a resulting trust.

General Principle: When a gift is reached without the use of all the money, the surplus is held on resulting trust.

Re Abbott Fund Trusts, Smith v Abbott [1900] 2 Ch 326
Facts: A trust was set-up following an appeal for funds to provide an income for two deaf and dumb women. The two women then died and the issue was what would happen to the remaining funds and it was held this was effectively a trust for maintaining the two women and when they died the purpose of the trust no longer remained and the trust effectively failed.
Ratio: Any remaining funds were held on resulting trust and the settlors were all the people that had contributed to the fund.
Application: The property was held for the contributors and subscribers of the fund in proportions to their contributions as resulting trust.

General Principle: Where the money is held upon trust and the trusts declared do not exhaust the fund it will revert to the donor or settlor under resulting trust.

Re Gillingham Bus Disaster Fund [1958] Ch 300
Facts: A fund was set-up following an appeal after an accident that killed several royal marine cadets. The Mayors raised over £9,000 which exceeded what was required. The question for the court was what should have happened to the surplus.
Ratio: To have a charitable trust, there must be compliance to the beneficiary principle so that there must be certainty in relation to the beneficiaries. Otherwise, the trust is not valid and the property goes *bona vacantia* to the Crown. Where the donor does part with the money *sub modo* to the intent that

the trust should be carried out into effect, once the effect is reached, the surplus still belongs to him.

Application: It turned out that the trust was invalid because it was said to be a purpose trust and because it was not charitable. The court stated that the money was held in a resulting trust for the contributors and that the Crown could not claim the surplus as *bona vacantia*.

General Principle: On closure of a fund for the benefit of third parties there is no resulting trust in favour of subscribers or outright donors.

Re West Sussex Constabulary's Benevolent Fund Trusts [1971] Ch 1

Facts: Members of the West Sussex Constabulary created a fund for granting allowances to widows and dependants of decease members. The funds had come from identifiable donations and legacies, members' subscriptions, collecting boxes and proceeds of entertainment, sweepstakes and raffles. The question for the court concerned the distribution of the remaining fund, once the purpose was no longer feasible. **Ratio: When the fund remains *bona vacantia*, there is no room for resulting trust and the fund simply goes to the Crown. The fund is not held bona vacantia if the contributors paid the money for a specific purpose that is no longer feasible so that they can receive the remaining fund back.**

Application: The court held that in a case of unincorporated associations where the association wound up the purpose failed and the money in the fund would be held on a resulting trust for the settlor, in this case identifiable donations and legacies. Members' subscriptions, collecting boxes and sweepstakes were not allowed to receive the remaining fund.

General Principle: Resulting trusts may be classified as 'presumed' resulting trusts or 'automatic' resulting trusts.

Vandervell v IRC [1967] 2 AC 291

Facts: A wealthy business man who wished to make a gift, in a way which was most tax efficient for him. This kind of operation led to a series of very complicated transactions by which he tried to make the gift by avoiding to generate any tax liability. A bank held certain shares as Vandervell's nominee. In 1958 Vandervell transferred them to the Royal College of Surgeons. The transfer was subjected to an option, for Vandervell to purchase the shares back within 5 years on payment of GBP 5,000 in favour of Vandervell Trustees Ltd, whose main function was to act as trustee of a settlement on Vandervell's children. Although the option was granted by the royal college of surgeons the court approached it on the basis that the potion was held on trust and then acquired by the Vandervell Trustees Ltd. It was clear that the option was granted on trust and Vandervell effectively created trust, because he instructed the college to grant the option. But Vandervell had at no time declared what the terms of the trust were since his plan was to declare subsequently what the terms of the trust would have been. **Ratio: Automatic resulting trusts are called automatic because the resulting trust for the settlor arises automatically by operation of law from the fact that the trust has failed or the settlor has failed to disclose the terms of the trust. Sometime what will happen is that the trust may be valid but incomplete in the sense it makes no provision for the eventuality of the beneficiary's death. Therefore, the resulting trust doctrine fills out what is left unsaid.**

Application: It was held to be a failed trust and that there was a resulting trust for Vandervell. Vandervell was assessed to surtax on the basis that the dividends which had been paid to the college were to be treated as his income. The court pointed out that when a trust has been created without specifying its terms, the interest will revert to the settlor through a resulting trust.

Conditional payment or loan

Payments contingent on the performance of actions or money lent by banks always result in resulting trusts.

General Principle: Conditional payments or loans fall into the category of resulting trusts. The money that represents the loan must not become part of the general asset of the borrower for the resulting trust to be created.

Barclays Bank Ltd v Quistclose Investment Ltd [1970] AC 567
Facts: Rolls Razor Ltd became liable to pay its shareholders. The company did not have enough available cash to pay its shareholders. They arranged to obtained a loan from Quitclose investment Ltd upon the terms that the money lent was to be used solely to enable Rolls Razor to pay the dividend to its shareholders. Rolls Razor sent the Quitclose cheque for the sum lent together with a covering letter revealing the purpose of the loan to their bank, which placed the money in a specially opened account named "No.4 ordinary dividend share account." At all material times Rolls Razor Ltd was heavily in debt to the bank. Before the payment of the dividend Rolls Razor Ltd went into voluntary liquidation. The bank claimed to be able to set-off the money in the No.4 account against Rolls Razors Co's indebtedness to it. The question arose as to who owned the money in the No. 4 account. Plowman J. upheld the bank's claim, but the Court of Appeal reversed his decision. The case went to the House of Lords. **Ratio: Where money is lent to the borrower for a specific purpose and the purpose fails, there is no beneficial interest in the money lent. The borrower holds the money upon resulting trust for the lender.**
Application: The court dismissed the bank's appeal on the following grounds:
(1) that not only was Rolls Razor Ltd under a legal contractual obligation to repay to Quitclose the money lent (which was not disputed), but since the and only purpose of the loan had failed the money was subject to a resulting trust for Quitclose and
(2) that it was plain that the bank knew of the purpose of the loan and was therefore a trustee of the money for Quitclose.

Presumed resulting trusts

Where someone gratuitously transfers property to another or purchases property which he puts in another persons' name, then under the doctrine of presumed resulting trusts, although that person receiving the property has legal title, the beneficial interest in the property lies with the person transferring or buying the property. There is a presumption when a gratuitous transfer of property takes place that when the recipient has not provided any consideration, then equity presumes that no gift was intended and that it was intended to appoint a nominal owner, a legal title owner where the beneficial title should remain with the person making the gift. This is called a presumed resulting trust because it is based on a presumption, that beneficial interest in the gift should be retained.

Presumptions of advancement

In some circumstances, under s. 60(3) Law of Property Act 1925, there is a contrary presumption of advancement and the presumption of advancement arises because of some special relationship between the parties. If a father makes a transfer of property to a child or if the father buys property on puts this in his child's name then instead of a presumption of a resulting trust, there is a presumption of advancement. Therefore, the child is the absolute owner of the property. A presumption of advancement arises as between a father and child and this stems from the legal responsibility of a father to support his children. These doctrines of presumptions are quite ancient. They date from the eighteenth century and before. Consequently, they tend to be old fashioned and traditionally there is no presumption of advancement in a case of transfer from a mother and a child, because traditionally maintenance of the child has been with the father and not the mother. Similarly, there is a presumption of advancement in the case of a transfer from a husband to his wife, but not the other way around.

Lord Diplock said in **Pettit v Pettit** [1970] AC 777 at 842:

"It would, in my view, be an abuse of the legal technique for ascertaining or imputing intention to apply to transactions between the post-war generation of married couples' "presumptions" which are based upon inferences of fact which an earlier generation of judges drew as to the most likely intentions

of earlier generations of spouses belonging to the propertied classes of a different social era."

The court will not rely on presumptions based on outdated social attitude, they will instead consider evidence on what the actual intention was, but it appears that traditional presumptions of that sort will be disregarded.

Evidence of an illegal purpose

Evidence of an illegal purpose refers to those circumstances where people have made transfers and rely on a resulting trust. Even where title to property has been acquired in a course of illegal conduct, a Claimant to an interest in it may still seek to assert his claim, so long as he does not plead, or rely on, an illegality.

General Principle: In those circumstances where a person enjoys an equitable interest by way of a resulting trust and only subsequently illegality occurs, illegality is not decisive.

Tinsley v Milligan [1993] 3 All ER 65
Facts: The parties were two women that purchased a house in the sole name of one, the Claimant, but on the understanding that they were both joint beneficial owners of the property. The purpose of the purchase was to perpetrate a social security fraud. When the parties fell out, the Claimant, in whose name the house was registered, asserted her right to sole ownership of the property. The Defendant argued that she had an equitable right in the property. The question for the court was whether the Claimant could rely on the presumption of a resulting trust, to try and assert ownership, first having made the transfer for fraud. The court allowed this, and the Claimant appealed.
Ratio: The most important application of an assumed resulting trust is the situation where a couple buy a property

together. The basic rule here is the person who provided the money is presumed to have intended to retain ownership of the property; this is the traditional presumption under the doctrine of presumed resulting trusts. Similarly, if a house is brought with equal proportions then the presumption is that they hold it under a resulting trust in the proportions to their contributions.

Application: The appeal was dismissed because, even though the property had been acquired for fraudulent purposes, the equitable right of the claimant would stand.

Constructive Trusts

Equity recognises the validity of constructive trusts when a person holds a property for the benefit of another moved by justice and good conscience. The circumstances in which constructive trusts may be recognised by the courts are several and they may increase in time on discretion of the court. Constructive trust usually requires the performance of only one duty, such as the transfer of the property to the beneficiary entitled to it. The beneficiary can obtain the property from the trustee by way of constructive trust.

Constructive trusts imposed for unconscionable conduct

A constructive trust is another category of trust, which arises by the operation of law. The basic notion is that a constructive trust arises to frustrate or as a remedy for fraudulent or unconscionable conduct.

"A constructive trust is one which arises by operation of the law, and not by intention of the parties, express or implied." Martin, Modern Equity.

"A constructive trust is a trust which is imposed by equity to satisfy the demands of justice and good conscience, without reference to any express or presumed intention of the parties." Carl Zeiss Stiftung v Herbert Smith No 2 (1969).

Furthermore,

"A constructive trust is the formula through which the conscience of equity finds expression. When property has been acquired in such circumstances that the holder of the legal estate may not in good conscience retain the beneficial interest, equity converts him into a trustee." Beatty v Guggenheim Exploration Co. (1919).

General Principle: Equity does not allow statute to be used as an instrument of fraud.

Rochefoucauld v Boustead [1897] 1 Ch 196

Facts: The Claimant conveyed property to the Defendant after he had agreed to hold the property on trust for the Claimant. The problem was that per the statutory provision under **Section 53(1)(b)** of the Law of Property Act 1925 *'A declaration of trust respecting any land or any interest therein must be manifested and proved by some writing signed by some person who is able to declare such trust or by his will'.* It appeared this was an invalid trust and therefore the Defendant argued he owned the property beneficially. The Defendant was trying to go back on his agreement of holding the property for the Claimant, and he evoked this statutory provision, which states a trust is invalid unless it is evidenced and documented.

Ratio: An arrangement between the parties may be looked at as a valid trust even if it does not comply with statutory formalities in the presence of an attempt of fraud.

Application: The court applied the maxim and held that the Defendant did in fact hold that property on trust for the Claimant.

General Principle: A constructive trust arises from the operation of law to prevent fraud and it is not subject to any requirement.

Bannister v Bannister [1948] 2 All ER 133

Facts: The Defendant inherited two cottages from the husband. Mrs Bannister sold both cottages to the Claimant, her brother-in-law under market value, on the oral undertaking by the Claimant to let her stay in one of the cottages rent free. Later, despite the oral agreement, the Claimant gave the Defendant notice to quit.

Since the widow did not leave the cottage, the Claimant claimed possession of the cottage. **Ratio: Fraud occurs as soon as the absolute character of the conveyance is set up for defeating the beneficial interest. Denial of the existence of the trust amounts to fraud.**

Application: The courts said there was a constructive trust. Since the Defendant sold the two cottages under market value on the faith of the oral undertaking and would not otherwise have done so, the court looked at the undertaking as having reserved the Defendant a benefit.

Situations where constructive trusts arise

The constructive trust, says Jill Martin, '*is usually regarded as a residual category; one which is called into play when the court desires to impose a trust and no other suitable category is available*'. The constructive trust arises in situations where the court will determine (a) the existence of a trusteeship or the terms of the trust. For instance:

- In cases of unauthorised profits by fiduciaries. For example trustees and company directors (**Boardman v Phipps** [1967] 2 AC 46).

- Where a statute has been used as an instrument of fraud **5Rochefoucauld v Boustead** [1897] 1 Ch 196).

- Where a purchaser has undertaken to recognise another's rights even only as licensees (**Lyus v Prowsa** [1982] 1 WLR 1044).

- The 'joint venture' constructive trust: where the claimant and defendant have entered into an arrangement whereby one acquires property for the benefit of both, but the agreement has not been properly evidenced (**Banner Homes Group plc v Luff Developments Ltd** [2000] Ch 371).

- Where a person acts as executor/administrator of an estate without obtaining proper authority (referred to as an executor/administrator *de son tort*) – **James v Williams** [1999] 3 All ER 309.

- Where a joint tenant kills joint tenant, or a beneficiary under a will kills the testator or the beneficiary under a life insurance policy kills the policy-holder.

- In cases of mutual wills (**Re Cleaver** [1981] 1 WLR 939).

- Where property has been stolen (Lord Browne-Wilkinson in **Westdeutsche Landesbank Girozentrale v Islington London Borough Council** [1996] AC 669).

- Co-ownership disputes where the beneficial interests have not been declared (**Stack v Dowden** [2007] UKHL).

Strictly speaking, liability as a constructive trustee exists only where the relevant property is vested in the defendant. If no property has been vested in the defendant, s/he may be subject to a duty to account which is a personal remedy; but the defendant is often, misleadingly said to be "liable to account as a constructive trustee" in this situation. Many writers, including **Sir Peter Millett** (then Millett LJ, eventually Lord Millett), have argued it would be more straightforward simply to say that the defendant is "liable to account".

Institutional v remedial constructive trusts

Within the Common Law world, constructive trusts may be seen either as a recognition by the court of a pre-existing interest in property or a remedy to give the property interest to the person who should have it. Thus, remedial constructive trusts have to be distinguished of institutional constructive trusts. As Hemsworth has put it: '*First there is the institutional constructive trust where the court's role is to declare or confirm an existing trust, usually where the constructive trustee seeks to refute the beneficiary's interest; and secondly there is the remedial constructive trust, where the court is asked as a matter of the exercise of its discretionary powers rooted in equity to impose a trust by way of remedy to the client'* ((2000) at 163).

Remedial constructive trusts are well-developed in Australia, New Zealand and Canada and arise *'where a person holding title to property is subject to an equitable duty to convey it to another on the ground that he would be unjustly enriched if he were permitted to retain it'* (**A. Scott,** (1955) 71 LQR 39), or to redress unconscionable behaviour – **Pettkus v Becker** (1980) 117 DLR (3d) 257 (wife entitled to a half-share in the house on the basis of extensive indirect contributions e.g. labour).

General principle: The remedial constructive trust has not been accepted in England.

Halifax BS v Thomas [1996] Ch 217 per Peter Gibson LJ at 226, 229
Facts: In this case, the defendant fraudulently obtained a mortgage; the flat was repossessed by the mortgagee and sold; the mortgagee sought to keep the profit to prevent the defendant from profiting from his fraud, but the CA refused to impose a remedial constructive trust.
Ratio: *'There is no English authority to support the proposition that a wrongdoing defendant will be required to account for a profit which is not based on the use of the property of the wronged plaintiff. ...English law has not followed other jurisdictions where the constructive trust has become a remedy for unjust enrichment'*
Application: In England, remedial constructive trust cannot be granted by Courts to provide remedy to give the property interest to the person who should have it.

However, there have been calls to introduce remedial constructive trusts. *'Although the resulting trust is an unsuitable basis for developing proprietary restitutionary remedies, the remedial constructive trust, if introduced in English law, may provide a more satisfactory road forward'* (**Westdeutsche v Islington LBC [1996] AC 669 per Lord Browne-Willkinson at 716**).

One problem with the remedial constructive trust is the effect it may have on the rights of third parties and namely for other creditors on an insolvency. In **London Allied Holdings Ltd v Anthony Lee [2007] EWHC 2061 Ch, Etherton** J noted that no English authority categorically denies the possibility of a remedial constructive trust, and added that ' ... *there still seems scope for real debate about a model more suited to English jurisprudence, borrowing from proprietary estoppel: namely, a constructive trust by way of discretionary restitutionary relief, the right to which is a mere equity prior to judgment, but which will have priority over the intervening rights of third parties on established principles, such as those relating to notice, volunteers and the unconscionability on the facts of a claim by the third party to priority*'.

Institutional constructive trusts which are currently recognized in England and Wales will only be imposed where the court recognises a proprietary interest held by someone other than the legal owner which exists prior to the court order, and will then be followed by a remedy to convey the property to the identified beneficial owner However, the trust is not the remedy itself. In contrast, the remedial constructive trust creates a new interest on the part of the 'rightful' owner. The idea behind an institutional constructive trust is quite simple: the court is required to identify certain facts which have occurred in the past which have given rise to the imposition of such a trust.

There is disagreement as to the breadth of the constructive trust jurisdiction. At present there is reluctance to apply equitable remedies in commercial situations because commercial relationships are conducted at arm's length with legal advice: parties to a contract do not generally owe each other fiduciary obligations But some authorities, namely Lord Millett, would like to extend the jurisdiction more into the commercial world. Many of the more recent cases on constructive trusts involve a background of commerce or investment, rather than what one might think of as a traditional private trust.

Bribes received by fiduciaries and constructive trusts

A bribe exists when property is received by a fiduciary in order to perform a service that betrays the trust bestowed on him by his principal.

Definition

Much judicial and academic learning has been devoted to attempts to define the term "fiduciary", particularly in Australia and Canada. In England, as usual, we have tried to muddle through without attempting a definition, believing that anyone can recognise a fiduciary when he sees one. The judiciary finally drawn a definition '*A fiduciary is someone who has undertaken to act for or on behalf of another in a particular matter in circumstances which give rise to a relationship of trust and confidence. The distinguishing obligation of a fiduciary is the obligation of loyalty*' (**Bristol & West Building Society v Mothew [1998]**).

The circumstances, not the role, are what give rise to a fiduciary relationship. The category of fiduciaries is not closed – **English v Dedham Vale Properties Ltd** [1978] 1 WLR 93; **Reading v A-G** [1951] AC 507.

Rationale

The principle is a strict one. As **Tang Han Wu**, puts it: 'Equity takes a harsh view of fiduciaries. Harsh profit-stripping rules were evolved to ensure that this underlying policy behind fiduciary law was achieved. In short, these rules were meant to act as a strong deterrent and have a prophylactic effect to discourage the fiduciary from breaching his duty'.

For many years there was uncertainty in English law as to the legal position if someone (F) who is a fiduciary - this will include employees working for an employer or other principal (P) - takes a bribe (or makes a secret profit, or takes a secret commission) in the course of their engagement. The cases all agreed that P could claim the value of any money, or other asset, that was given to F. What was unclear was whether F was simply 'liable to account' to P (i.e. F was under a personal liability), or whether F held the money or other property 'on constructive trust', in the sense that P had a proprietary claim to the money or property.

An important evolution of jurisprudence of the UK courts occurred on this issue. A first range of cases established that the procurement of the bribe was involving a debtor/creditor relationship as the property in the bribe has passed to the recipient. A personal claim to account lay against the recipient of the bribe. This was the initial, and now out of date, basis for liability (see **Heiron 1880**). Recently, the Supreme Court overruled this solution in **European ventures 2014**, by enshrining that a proprietary claim based on a constructive trust arose in favour of the principal or claimant, as the bribe represents money or assets belonging to the principal.

General principle: The liability of the fiduciary was personal and involved a duty to account.

Metropolitan Bank v Heiron (1880) 5 ex D 319
Facts: A director of company received a bribe and pleaded a limitation defence on the ground that the company could not treat the bribe as its property. **Ratio: "The ground of this suit is concealed fraud. If a man receives money by way of a bribe for misconduct against a company or any person against whom he stands in a fiduciary position, he is liable to have that money taken from him by his principal. But it must be borne in mind that that liability is a debt only differing from ordinary debts in the fact that it is merely equitable, and in dealing with equitable debts of such a nature Courts of Equity have always followed by analogy the provisions of the Statute of Limitations".**
Application: The director of a company receiving a bribe is able to plead a limitation defence, he is personally liable since his liability involves a duty to account.

General principle: The bribes and the subsequent property acquired by the fiduciary are subject to the claims of the injured party.

A-G for Hong Kong v Reid [1994] 1 AC 324
Facts: The DDP of Hong Kong government, Mr. Ried, had a proprietary claim over houses purchased in New Zealand with bribes taken by a prosecutor in HK. In the meantime the properties had decreased in value. The question in issue concerned the status of a fiduciary who received a bribe, in particular, whether such a fiduciary became a mere debtor for the innocent party or alternatively a trustee for the aggrieved party.
Ratio: Lord Templeman: "When a bribe is offered and accepted in money or in kind, the money or property constituting the bribe belongs in low to the recipient. As soon as the bribe was received, whether in cash or in kind, the false fiduciary geld the bribe on a constructive trust for the person injured".
Application: Since the representative property had decreased in value, the fiduciary was liable to account for the difference between the bribe and the undervalue.

However, in **Sinclair Investments (UK) Ltd v Versailles Trade Finance Ltd** (In Administration) [2011] EWCA Civ 347; [2011] 3 WLR 1153 the Court of Appeal followed Lister v Stubbs and declined to follow **A-G HK v Reid**. Although the case involved secret profits made from a commercial fraud rather than bribes, the CA held that profits obtained in breach of a fiduciary duty were subject to a personal liability to account, but not to a proprietary claim. This case prompted widely divergent comments from academics.

FHR European v Mankarious [2013] EWCA Civ 17 illustrates the difficulties the courts were encountering in applying the old law in general and Sinclair v Versailles in particular. At first instance Simon J stated that he was applying **Sinclair v Versailles** and held Cedar Capital Partners accountable in equity, but did not find a constructive trust. The Court of Appeal reversed him on this, saying that they were also following Sinclair v Versailles, but that the facts in the instant case were distinguishable from those in Sinclair v Versailles, so it fell within one of the exceptions mentioned in that case: the Court of Appeal therefore found that there was a constructive trust.

General principle: The principal is entitled to the benefit of the fiduciary's unauthorized acts in the course of his agency.

FHR European Ventures LLP v Cedar Capital Partners LLP [2014] UKSC 45
Facts: The claimants asked the defendants to negotiate with a third party to negotiate and conclude a very onerous contract with a third party. The defendants and the third party entered into a brokerage agreement to facilitate the conclusion of the agreement with the claimant in return for a €10 million commission. The defendant claimed for a traditional debtor/creditor relationship, despite his fiduciary's duties relying on **Heiron.**
Ratio: "The principal is entitled to the benefit of the agent's unauthorised acts in the course of his agency, in just the same way as, at law, an employer is vicariously liable to bear the burden of an employee's unauthorised breaches of duties in the course of his employment. The agent's duty is accordingly to deliver up to his principal the benefit, which he has obtained, and not simply to pay compensation for having obtained it in excess of his authority. The way that legal effect can be given to an obligation to deliver up specific property to the principal is by treating the principal as specifically entitled to it".
Application: The Supreme Court declared that the secret commission of € 10 million was held on constructive trust for the claimant.

The Supreme Court therefore overruled Lister v Stubbs and Sinclair v Versailles and held that bribes and secret commissions should and would be held on a proprietary constructive trust. Although it was conceded that allowing a proprietary claim would work against the unsecured creditors of F, there was no real injustice to them here, as the bribe ought never to have been an asset of F [43].

The decision in **FHR European Ventures LLP v Cedar Capital Partners LLC** resolves the question of whether a covert profit or gratuity resulting from a transgression of fiduciary duty is held on constructive trust (the answer is yes), but that its reasoning has been criticised. In **Crown Prosecution Service v. Aquila Advisory Service Ltd [2021]** UKSC 49, the Supreme Court employed this principle without criticism in determining the consequences of imposing a constructive trust. It was determined that, as a result of the existence of a constructive trust, the beneficiaries of the trust (the person to whom the fiduciary duty was owed) could claim the covert commission/bribe from the constructive trustee ahead of those who had a personal claim against the trustee.

According to other case law; some profits are unauthorized because of the position of the beneficiary. A fiduciary must not take advantage of his position to make an unauthorised benefit for himself or herself (**Boardman v Phipps** [1967] 2 AC 46). This duty has been extended to trustees of the home – **Protheroe v Protheroe** [1968] 1 WLR 519 – and to business partners – **Thompson's Trustee v Heaton** [1974] 1 WLR 605; **Popat v Shonchhatra** [1995] 1 WLR 908.

Purchase of trust property

The courts have developed a rule prohibiting trustees and other fiduciaries, without authority, from purchasing the trust property. If the purchase takes place the transaction is treated as voidable at the instance of the beneficiary. If a trustee or retired trustee purchases his beneficiary's beneficial interest, the beneficiary can have the sale set aside unless the trustee can establish the propriety of the transaction – **Tito v Waddell (No 2)** [1977] Ch 106 (the 'fair-dealing rule'). The trustee must show that:

1. He took no advantage of his position

2. The beneficiary was fully informed, and
3. The beneficiary received full value.

General principle: The fiduciary is prohibited from taking personal profits from any activity connected with his status as a fiduciary.

Regal (Hastings) Ltd v Gulliver [1942] 1 All ER 378

Facts: The Company received an offer from one of its subsidiaries to sell shares.

The company did not buy them but four of its directors subscribed for the shares personally and sold later them for a profit. All the transactions were *bona fide*. The company claimed that the directors were accountable for their profit.

Ratio: 'The rule of equity, which insists on those, who by use of a fiduciary position make a profit, being liable to account for that profit, in no way depends on absence of bona fides; or upon such questions or considerations as whether the profit would or should otherwise have gone to the plaintiff, or whether the profiteer was under a duty to obtain the source of the profit for the plaintiff, or whether he took a risk or acted as he did for the benefit of the plaintiff, or whether the plaintiff had in fact been damaged or benefited by his action. The liability arises from the mere fact of a profit having, in the stated circumstances, been made. The profiteer, however honest and well intentioned, cannot escape the risk of being called upon to account' (per Lord Russell).

Application: Company directors must not take advantage of their position to make personal profit. Trustees may retain directors' fees if they are appointed trustee independently of their shareholding capacity or if they were a director before they were a trustee.

Summary

- Resulting or constructive trusts arise by the operation of the law.

- A resulting trust is a trust which arises in favour of the settlor. When the settlor transfer a property to a person, but something occurs to trigger the trust, the property is then held by that person on trust for the settlor.

- 'Resulting' refers to the fact that the beneficial interest in the property returns to the settlor.

- Resulting trusts may be created in miscellaneous sets of circumstances.

- An automatic resulting trust is a trust that arises when an express trust has been established but it fails in whole or in part.

- Payments contingent on the performance of actions or money lent by banks represent resulting trusts.

- Where someone gratuitously transfer property to another or purchases property which he puts in another persons' name, then under the doctrine of presumed resulting trusts, although that person receiving the property has legal title the beneficial interest in the property lies with the person transferring or buying the property.

- A contrary presumption of advancement may occur in some circumstances where there is a special relationship between the parties.

- Evidence of an illegal purpose refers to those circumstances where people have made transfers and rely on a resulting trust.

- Equity recognises the validity of constructive trusts when a person holds a property for the benefit of another moved by justice and good conscience.

- Trusts of the matrimonial or quasi-matrimonial home concern shared properties such as matrimonial homes shared by husband and wife that courts may allocate as they think appropriate amongst married couple in the eventuality of divorce.

- Normally during the purchase of a house, a solicitor produces a written declaration of trust that states who owns the property and in what shares.

- Per the new doctrine developed by the court, there are two circumstances in which a constructive trust may arise despite the absence of a written declaration.

- The court will find a Resulting or Constructive trust if it can be shown that there is an agreement or common intention with detrimental reliance between the parties.

Chapter 11 –
Trusts for Family Home

Introduction

Trusts for family home relate to those circumstances where there is a dispute as to the ownership of a property between couples (married or unmarried). The property dispute may stem from a breakdown in the relationship between the parties. But if the dispute arises on the bankruptcy or death of one of the parties this may involve the rights of third parties.

In the context of family assets, it may happen that the purchase of a property is under the name of one party that retains the legal title. The question that may arise is whether the other party has a beneficial interest in the property. To settle the dispute the court will look at all the circumstances related to the purchase of the property, considering any express intention of the parties and expense at the time of the purchase. The court may also impose a common intention constructive trust or a resulting trust in case of investment properties. Finally, the Court may apply the statutory principles of the Matrimonial Causes Act 1973 in the event of a divorce, decree of nullity or judicial separation.

Trusts of the matrimonial or quasi-matrimonial home

This type of trust concerns shared properties such as matrimonial homes shared by husband and wife. The questions that arise when looking at this type of trusts are the following: How is the property owned? Who does it belong to? To the man, to the woman or to both? The Matrimonial Causes Act 1973 applies in in the event of a divorce, decree of nullity or judicial separation. Under Sections 23 and 24 of the Act, courts have special powers to allocate property as they think appropriate amongst married couple in the eventuality of divorce. There are many situations in which the Act will not apply, for example, if a couple is not married or if one of them dies or if one member of the couple has a dispute with an outsider. To determine the prospective interests of the parties, the law of resulting and constructive trusts must be applied. What has happened is that the courts have developed a doctrine that applies in this type of case. The origins of the doctrine come from the two lines of authority mentioned, presumed resulting trusts and constructive trust to prevent fraud. The courts have effectively moulded a new doctrine that applies in this type of situation, but the clear origins of the two doctrines are apparent in the new doctrine.

Written declaration of trust and oral declaration of trust

When assessing the ownership of a family home, the first step is to trace the conveyance or transfer of the legal title. When two parties buy a house, a competent solicitor normally produces a written declaration of trust, that will state who owns the property and in what shares. Equity follows the law so that if the legal title has been transferred in the joint names of the parties, the equitable interest will be *prima facie* enjoyed by the same parties.

General Principle: If there is a written declaration in the trust, this will be conclusive of the equitable interest of the parties.

Goodman v Gallant [1986] Fam 106
Facts: The parties bought a property into joint names. 'upon trust to sell (…) and until sale upon trust for themselves as joint tenants'. After a dispute arisen between the parties, the Defendant left the property. The Claimant gave written notice of severance of the joint tenancy. The Claimant brought an action claiming to be entitled to a three-quarters share in the house.
Ratio: Where a conveyance into joint names contained an express declaration of trust that the parties hold the sale of a property on trust for themselves as joint tenants, on severance of the tenancy, a tenancy in common in equal shares arises.
Application: The court dismissed the appeal on the ground that the declaration of joint tenancy made by the parties was exhaustive and conclusive so that a constructive trust could not arise.

The New Doctrine: Common intention of Constructive Trust

Generally, a constructive trust arises where it can be shown that it would be unconscionable for the legal owner of property to enjoy the whole beneficial interest without the other. The courts have developed a new doctrine that is referred to as the doctrine of 'common intention' of constructive trusts. Its development began in the two big cases of **Gissing v Gissing** [1971] AC 886 and **Pettit v Pettit** [1970] AC 777 and it was culminated in the case of **Lloyds Bank v Rosset** [1989] Ch 350.

The doctrine says the court will find a Resulting or Constructive trust, if two conditions are satisfied:

There must be an agreement or common intention that the beneficial interest of the house is to be shared. The agreement or common intention must be expressed or implicit.

Party who acquires an interest or whose interest is to be enlarged by this agreement or common intention must have suffered the detriment in reliance on the common intention.

- **Finding a trust**

When the purchase of a property is under the name of one party that retains the legal title, the second party may claim a beneficial interest in the property. To successfully argue the existence of a resulting or constructive trust, the Claimant must show an agreement or common intention with detrimental reliance. Typically, a woman who tries to assert her interest in the house must show that both conditions are present.

General Principle: When the legal title has been conveyed in the name of one party, the one without legal title has the legal burden of giving evidence of a common intention the reliance on which has caused detriment.

Pettitt v Pettitt [1970] AC 777
Facts: Mrs Pettit retained the legal title of a cottage bought with her own money. Mr Pettit contributed to the decoration of it by

expending £725. After the divorce, the husband claimed to be beneficially entitled to a share in the sale of the cottage.

Ratio: If there is not clear agreement or common intention in the attribution of a beneficial interest, the spouse that expends money upon the property has no claim.

Application: The court held that there was no common intention of the parties to benefit the husband of an interest in the property. The works carried out by the husband represented ordinary improvements to a family property for the common enjoyment of the parties.

General Principle: It is burden of the Claimant to show that both conditions are satisfied for the court to validly recognise resulting or constructive trust.

Gissing v Gissing [1971] AC 886

Facts: Mrs Gissing had been married to Mr Gissing for 16 years, and had paid a substantial sum towards furniture and the laying of a lawn, but the house had been conveyed into the name of Mr Gissing alone, and Mrs Gissing had made no direct contributions towards its purchase. On their divorce, she claimed a beneficial interest.

Ratio: When common intention between the parties in relation to the attribution of a beneficial interest cannot be shown, the beneficial interest in the property cannot be recognised by way of constructive trust.

Application: The court held that it was not possible to draw an inference that there was any common intention that the wife should have has any beneficial interest in the matrimonial home.

- **Express and inferred common intention constructive trusts (CICT)**

General Principle: Two are the categories of trust that can arise under the new doctrine. Each category represents a peculiar way in which the condition may be satisfied.

Lloyds Bank v Rosset [1989] Ch 350

Facts: Lloyds Bank appealed against a decision upholding Rosset's beneficial right to occupy property over which the bank had a registered charge. The Defendant had carried out decorating work and supervised restoration on property purchased in the sole name of her husband. Rosset was in possession on 7 November 1982 but contracts were not exchanged until 23 November and completion took place on 17 December. On 14 December, the husband executed a charge in favour of the bank unbeknown to Rosset. The charge was registered on 7 February 1983. The husband defaulted on the loan.

Ratio: Lord Bridge stated that two are the conditions that must be satisfied to have a trust arisen under the new doctrine:

- **Inferred CICT: where there is no evidence of oral statement or discussion between parties about ownership, but the court can infer common intention to share beneficial ownership, from the fact that both parties have made referable contributions.**

- **Express CICT: where there is an actual oral statement about beneficial ownership, therefore the parties have discussed beneficial ownership or one of them has made a representation or statement and this provides the evidence of common intention. But of course, the mere statement is not detrimental reliance, so in this case a separate detrimental reliance must be found. The detrimental reliance need not amount to a referable contribution.**

Application: The relevant date for determining whether the Defendant was in occupation of the property for creation of an overriding interest in terms of the **Land Registration Act 1925 Section 70** was the date of the creation of the charge, 17 December. The bank correctly challenged whether Rosset had any beneficial interest in the property. There was no express agreement between Rosset and the husband between November and 17 December that Rosset would have a beneficial interest in the property and no express evidence of discussions to that effect. The work Rosset did on the property was insufficient to create the inference of beneficial ownership or creation of a constructive trust. Conduct such as payment towards the purchase price by the party who was not the legal owner was required before such an inference would be drawn.

Concerning inferred CICT, as an alternative to finding an express common intention, the common intention may be inferred from the legal owner's conduct. The supposed requirement of a 'direct financial contribution' necessarily means that indirect contributions are not recognised. Direct financial contributions mean financial contribution, which is referable to the purchase. Indirect financial contributions means where the household expenditure is split between the parties so that the legal owner of the home pays the mortgage instalments and the claimant pays other expenses. The contribution is indirect because the claimant does not directly pay towards the mortgage, but makes it easier for the legal owner to do so.

For express CICT, evidence of express discussion between the parties has to be shown, identical intentions held by each party, but not communicated, will not suffice. This often comes to the fore in cases where 'excuses' are used. In **Grant v Edwards [1986] Ch 638** at the time of her partner's purchasing of a family home, the claimant was in the process of divorcing her husband; the man put the deeds in his name only, though the reason for not including her as a party to the conveyance was that this might cause problems in the divorce proceedings; it was not difficult to construe conversations about this as an agreement that she should have an interest in the land, albeit that it would be better for her name not to appear on the deeds.

Application of the new doctrine

Courts have dealt with the development and application of the new doctrine in several circumstances. The question for the court is to decide whether or not the duties undertaken by a party are connected with a common intention to attribute a beneficial interest in the property. Without this common intention, the court cannot allow claim for beneficial interest in the property.

General Principle: Domestic duties such as looking after children or the house are insufficient to create a beneficial interest in the property.

Burns v Burns [1984] Ch 317
Facts: The Claimant, Valerie Burns, had been living with the defendant for 17 in the house. She and the Defendant, Patrick Burns, had never married. The house had been purchased in the name of the Defendant that paid the purchase price. The Claimant made no contribution to the purchase price or the mortgage repayments, but had brought up their two children, performed domestic duties and recently contributed from her own earnings towards household expenses. She also bought various fittings, and a washing machine, and redecorated the interior of the house. The Claimant left the Defendant and claimed a beneficial interest in the house.
Ratio: Common intention does not lead to the creation of an equitable interest only on the basis of that the parties have lived together or have undertaken domestic duties.
Application: In the absence of a financial contribution which could be related to the acquisition of the property, for example to the mortgage repayments, or a contribution enabling Patrick Burns to pay the mortgage instalments, she was not entitled to a beneficial interest in the house.

General Principle: Where common intention is inferred from an unenforceable oral declaration or from actual statements of intention.

Eves v Eves [1975] 1 WLR 1338
Facts: Janet and Stuart Eves purchased a house in which it was intended both should live. The house was conveyed into his name alone, and he provided the entirety of the purchase money. However, he told her that if she had been 21 years of age he would have put the house into their joint names, as it was to be their joint home, but that as she was under 21 it would have to be put into his name alone. She believed him, but he later admitted that this was an excuse, and that he never intended her to have a share. She did a lot of heavy work in reliance on the statement; because the house

was in a very bad state, she helped to do it up. On the breakdown of the relationship four and a half years later, the question arose as to whether Janet had a share in the house, and if so, in what proportions.

Ratio: When attributing a beneficial interest in disputes involving the family home, the court gives interpretation on a case-by-case basis aiming at fairness.

Application: Stuart Eves (the Defendant) held the legal estate on trust for sale for himself and Janet, in the proportions of one-quarter to Janet and three-quarters to himself.

General Principle: Indirect contributions to the purchase of a house may give right to a beneficial interest in the property.

Grant v Edwards [1986] 2 All ER 426

Facts: In 1969 a house was purchased for the Claimant, Mrs Linda Grant, and the Defendant, George Edwards, to live in as if married (although Linda Grant was actually married to someone else). The house was purchased in the name of Edwards and his brother. Edwards told Grant that her name would not go on the title for the time being because it would cause prejudice in the matrimonial proceedings pending between Mrs Grant and her husband. He had no intention of conveying any legal title to the Claimant. The Defendant paid the deposit on the house, and most, but not all, of the repayments on the two mortgages. The Claimant also contributed towards general household expenses, provided housekeeping and brought up the children. In 1980 the couple separated, and the Claimant claimed a beneficial interest in the property.

Ratio: Indirect contributions such as actions done relying on the acquisition of an equitable interest in the property may allow the identification of common intention between the parties.

Application: Edwards' statement that Mrs Grant's name would have appeared on the title except that it could cause prejudice in the matrimonial proceedings was evidence of a common intention that Mrs Grant should have beneficial interest (a half share) in the property. Mrs Grant had relied to her detriment on the common intention, so that she was entitled to a half share on a resulting or constructive trust.

General Principle: Oral discussion between the parties may support the identification of common intention, but the court will also look at the conduct of the parties.

Hammond v Mitchell [1991] 1 WLR 1127
Facts: The parties were a couple that lived together in a bungalow bought by the husband through a mortgage. The property was in the name of the husband but he guaranteed that half of the property would have been of the wife anyway. Later, the husband bought a house in Spain where the couple lived for a little while. When the relationship terminated, the wife claimed a beneficial interest in the properties and other assets.
Ratio: The discussion the couple had in the purchase of the bungalow clearly showed the common intention of the parties to grant a beneficial interest in the property to the wife.
Application: The court held that the wife was granted a half share in the bungalow on the basis of the statements made by the man that amounted to an enough clear express common intention. Nevertheless, the same intention could not be ascertained in relation to the property in Spain.

- **Apportionment of beneficial interest**

General Principle: Absence of express agreement between the parties does not authorise to validate the presence of a beneficial interest.

Gissing v Gissing [1971] AC 886
Facts: Mrs Gissing had been married to Mr Gissing for 16 years, and had paid a substantial sum towards furniture and the laying of a lawn, but the house had been conveyed into the name of Mr Gissing alone, and Mrs Gissing had made no direct contributions towards its purchase. On their divorce, she claimed a beneficial interest.
Ratio: A beneficial interest cannot be attributed when it is not possible to draw an inference that there is common intention

that the party should have the beneficial interest in the matrimonial home.

Application: The House of Lords held that she had no interest because she did not contribute to the purchase price of the property.

- **Valuation of the interest**

Once common intention to attribute a beneficial interest to the party has been proved and that one of the parties has suffered detriment relying on that intention, the next step is to quantify the beneficial interest.

General Principle: When an investment is made jointly, the amount of the contribution is the means to determine the extent of the interest.

Sekhon v Alissa [1989] 2 FLR 94

Facts: A mother (Claimant) and a daughter (Defendant) purchased a property conveyed into the daughter's sole name. The daughter contributed £15,000. The mother paid the remaining balance. The mother brought a claim alleging that the purchase of the property was a joint commercial venture. The daughter argued that the money was a gift or an interest free loan. The evidence showed that the mother's contribution represented the sum total of her life savings, that she believed a joint conveyance would have adverse capital gains tax implications, that she regarded the purchase as a joint venture to give her a better return on her money as an investment, that no member of the family thought it was a gift, that the daughter had accounted to the mother for some of the rents received from the property and that at one stage the daughter had sought legal advice on giving the mother an interest in the property. **Ratio: The law presumes a resulting trust in favour of the mother unless there is evidence to rebut it.**

Application: The evidence did not show that the money was a gift or a loan. The mother was to have some interest in the property. The amount of her contribution was the means to determine the extent of her interest.

<u>**Recent developments**</u>

In the absence of written evidence of ownership of a property, but with conveyance of the legal title in the joint names of the parties, the beneficial interest follows the legal title. Therefore, the parties will *prima facie* enjoy the beneficial interest. The question for the court may be to which extent. If the transfer of the title is in joint names, the parties will enjoy the beneficial interest in equal shares. If one of the party claims that the beneficial interest differs from the legal title, it will be his burden to give evidence in support of the assumption. Nowadays, the court assesses valuate the extent of the beneficial interest more in the light of the common intention of the parties, rather than strictly calculating who paid what.

General Principle: A receipt for capital money arising on a disposition of the land does not amount to an express declaration of a beneficial joint tenancy.

Huntingford v Hobbs [1993] 1 FLR 736
Facts: The parties decided to move to a property that was purchased partially with the money obtained by the sale of the former home of the Defendant, partially through a loan for which the Claimant gave service. The transfer contained no declaration as to the trusts on which the beneficial interest would be held but did contain a declaration that: "the transferees declare that the survivor of them can give a valid receipt for capital money arising on a disposition of the land." In August 1988, the man left to marry another woman. In 1989, he sought a sale of the property and a declaration as to the trusts in relation to the equitable interests. At first instance, the judge considered the contributions, which each party had made to the house. The judge approved the sale of the property and granted Mr Hobbs a sum of £3500. The man appealed, claiming that as joint tenants they should have beneficially enjoyed the property in equal shares.
Ratio: In order to establish whether or not the parties were entitled to the sale of the property in equal shares, it is essential to consider if the transfer of the property contained a declaration of trust.

Application: The court had to decide whether the declaration in the transfer that the survivor could give a valid receipt for capital amounted to a declaration of trust. The court held that the words used did not amount to a declaration of trust. Nevertheless, the court agreed that between the parties there was a common intention to give the man some beneficial ownership in the property. The difficulty was to assess the extent of the beneficial interest in the absence of a written declaration of trust. The court held that the basic proportions that should have governed the calculation of the beneficial interest had to refer to the cash contribution given by the lady and the money raised on mortgage by the man.

General Principle: Both in joint and sole legal ownership cases, when there is direct contribution to the purchase of the property the court may adopt a broader view of the conduct of the parties in order to quantify their shares.
Midland Bank v Cooke [1995] 4 All ER 565
Facts: In 1971, shortly before Mr and Mrs Cooke's marriage, their matrimonial home was purchased by Mr Cooke, and registered in his name alone. The only financial contribution which she could argue was half a wedding present, of £1,100, from Mr Cooke's parents. She did not make any contributions to the mortgage instalments, but discharged other household outgoings, and devoted much time and energy to the improvement of the house and garden. In 1978, the original mortgage was replaced by a new mortgage in favour of Midland Bank, granted to Mr Cooke in his sole name, which also secured repayment of the business overdraft of Mr Cooke's company. In 1981, Mrs Cooke signed a consent form postponing her rights in the property, if any, to the bank. Later that year, a second charge was executed on the property to secure their liability under a joint guarantee, as security for a business loan. In 1984, the property was conveyed into the joint names of Mr and Mrs Cooke. In 1987, the bank brought possession proceedings, claiming outstanding amounts due under the mortgage. Mrs Cooke claimed a one half beneficial interest in the property, overriding any interests of the bank. It was common ground that at the time of purchase there had been no discussion between the parties as to how the property should be owned

beneficially. At first instance, Mrs Cooke claimed a beneficial interest in the property, which was binding on the bank notwithstanding the 1981 consent form, which she claimed, had been obtained by undue influence. The judge decided that Mrs Cooke had a 6.47% share, based on her financial contributions (one half of the wedding present from Mr Cooke's parents). He also found in her favour on the undue influence issue. Mrs Cooke appealed on the quantification of her interest, and there was no cross-appeal by the bank on the undue influence finding.

Ratio: When determining the proportions of the contribution of the parties in the property, the court is allowed to consider all the conducts that show the intention of the parties in relation to the beneficial shares in the property.

Application: The Court of Appeal held that the beneficial interests in the property should be shared equally. The valuation was based not on the resulting trust contributions to the purchase price of the parties, but to the common intention constructive trust that the parties showed when living in the property.

General Principle: In assessing the beneficial interest of the parties in the property, the court looks at the whole course of dealing between the parties and decides the fair share for each of them.

Oxley v Hiscock [2004] EWCA Civ 546

Facts: The parties were an unmarried couple that purchased a house in the name of the Defendant. The cost of the property was £127,000. The amount of £30,000 was provided by a building company. The remaining money came from the sale of the Claimant's former house (£36,600) and the direct contribution of the Defendant (£60,700). The relationship terminated. The Defendant sold the property. The Claimant brought an action claiming a beneficial interest in the property in equal shares. At first instance, the judge found in favour of the Claimant and approved the division in equal share of the sale of the property. The Defendant appealed.

Ratio: In the absence of clear agreement in relation to the extent of the beneficial interest between the parties, the court looks at the direct contribution of the parties to the purchase price of the house and establishes the percentage of beneficial shares.

Application: The Court of Appeal found in favour of the Defendant assessing that the fair division of the proceeds was 60 per cent to the Defendant and 40 per cent to the Claimant. The percentage was assessed on the basis of the contribution of money provided by the parties. The Defendant gave a substantially greater amount of money.

General Principle: It is still essential to show that there was an express communication between the parties of a shared common intention to attribute the beneficial interest in order to create a constructive trust.

Lightfoot v Lightfoot-Brown [2005] EWCA Civ 201

Facts: The Claimant owned a property. The parties got married and they moved in the property together. On divorce, they recognised to be joint beneficial owners of the property. They agreed that the Defendant would have paid all mortgage instalments in respect of the property in exchange of the Claimant's interest. The property was transferred to the Defendant. At some point the parties tried reconciliation and the Claimant lived in the house, paying some mortgage instalments and a capital repayment of one mortgage of £41,000. The relationship ended and the Claimant brought an action arguing to be entitled of a 50 per cent beneficial interest in the property. At first instance, the judge held in favour of the Defendant on the ground that there was a lack of common intention between the parties since the Defendant was unaware of the capital mortgage repayment. The Claimant appealed.

Ratio: In order to assess the attribution of a beneficial interest, there must be an express agreement between the parties that the property must be shared beneficiary or in the absence of such express agreement, the conduct of the parties must show intention to share the beneficial interest. The intention must be reasonably understood by a manifested conduct or words.

Application: The Court of Appeal agreed with the judge at first instance that there was no evidence of common intention between the parties since the Defendant did not know that the Claimant had paid the capital mortgage of £41,000.

General Principle: In order for the court to allow a constructive trust, the Claimant must show to have relied on an express or implied intention to share the property that has caused detriment.

Stack v Dowden [2005] EWCA Civ 857
Facts: The parties bought a house in their joint names. The purchase price was reached thanks to a mortgage advance of 65,000 for which both parties were liable, the sale of the previous house and savings of £58,000 from the Defendant's account. There was not a declaration of trust, but the parties agreed that the survivor of the two would have been entitled to a valid receipt for capital moneys. When the relationship ended, the Defendant excluded Mr. Stack from the house but she paid him £900 to cover the cost of alternative accommodation under a time-limited order. When the order expired, Ms Dowden was still in exclusive occupation of the house and Mr Stack continued living in an alternative accommodation. He brought an action claiming that the property was held upon trust for the parties as tenants in common in equal shares.
Ratio: It is on the Defendant's to show that the common intention of the parties was to hold the properties otherwise than as beneficial joint tenants. Ms Dowden's contributions to the acquisition of the property and to the capital repayment of the loan must be considered.
Application: The House of Lords confirmed the Court of Appeal's decision that in the light of the contributions provided when purchasing the property, the beneficial ownership of the parties had to be split in the proportion of 65 per cent in favor of the Defendant.

General Principle: When the parties are joint tenants of an estate and in the absence of the contrary, the equitable interests would follow the legal interests.

Crossley v Crossley [2005] EWCA Civ 1581

Facts: The parties were Mrs Crossley and her son. The both lived in the family home. After the death of the husband (and father) the legal title of the property was registered in the joint names of the parties. Later, the wife of the son moved in the property. The relationship between mother and son deteriorated. The son brought an action claiming to have a beneficial interest in the house in equal share. The County Court found in his favour and the mother appealed arguing that there was no agreement to support the attribution of the beneficial interest in equal share.

Ratio: The Court will put under discussion the presumption that equitable title follows legal title in those circumstances where the parties own a property as joint tenants only if there are evidence of the contrary.

Application: The Court of Appeal agreed that the son was entitled to the beneficial interest. The legal estate was transferred into joint names and the mother was not able to give evidence contrary to the assumption.

General Principle: In the absence of an express agreement the court must look not only at the financial contributions given to the purchase but also to the whole relationship between the parties.

Fowler v Barron [2008] EWCA Civ 377

Facts: The parties were an unmarried couple that lived together for about seventeen years. Mr Fowler was a retired fireman for medical reasons. The couple had a son and a daughter. The bought the property in their joint names. There was no signed transfer document or agreement in relation to beneficial interest in the property, but a declaration that the survivor of the two could have given a valid receipt for capital money on the disposition of the property.

Ratio: It is burden of Mr Fowler to show that the parties did not intend to own the property in equal shares. The court must consider the whole course of conduct in relation to the property and the whole of the parties' relationship so far as it

helps in identifying their intentions to equally share the beneficial interest.

Application: On the basis that many more factors than financial contributions should have been considered relevant in the definition of the parties' intention towards the ownership of the property, the court held the parties had both equal interests in the property. The factors to consider include, among others, the reasons why the parties bought the property as joint tenants, the nature of their relationship and the presence of children to whom guarantee a home.

General Principle: In joint legal ownership cases where the intention of the parties is disputed, the Court will strive to construct an intention that is fair and just in order to quantify the interests of the parties.

Jones v Kernott [2012] 1 AC 776

Facts: The parties were an unmarried couple that bought in joint names a property. The purchase price of the house was £30,000. The Claimant contributed £6,000. The rest was raised by a mortgage paid by the Claimant. The Defendant gave £100 per week to cover the household expenses. The relationship ended and the Defendant left the property. The Claimant stayed in the property with the children. The Claimant assumed sole responsibility in the maintenance of the property. At the time of the separation it was accepted that the parties held the property in equal shares. Nevertheless, few years later the Defendant started a correspondence claiming his interest in the property so that the Claimant brought an action claiming that she owned the entire beneficial interest in the property.

Ratio: The presumption that equitable title follows legal title can be displaced by showing that the parties had a different common intention in relation to the beneficial interest in the property. The intention of the parties was held to have changed Application: The court held in favour of the Claimant that was held sole benefit of any capital gain in the joint property.

Summary

- Where the transfer of property is subject to an express agreement or understanding between the parties, this is conclusive as to their intentions.

- In the absence of such an express intention the courts may enforce an implied intention between the parties as to their beneficial interests.

- Where a family home had been bought in the joint names of an unmarried cohabiting couple who were both responsible for any mortgage, but without any express declaration of their beneficial interests, the starting point was that equity followed the law so that the presumption was that they were joint tenants both in law and in equity.

- The presumption of joint ownership could be displaced by showing that the parties had had a different common intention at the time when they had acquired the home or that they had later formed a common intention that their respective shares would change; that the primary search was for what the parties had actually intended and their common intention was to be deduced objectively from their words and conduct; that where it was clear that the parties had not intended a beneficial joint tenancy at the outset or that they had changed their original intention, financial contributions will only be one factor amongst many others.

Chapter 12 –
Duties and Powers

Introduction

The exercise of trustee's functions is limited by a range of duties. As having the control of the trust property he owes several duties to the beneficiaries. The list of duties is so long that we do not intend, in this Chapter, to provide an extensive one.

The most important principle leading his actions is that the interest of the beneficiaries must prevail and not conflict with his own interests. This is also the subject of the next chapter. Then, according to general principles of contract Law, the trustee must obey the terms of the trust.

In making decisions, trustees must act in good faith, responsibly and reasonably. They must ensure that they are in possession of all relevant facts and information before making a decision. This may include taking advice from appropriate experts, such as solicitors and accountants. However trustees must always remember that advisers only advise. It is the trustees' responsibility to make the decisions.

Conversely, trustees are endowed with a variety of powers in order to equip them for the management of the trust property. The powers mainly concern exceptional situations or changes of circumstances since the creation of the trust. However, the powers are not unrestricted; the trustee must act in accordance with the source and scope of the power.

Duties of trustees

The "ordinary prudent man of business"

Throughout the administration of the trust the trustee is required to exhibit an objective standard of skill as would be expected from an ordinary prudent man of business. The courts have thus developed the "ordinary prudent man of business" test. The expression duty of prudence is not entirely accurate nowadays however it has always been called this in the past.

General Principle: The "ordinary prudent man of business" test is satisfied when the trustee had exercised the same care he would have done in relation to his own money.

Speight v Gaunt (1883) 9 App Cas 1
Facts: In this case a trustee had entrusted funds to a stockbroker, the stockbroker defrauded the trust and the question was whether the trustee was in breach of his duty of prudence.
Ratio: The court held that the trustee had exercised the same care he would have done in relation to his own money, he had no reason to question the honestly of the broker, thus the trustee was not in breach. The leading original authority this case in which the House of Lords stated: "As a general rule the trustee sufficiently discharges his duty is he takes in managing trust affairs all those precautions which an ordinary prudent man of business would take in managing similar affairs of his own".
Application: The "ordinary prudent man of business" test like all such tests including the reasonable man test is not really enlightening because it all depends on its application to any particular facts.

The rule that emerged from this case was that a trustee is bound to conduct the business of the trust in the same way in which an ordinary prudent man of business conducts his own, and has no further obligation. He may employ brokers and agents in cases in which they are employed in the ordinary course of business.

Duty and standard of care at common law

This principle was found in the Trustee Investment Act 1961 and now found in the Trustee Act 2000, it is essentially the same principle and when you consider the principle you really have to consider the case law. The duty of care is essentially objective, but as the passage below indicates, the trustee's 'special knowledge or experience' holds him to a higher standard and degree skill. On the other hand there is no concession made for a trustee who is particularly ignorant, this is an important question because some trustees are just friends of the family and some people appointed as trustee don't understand what is involved and may have a very limited understanding of investment. Thus on one hand we have a higher duty through special skill and no allowance for unfamiliarity of business investment, this has an asymmetrical approach.

The idea of a higher standard for someone with special knowledge or experience was recognised in the case of **Bartlett v Barclays Bank** (no 2), prior to the Trustee Act.

General Principle: Where the trustee is a professional such as a bank or an insurance company, the standard of care is higher than the degree of diligence expected from a non-professional trustee.

Bartlett v Barclays Bank (1980) CH 515
Facts: Here the bank was trustee of a settlement, which consisted of all the debenture stock and shares in a private company. Without the bank's knowledge, the board embarked on hazardous property speculation, and lost a great deal of money. The bank did not attend board- meetings, and the only information it had was gleaned at annual general meetings.
Ratio: The bank was held to the standard of that of a competent bank, and as an expert on trustee investment, here they were found to be in breach of trust, and liable for the loss occasioned. The professional trustee is required to administer the trust with such a degree of expertise as would be expected from a specialist in trust administration.
Application: This objective standard is applied but the courts after due consideration of the facts of each case.

Section 1of the Trustee Act 2000 provides that:

"Whenever the duty under this subsection applies to a trustee, he must exercise such care and skill as is reasonable in the circumstances, having regard in particular-

(a) to any special knowledge or experience that he has or holds himself out as having, and
(b) if he acts as trustee in the course of a business or profession, to any special knowledge or experience that it is reasonable to expect of a person acting in the course of that kind of business or profession.
(2) In this Act the duty under subsection (1) is called "the duty of care".

Duty to safeguard trust assets

The duty to safeguard the trust assets is a continuing and onerous one that is strictly applied. If any part of the trust property is outstanding the trustees are under a duty to press for payment.

General Principle: The trustee will be liable for not having brought legal proceedings where it was necessary to safeguard the trust assets.

Re Brogden (1888) 38 Ch D 548 (CA)
Facts: Under the terms of his will John Brogden covenanted to pay £10,000 to the trustees in respect of his daughter's marriage settlement within 5 years of his death. He died and the money was not paid. Whilst the trustees requested payment on several occasions they did not take action in order to avoid family upset. The monies were never paid and the securities proved inadequate.
Ratio: The trustees were liable for breach of trust – on the basis that they should have taken active proceedings. Further, once it is shown that the trustee has neglected to do his duty he is prima facie liable for all the consequences of the breach.
Application: This case laid down the principle that the only excuse for not taking action to enforce payment was a well-founded belief on the part of the trustees that such an action would be fruitless, with the onus of proof on the trustees.

It should be noted, however, that trustees have extensive discretion to settle claims by and against the trust under Trustee Act s. 15 and will not be liable where such powers have been exercised in good faith. It is suggested that following the enactment of Trustee Act 2000 it now seems that under s. 15 trustees who discharge their statutory duty of care under s 1(1) of the Trustee Act 2000 will not be liable where failure to sue is the result of the positive exercise of their discretion as opposed to a passive attitude of doing nothing.

Duty to act unanimously

It is the general rule that unless there is a contrary provision in the trust instrument, any exercise by trustees of their powers or discretions, must be by the unanimous decision of all the trustees. Consequently, once a trust decision is made, the trustees become jointly and severally liable to the beneficiaries in the event of a breach of trust. This rule does not apply to trustees of charities and occupational pension trusts.

In **Bahin v Hugues** (1886) 31 Ch D 390, "passive" trustees were liable to the beneficiaries for breach of trust along with an active trustee. As Cotton LJ has put it:

"Miss Hugues was the active trustee and Mr Edwards did nothing, and in my opinion it would be laying down a wring rule to hold that where one trustee acts honestly, though erroneously, the other trustee is to be held entitled to indemnity who by doing nothing neglects his duty more than the acting the trustee ... In my opinion the money was lost just as much by the default of Mr Edwards as by the innocent though erroneous action of his co-trustee, Miss Hugues. All the trustees were in the wrong, and everyone is equally liable to indemnity the beneficiaries".

Duty to act impartially

A trustee is under a general duty to maintain equality between beneficiaries, that is, no one beneficiary benefits at the expense of another. Particular difficulties arise in maintaining a balance between rights of tenants for life and remaindermen. This duty is particularly important in relation to the duty to convert and apportionment.

General Principle: The trustee cannot act in favour of a beneficiary or a group of beneficiaries when it is not stipulated in the trust.

Lloyds Bank v Duker (1987) 3 All ER 193
Facts: The Court refused an application requiring the trusteed to transfer to a beneficiary his share of a trust fund, namely 46/80 of shares of a private company. **Ratio: The Court rejected the claimant's application because the trustee would have acted partially by transferring a majority holding in a company exceeding the value of the remaining shares subject to the trust. As Mowbray QC puts it in this case: "I mean the principle that trustees are bound to hold an even hand among their beneficiaries, and not favour one as against another, stated for example in Snell's Principles of Equity, opt cit, p. 225."**
Application: The claimant, most probably the beneficiary, will have to prove that the trustee has acted in breach of his duty of impartiality. Yet, it is not an easy task to challenge the exercise by a trustee of discretion.

Duty to act personally

The reason for this rule lies on the fact that the settlor appoints a particular trustee because of his personal qualities. Therefore, the trustee should act personally when administrating the trust. The general rule is *delegatus non potest delegare,* A delegate cannot delegate his duty. However, this duty is not strictly required in all situations, since the contemporary commercial climate requires some special skills and knowledge in particular situations. Therefore trustees are entitled to appoint agents to perform acts in respect of the trust. A section 11 to 20 of the Trustee Act 2000 provides the trustee with several powers of appointment that we will examine in details in the section on powers of trustees.

Duty not to make a profit

A trustee is undoubtedly a fiduciary and therefore is subjected to fiduciaries duties. The justification for this rule is that the trustee has control over the trust, which he is required to use solely for the benefit of the beneficiaries.

In **Bray v Ford [1896] AC 44 Lord Hershell** said *"it is an inflexible rule of a Court of Equity that a person in a fiduciary position ... is not, unless otherwise expressly provided, entitled to make a profit; he is not allowed to put himself in a position where his interest and duty conflict"*. Liability arises from the mere fact that a profit has been made by the fiduciary, it does not depend on dishonesty or negligence.

Duty to account and give information

A trustee must keep accounts and be ready to provide them to the beneficiaries for inspection: **Pearse v. Green** (1819) 1 J&W 135. The beneficiaries are only entitled to inspect – if they want a copy they can be required to pay for it. The beneficiaries are entitled to see the "trust documents", such as title deeds, share certificates, &c relating to the trust property. The trustees must give reasonable information to the beneficiaries concerning the trust, as well as providing relevant information to new or successor trustees.

Duty to distribute

It is an elementary principle of trusts law that the trustees are required to distribute the trust property to the beneficiaries properly entitled to receive the same. In other words, trustees are under an absolute duty that they pay, in relation to both income and capital, the right amount to the right person. Failure to do will be a breach for which they will be liable.

General Principle: An aggrieved beneficiary may, in addition to his right to sue the trustee, trace his property in the hands of the wrongly paid person.

Woolwich Building Society v IRC No. 2 1992 3 All ER 737
Facts: Instead of paying a beneficiary, a trustee paid a public authority in the form of taxes paid, pursuant to an *ultra vires* demand by the authority.
Ratio: The Court considered that the taxes paid were *prima facie* recoverable by the member of the public as of right.
Application: This right of the beneficiary to trace his property wrongly given to another person is available even when this person is a public authority.

Duties with regard to investment

As we have seen it is a basic duty of trustees to act fairly between the different classes of beneficiary. Thus, when they are choosing investments trustees are under a duty to hold a balance between them and must take care not to favour the tenant for life over the remainderman and *vice versa*. Trustee must invest so as to provide a reasonable income for the tenant for life, while protecting the value of the capital for the remainderman.

However, it has been suggested that the trustees should also take into account the personal circumstances of the individual beneficiaries. In **Nestle v National Westminster Bank plc** (1988) Staughton LJ observed *"If a life tenant is living in penury and the remainderman already has ample wealth, common sense suggests that a trustee should be able to take that into accou*nt." Hoffman J added in this case that the balance principle is better expressed as a requirement that the trustees must act fairly in making investment decisions which might have different consequences for different classes of beneficiaries: *"It would be an inhuman law which required trustees to adhere to some mechanical rule for preserving the real value of the capital when the tenant for life was the testator's widow who had fallen on hard times and the* *remainderman was young and well off*". Another question that needs to be considered is whether trustees can take into account non-financial considerations when making investment decisions.

General Principle: Trustees have a duty of investment in the best interests of present and future beneficiaries.

Cowan v. Scargill [1984] 2 All ER 750
Facts: This case involved a pension scheme established by the National Coal Board and managed by a committee of trustees. In 1982 a new investment plan was put before the committee, but the 5 NUM trustees refused to agree on the plan unless it was amended so that overseas investment was restricted, and no investments were made in energies competing with coal.
Ratio: The trustees were in breach of their duty to use their powers of investment in the best interests of present and future beneficiaries. If the purpose of the trust was to provide financial benefits, then "best interests" of the beneficiaries normally, though not inevitably, meant "best financial interests".
Application: This case also adds that personal interest and social and political views should be put to one side when deciding to invest abroad or in controversial areas such as armaments or tobacco. However, following the enactment of the Trustee Act 2000, this has changed since it has introduced *"the standard investment criteria"*. The explanatory notes to the Act specifically state that the suitability of investments *"will include any relevant ethical considerations as to the kind of investment which it is appropriate for the trust to make"*.

Exclusion Clauses in the Trust Instrument

Exclusion clauses which are validly inserted in trust instruments may have the effect of limiting the liability of trustees. They are usually introduced by professional trustees is that professional trustees will require themselves to be appointed on their own standard terms and conditions. Their terms and conditions will include an exclusion clause, to the effect that the bank will not be liable for any breach of duty unless it amounts to a wilful default. The effect of this in practice, although the law says that a bank (professional trustee) is held to a higher standing than an ordinary average trustee, it seems to be effective in excluding liability except for wilful default.

General Principle: A clause in a settlement providing that a trustee was exempted from liability for loss or damage to the fund or its income "unless such loss or damage shall be caused by his own actual fraud" could validly exclude liability for gross negligence.

Armitage v Nurse [1998] Ch 241
Facts: In this case, an exclusion clause was validly introduced, excluding the trustees' liability "unless such loss or damage shall be caused by their own actual fraud".
Ratio: The Court that the clause validly protected the trustees from liability. The trustees were not guilty of actual fraud and could enlist the protection of the exemption clause.
Application: Since the clause is validly introduced, the trustee can secure the exclusion of his liability in almost every case.

For a trustee to be guilty of fraud, there had to be a fraudulent intention and proof of dishonesty, **Derry v Peak (1889)** 14 App. Cas. 337 applied, so that even if trustees deliberately committed a breach of trust, if they did so in good faith, honestly believing that they were acting in the best interests of the beneficiary, there could be no fraud.

Powers of trustees

Power to appoint nominees

Under Section 16 of the Trustee Act 2000, trustees are entitled to appoint nominees in relation to the trust asset as they may determine. Moreover, the trustee may take steps to ensure the vesting of those assets in the nominee. Such appointment must be written.

Power to appoint custodians

In relation to specified assets, the trustee may appoint a custodian under section 17 of the Trustee Act 2000. Custodian is a person undertaking the safe custody of an asset or any documents or records concerning this asset. Such appointment must be written.

Persons who may be appointed as nominees or custodians

Section 19 of the Trustee Act 2000 requires that the nominee or custodian must carry a business, which consists of or includes acting as nominees or custodians. In the alternative, the nominee or custodian must be a body corporate controlled by the trustees.

Powers of investment

Trustees have a general power of investment section 3 of the Trustee Act 2000. Under this provision, trustees can invest in the same kinds of investments as an absolute owner. An "investment" for these purposes refers to property which will produce an income yield.

However, trustees must comply with their general duty of car, as provided by section 3 (3):

"(i)   the power does not relate to all possible investments, as it does not authorise investments in land other than loans secured on land. Investment in land, which I mention in the preceding section, is dealt with separately under Part III of the Act.

(ii)   Trustees are not given an unfettered discretion in their choice of investments.

(iii)   The statutory duty of care will apply in the case of both statutory and express investment powers.

(iv)   Other pre-existing fundamental duties will apply such as a duty to act in the best interests of the beneficiaries."

Ss. 4 requires the trustees to have regard to 'standard investment criteria'.

The standard investment criteria are:

*"(i)   the suitability to the trust of the investment of the same
         kind as any particular investment proposed to be made or
         retained and of that particular investment as an
         investment of that kind, and*

*(ii)   the need for diversification of investments of the trust, in
         so far as it is appropriate to the circumstances of the trust.*

*'Suitability includes consideration of both size and risk of the
investment and the need to balance income with capital growth. It
is suggested that it will also include any relevant ethical
considerations as to the kind of investments that it is appropriate
for the trust to make."*

Ss. 4 and 5 also apply in the case of express powers of investment
in the trust instrument. The new power of investment will apply
to existing trusts. However it will not generally apply to trusts
which have a power of investment conferred by the Trustee
Investment Act 1961. The Act requires trustees to review the
investments of the trust from time to time. During such reviews
the trustees must consider whether, having regard to the standard
investment criteria, the investments should be varied.

S 5(1) Trustee Act 2000 provides that before exercising any power
of investment trustees must obtain and consider proper advice
about the way, having regard to the standard investment criteria,
the power should be exercised. Section 5(2) provides that when
reviewing the existing trust investments, trustees must obtain and
consider proper advice about whether, having regard to the
standard investment criteria, the investments ought to be varied.
This section provides as it follows: *"Proper advice is the advice
of a person who is reasonably believed by the trustee to be
qualified to give it, by virtue of his ability in and practical
experience of financial and other matters relating to the proposed
investment"*.

The trustee is not required to follow the advice, but he cannot
reject it merely because he disagrees. He could perhaps reject it,
if by so doing he was acting as an ordinary prudent man of

business. If the trustee does follow the advice he is not automatically protected from being in breach of trust. However, it will probably be difficult for a beneficiary to establish a breach of trust if the trustee acted in a bona fide manner. The court would probably grant relief under s 61 Trustee Act 1925. (We will consider this in more detail when looking at beneficiaries' remedies.) Section 5(3) provides that a trustee need not obtain advice if he reasonably concludes that in all the circumstances it is unnecessary or inappropriate to do so. This would apply where the trustee is perhaps an investment adviser and has the skill and knowledge already.

Powers of maintenance and advancement

Powers of maintenance and advancement may be expressly conferred by the trust instrument. Both these have the object of providing for infant (that is, people below the age of 18) beneficiaries who are not as yet entitled to any of the income or capital, but who require financial support during their minority. A power to maintain an infant beneficiary is not implied into the trust instrument, and thus it must be expressly given or advantage taken of the power in s. 31 Trustee Act 1925. The statutory power operates provided no contrary intention is expressed, but where the statutory power is expressly excluded it can't be used, even if an express power turns out to be useless. In **Re Erskine's ST** [1971] 1 WLR 162, a settlement contained a provision for accumulation which was void for perpetuity. But since the statutory power was excluded by the provisions of the trust instrument, the income which the trustees had accumulated could not be applied for the beneficiary, and resulted to the settlor's estate.

- **Power of maintenance**

The power to maintain under section 31 of the Trustee Act 1925 can only arise where the beneficiary is "entitled to receive intermediate income" under the trust. What does this mean? Suppose a testator in her will has left all her shares in a particular company to her daughter, A, if she reaches the age of 18. A is seven years old at the time of her mother's death. The trustees keep the shares and wait to see if A fulfils the condition and enables them to pass the shares to her. Six months after the testator's death, the trustees receive a dividend of £30 from the company. To whom does this money belong? The general rule is that when a person has a contingent interest in property, any income earned by the property between the date of the gift and the time when the interest vests belongs to the done, provided she attains a vested interest. When this is the position, we say that the gift "carries the intermediate income", that is, the gift of capital carries with it the income earned up to the time when the gift vests. So, assuming the gift to A carries the intermediate income, when A reaches 18 the trustees will pass to her not only the shares but also the accumulation of money from the dividends.

Assuming income to be available, the trustees have discretion as to whether to maintain the beneficiary. The courts will not interfere if the trustees exercise their power in good faith and have applied their minds to what should be done. Trustees cannot be compelled to maintain. Section 31 directs them to have regard to the age and requirements of the infant, whether any other income is available for his maintenance, and generally to the circumstances of the case. The money may be paid to the parent or guardian or directly for his benefit, such as school fees. If the infant is married, it may be paid directly to him. Subject to a contrary intention in the trust instrument, the power to maintain ceases when the beneficiary reaches the age of majority. Even if his interest is still contingent, the trustees must pay the whole of the income to him until he obtains a vested interest or dies.

The Court has inherent jurisdiction to approve the use of income or even capital for the maintenance of infant beneficiaries, but in practice this is rarely necessary.

- **Power of advancement**

The trustee's power of advancement is enshrined by section 32 of the Trustee Act 2000. Payments by way of advancement are sums advanced from capital, in theory to cover major costs such as setting up the beneficiary in her profession, though unlike maintenance it is not restricted to infant beneficiaries.

The power of advancement may arise in three ways:

- By an express power contained in the trust instrument, in which case the provision is a matter for strict construction. This is usually used where the settlor considers the statutory provision to be inadequate.
- Trustee Act 1925, s. 53 – the court has the power to order the use of capital for the infant's maintenance, education or benefit.

- Trustee Act 1925, s. 32 - This power confers on trustees an absolute discretion to pay or apply capital money of the trust for the "advancement or benefit" of a beneficiary entitled to such capital, whether or not that interest is vested or contingent.

- The word "advancement" clearly connotes some substantial payment with a view to establishing the beneficiary in life such as for example, to enable the beneficiary to buy a house or business. The term "benefit" may be read disjunctively and has a clearly wide meaning. In **Pilkington v. IRC** [1964] AC 612, it was held by Lord Radcliffe that the combined phrase means *"any use for the money which will improve the material situation of the beneficiary."* It will thus include the discharge of the beneficiary's debts and also the re-settlement of capital to avoid tax. There is no need to show that the advancement was to meet some personal need of the beneficiary, but must not be casual payment.

The Trustee Act provides with a couple of restrictions on the power of advancement:

- o S. 32(1)(a) – the trustees must not advance more than ½ of the beneficiary's presumptive or vested share or interest.

- o S. 32(1)(b) – when the beneficiaries become absolutely entitled to their interest, the previous advancement must be taken into account (such as, I gave you £5000 already),

- o S. 32(1)(c) – the advancement must not prejudice any beneficiary entitled to any prior interest, for example, a life tenant whose income would be reduced, unless the person with such an interest gives consent to the advancement.

- o S 32(2) – the trust fund must consist of money or securities or property held on trust for sale – **Re Stimpson Trusts** [1931] 2 Ch 77 – but not settled land.

Finally, the trustees must ensure that the advancements are applied for the purpose for which they are made and if they fail to do so they may be required to account to the trust for the money improperly advanced (see **Re Pauling's Settlement Trust** [1964] Ch 303).

Summary

- The most important principle leading the actions of the trustee's actions is that the interest of the beneficiaries must prevail and not conflict with his own interests.

- Then, according to general principles of contract Law, the trustee must obey the terms of the trust. In making decisions, trustees must act in good faith, responsibly and reasonably.

- The "ordinary prudent man of business" test is satisfied when the trustee had exercised the same care he would have done in relation to his own money.

- Where the trustee is a professional such as a bank or an insurance company, the standard of care is higher than the degree of diligence expected from a non-professional trustee.

- The trustee will be liable for not having brought legal proceedings where it was necessary to safeguard the trust assets.

- It is the general rule that unless there is a contrary provision in the trust instrument, any exercise by trustees of their powers or discretions, must be by the unanimous decision of all the trustees.

- The trustee cannot act in favour of a beneficiary or a group of beneficiaries when it is not stipulated in the trust.

- The trustee should act personally when administrating the trust. The general rule is *delegatus non potest delegare,* A delegate cannot delegate his duty.

- It is an elementary principle of trusts law that the trustees are required to distribute the trust property to the beneficiaries properly entitled to receive the same.

- As we have seen it is a basic duty of trustees to act fairly between the different classes of beneficiary. Thus, when they are choosing investments trustees are under a duty to hold a balance between them and must take care not to favour the tenant for life over the remainderman and *vice versa*.

- Trustees have a duty of investment in the best interests of present and future beneficiaries.

- Exclusion clauses which are validly inserted in trust instruments may have the effect of limiting the liability of trustees.

- Conversely, trustees are endowed with a variety of powers

in order to equip them for the management of the trust property.

- Under Section 16 of the Trustee Act 2000, trustees are entitled to appoint nominees in relation to the trust asset as they may determine.

- In relation to specified assets, the trustee may appoint a custodian under section 17 of the Trustee Act 2000.

- Section 19 of the Trustee Act 2000 requires that the nominee or custodian must carry a business, which consists of or includes acting as nominees or custodians. In the alternative, the nominee or custodian must be a body corporate controlled by the trustees.

- Trustees have a general power of investment section 3 of the Trustee Act 2000. Under this provision, trustees can invest in the same kinds of investments as an absolute owner.

- Ss. 4 requires the trustees to have regard to 'standard investment criteria'.

- Powers of maintenance and advancement may be expressly conferred by the trust instrument. Both these have the object of providing for infant (that is, people below the age of 18) beneficiaries who are not as yet entitled to any of the income or capital, but who require financial support during their minority.

Chapter 13 –
Fiduciary Duty

Introduction

Trustees have a variety of duties, namely on first being appointed. These obligations have been presented in several other chapters. However, in addition to those duties, a trustee is said to have overarching fiduciary duties to the beneficiaries. These do not stem from the trust instrument or terms of the trust itself, but rather from the special relationship of trust he is in. Fiduciary duties are essentially duties of good faith, to act solely in the interests of the other party.

As Millet LJ has famously put it in the case **Bristol & West Building Society v Mothew** [1998] Ch 1: "A fiduciary is someone who has undertaken to act for or on behalf of another in a particular matter in circumstances which give rise to a relationship of trust and confidence. The distinguishing obligation of a fiduciary is the obligation of loyalty. The principal is entitled to the single-minded loyalty of his fiduciary. This core liability has several facets: a fiduciary must act in good faith; he must not make a profit out of his trust; he must not place himself in a position where his duty and his interest conflict; he may not act for his own benefit or the benefit of a third person without the informed consent of his principal. This is not intended to be an exhaustive list, but it is sufficient to indicate the nature of fiduciary obligations."
General principle: A fiduciary is generally not entitled to make a profit by taking advantage of his position.

Bray v Ford [1896] AC 44 at 51
Facts: Mr Bray was a governor of Yorkshire College. Mr Ford was the vice-chairman of the governors and had also been working as a solicitor for the college. Bray sent him a letter, and circulated it to others, stating that Mr Bray, whilst holding a fiduciary position, illegally and improperly made profit as its paid solicitor. The question of the fiduciary duties arose for the first time.
Ratio: The House of Lords held that the fiduciary cannot, in principle, make profit if his interests are conflicting. In this case, Lord Herschell stated that: "It is an inflexible rule of a court of equity that a person in a fiduciary position is not, unless expressly

provided, entitled to make a profit; he is not allowed to put himself in a position where his interest and his duty conflict. It does not appear that this rule is founded on principles of morality. I regard it rather as based on the consideration that, human nature being what it is, there is danger of the person holding a fiduciary position being swayed by interest rather than duty, and thus prejudicing those whom he was bound to protect."

Application: Fiduciary duties are wide-ranging, but the essential basis is that a fiduciary may not personally profit from his position and has an overriding duty to avoid a conflict between his personal interests and the duties he owes to his principle. The main duty of fiduciaries is loyalty.

Who is a fiduciary?

English law does not provide a comprehensive list of the types of relationships that are fiduciary. Some relationships have come to be recognized as fiduciary *per se* for example trustee to beneficiary, solicitor to client, company director to company, business partner to co-partners, principal to agent, mortgagee to mortgagor.

General principle: A member of the security services has a fiduciary duty to the Crown to refrain from disclosing confidential information.

A-G v Blake [2001] 1 AC 268

Facts: A former member of the security services who disclosed information in his autobiography did not owe a continuing fiduciary duty to the Crown where the information was no longer confidential.

Ratio: The Court held that the defendant was ordered to pay over his profits from the book as damages for breach of his contract with the crown not to disclose information without consent.

Application: This was an exceptional case where an account of profits was ordered as damages for breach of contract. Normally, they are only ordered as a remedy for breach of fiduciary duty.

General principle: A fiduciary relationship can exist in the context of a joint property venture.

Murad v Al-Saraj [2005] EWCA Civ 959

Facts: Mr Al-Saraj persuaded Aysha and Layla Murad to enter into a joint venture, in which they would buy and run a hotel. He persuaded them by fraudulently representing to them that he would contribute £500,000 in cash towards the purchase. In fact, his contribution mainly consisted of setting off a secret commission that the hotel vendor agreed to pay him.

Ratio: The court held that there was a fiduciary relationship between the Murads and Mr Al –Saraj in relation to the joint venture. It was held that Mr Al-Saraj was in breach of that fiduciary duty in not disclosing to the Murads how he was actually making his contribution. He was ordered to pay over his profits from the venture to the Murads.

Application: In this case, the special circumstances of a pre-arranged relationship of trust and confidence led the Court to held that a fiduciary relationship existed.

Hence it can be seen that in most cases a fiduciary duty is imposed where there is a pre-arranged relationship of trust and confidence, in which one party is expected to act in the interests of another. The above considerations show that it is not just a trustee who has fiduciary duties. A fiduciary duty can arise in all sorts of other situations of trust and confidence. However, in the next section, we shall look mainly at the position of a trustee's fiduciary duty. Having a fiduciary duty involves a whole list of things that a trustee cannot do.

Unauthorised profits

According to the case law; some profits are unauthorized because of the position of the beneficiary. A fiduciary must not take advantage of his position to make an unauthorised benefit for himself or herself (**Boardman v Phipps** [1967] 2 AC 46). Therefore, the main rule is that a trustee may not profit from his trust. He is taken to accept office gratuitously and is not entitled to remuneration for his services. This rule has been applied rigorously, so that a trustee who ran a business on behalf of the trust was not entitled to remuneration for doing so (**Barnett v Hartley** (1866) LR 2 Eq 789).

The courts have been encouraged to adopt a less strict test where the fiduciary gain could not have been used by the principal, but have not yet done so: "It may be that the time has come when the court should revisit the operation of the inflexible rule of equity in harsh circumstances, as where the trustee has acted in perfect good faith and without any deception or concealment, and in the belief that he was acting in the best interests of the beneficiary. I need only say this: it would not be in the least impossible for a court in a future case, to determine as a question of fact whether the beneficiary would not have wanted to exploit the profit himself, or would have wanted the trustee to have acted other than in the way that the trustee in fact did act. Moreover, it would not be impossible for a modern court to conclude as a matter of policy that, without losing the deterrent effect of the rule, the harshness of it should be tempered in some circumstances" – **Murad v Al-Saraj** [2005] EWCA Civ 959.

General principle: A trustee must not take a commission for introducing trusts to businesses.

Williams v Barton [1927] 2 Ch 9
Facts: A trustee introduced some trust business to a stockbroking firm of which he was a member. His company granted him a commission for this service. **Ratio: The Court held that he had to hand over to the trust the commission that he received from his firm for the introduction.**
Application: The trustee his always bound by an obligation of loyalty to the trust, in other words the interests of the trust should always over his own interests.

Bribes and other "secret profits" obtained in breach of a fiduciary duty

A bribe exists when property is received by a fiduciary in order to perform a service that betrays the trust bestowed on him by his principal.

General principle: A fiduciary accepting a bribe is breaching his obligation of loyalty.

Attorney General for Hong Kong v Reid [1994] 1 AC 324

Facts: The acting DPP of Hong Kong accepted bribes, and used the bribe money to purchase properties in New Zealand. **Ratio: The Privy Council held that the money was received in breach of his fiduciary duty to the Crown, and accordingly the properties purchased with the money were held on constructive trust for the Crown.**

Application: The fiduciary cannot make profit for his own interest when they are conflicting with the interests of the trust.

For many years there was uncertainty in English law as to the legal position if someone (F) who is a fiduciary - this will include employees working for an employer or other principal (P) - takes a bribe (or makes a secret profit, or takes a secret commission) in the course of their engagement. The cases all agreed that P could claim the value of any money, or other asset, that was given to F. What was unclear was whether F was simply 'liable to account' to P (i.e. F was under a personal liability), or whether F held the money or other property 'on constructive trust', in the sense that P had a proprietary claim to the money or property.

An important evolution of jurisprudence of the UK courts occurred on this issue. A first range of cases established that the procurement of the bribe was involving a debtor/creditor relationship as the property in the bribe has passed to the recipient. A personal claim to account lay against the recipient of the bribe. This was the initial, and now out of date, basis for liability (see **Heiron 1880**). Recently, the Supreme Court overruled this solution in **European ventures 2014**, by enshrining that a proprietary claim based on a constructive trust arose in favour of the principal or claimant, as the bribe represents money or assets belonging to the principal.

General principle: The liability of the fiduciary is personal and involves a duty to account.

Metropolitan Bank v Heiron (1880) 5 ex D 319

Facts: A director of company received a bribe and pleaded a limitation defence on the ground that the company could not treat the bribe as its property.

Ratio: "The ground of this suit is concealed fraud. If a man receives money by way of a bribe for misconduct against a company or any person against whom he stands in a fiduciary position, he is liable to have that money taken from him by his principal. But it must be borne in mind that that liability is a debt only differing from ordinary debts in the fact that it is merely equitable, and in dealing with equitable debts of such a nature Courts of Equity have always followed by analogy the provisions of the Statute of Limitations".

Application: The director of a company receiving a bribe is able to plead a limitation defence, he is personally liable since his liability involves a duty to account.

General principle: The bribes and the subsequent property acquired by the fiduciary are subject to the claims of the injured party.

A-G for Hong Kong v Reid [1994] 1 AC 324

Facts: The DDP of Hong Kong government, Mr. Ried, had a proprietary claim over houses purchased in New Zealand with bribes taken by a prosecutor in HK. In the meantime the properties had decreased in value. The question in issue concerned the status of a fiduciary who received a bribe, in particular, whether such a fiduciary became a mere debtor for the innocent party or alternatively a trustee for the aggrieved party.

Ratio: Lord Templeman: " When a bribe is offered and accepted in money or in kind, the money or property constituting the bribe belongs in low to the recipient. As soon as the bribe was received, whether in cash or in kind, the false fiduciary geld the bribe on a constructive trust for the person injured".

Application: Since the representative property had decreased in value, the fiduciary was liable to account for the difference between the bribe and the undervalue.

However, in **Sinclair Investments (UK) Ltd v Versailles Trade Finance Ltd** (In Administration) [2011] EWCA Civ 347; [2011] 3 WLR 1153 the Court of Appeal followed Lister v Stubbs and declined to follow **A-G HK v Reid**. Although the case involved secret profits made from a commercial fraud rather than bribes, the CA held that profits obtained in breach of a fiduciary duty were subject to a personal liability to account, but not to a proprietary claim. This case prompted widely divergent comments from academics.

FHR European v Mankarious [2013] EWCA Civ 17 illustrates the difficulties the courts were encountering in applying the old law in general, and Sinclair v Versailles in particular. At first instance Simon J stated that he was applying **Sinclair v Versailles** and held Cedar Capital Partners accountable in equity, but did not find a constructive trust. The Court of Appeal reversed him on this, saying that they were also following Sinclair v Versailles, but that the facts in the instant case were distinguishable from those in Sinclair v Versailles, so it fell within one of the exceptions mentioned in that case: the Court of Appeal therefore found that there was a constructive trust.

General principle: The principal is entitled to the benefit of the fiduciary's unauthorised acts in the course of his agency.

FHR European Ventures LLP v Cedar Capital Partners LLP [2014] UKSC 45
Facts: The claimants asked the defendants to negotiate with a third party to negotiate and conclude a very onerous contract with a third party. The defendants and the third party entered into a brokerage agreement to facilitate the conclusion of the agreement with the claimant in return for a commission of €10 million. The defendant claimed for a traditional debtor/creditor relationship, despite his fiduciary's duties relying on **Heiron**.
Ratio: "The principal is entitled to the benefit of the agent's unauthorised acts in the course of his agency, in just the same way as, at law, an employer is vicariously liable to bear the burden of an employee's unauthorised breaches of duties in the course of his employment. The agent's duty is accordingly

to deliver up to his principal the benefit, which he has obtained, and not simply to pay compensation for having obtained it in excess of his authority. The way that legal effect can be given to an obligation to deliver up specific property to the principal is by treating the principal as specifically entitled to it".

Application: The Supreme Court declared that the secret commission of € 10 million was held on constructive trust for the claimant. The Supreme Court therefore overruled **Lister v Stubbs** and **Sinclair v Versailles** and held that bribes and secret commissions should and would be held on a proprietary constructive trust. Although it was conceded that allowing a proprietary claim would work against the unsecured creditors of F, there was no real injustice to them here, as the bribe ought never to have been an asset of F.

Director's fees

General principle: Where a trustee gains a directorship of a company from a trust, he is obliged to hand over to the beneficiaries any directors' fees he receives.

Re Macadam [1946] Ch 73
Facts: In this case, the trustees of a trust were empowered to appoint directors of a company. They appointed themselves and received directors' fees. **Ratio: The Court held that the trustees were accountable to the beneficiaries for the directors' fees, even though they did not act improperly. Application:** In order to determine whether this rule applies, the fact that the trustee acquired the directorship because he is a trustee is a crucial factor.

In **Re Gee [1948]** Ch 284; the courts added a further restriction to a trustee's entitlement to retain director's fees: "A trustee who has power, by the use of trust votes, to control his appointment to a remunerative position, and refrains from using them with the result that he is elected to the position of profit, would also be accountable" (See at 295 in this case). However, the trustee may retain the director's fee if he was appointed director before he became a trustee or if the trust itself allows the trustees to appoint themselves directors and to retain remuneration.

Authorized remuneration

First of all, the court has an inherent jurisdiction to order the payment of trustees, or increase the remuneration allowed under the trust deed, if so doing would be beneficial to the trust – e.g. effort beyond the call of duty, **Re Duke of Norfolk's ST** [1982] Ch 61.

General principle: Courts can order payment of trustees where it cannot have the effect of encouraging trustees in any way to put themselves in a position where their interest conflicts with their duties as trustees.

Guinness plc v Saunders [1990] 2 AC 663

Facts: In that case, a director of Guinness received a fee for providing his services in connection with Guinness's take-over of another company. **Ratio: This was held to be a breach of fiduciary duty, and the House of Lords refused to authorise remuneration to be paid to him for his work. As summarized by Lord Goff: "the exercise of the jurisdiction is limited to those cases where it cannot have the effect of encouraging trustees in any way to put themselves in a position where their interest conflicts with their duties as trustees".**

Application: In this case, the House of Lords clarified and restricted the power of courts to order payment of the trustees.

In addition to this, if all the beneficiaries are *sui juris*, they may authorised the trustees to be remunerated from the trust fund, but this will be viewed with suspicion as it may be tainted by undue influence. Finally, the rule in **Cradock v Piper (1850)** 1 Mac & G 664 permits a solicitor- trustee to be remunerated for court work undertaken for himself (as trustee) and his co-trustees, as long as this does not increase his costs over and above the costs he would have charged if he had not been a trustee.

The Trustee Act 2000 codified several rules concerning the payment of professional trustees. Its part V contains new provisions relating to remuneration of professional trustees. They relate to all services provided or expenses incurred after the Act came into force, irrespective of the date of creation of the trust – s33 (1). Therefore, under the current state of law, a trustee is entitled to payment if:

- There is a provision in the trust instrument entitling him to receive payment out of trust funds for services provided on behalf of the trust; and

- The trustee is a trust corporation or acting in a professional capacity – Trustee Act 2000 s.28.

- A trustee is entitled to receive reasonable remuneration out of trust funds for services provided to the trust if:

o The trustee is a trust corporation, but the trust is not a charitable one, or

o The trustee acts in a professional capacity but is not a trust corporation or a sole trustee, and the trust is not charitable – but only if the other trustees agree in writing that he may be remunerated – Trustee Act 2000 s.29.

Purchase of trust property

The courts have developed a rule prohibiting trustees and other fiduciaries, without authority, from purchasing the trust property. If the purchase takes place the transaction is treated as voidable at the instance of the beneficiary.

If a trustee or retired trustee purchases his beneficiary's beneficial interest, the beneficiary can have the sale set aside unless the trustee can establish the propriety of the transaction – **Tito v Waddell (No 2) [1977] Ch 106** (the 'fair-dealing rule'). The trustee must show that:

- He took no advantage of his position
- The beneficiary was fully informed, and
- The beneficiary received full value.

General principle: The fiduciary is prohibited from taking personal profits from any activity connected with his status as a fiduciary.

Regal (Hastings) Ltd v Gulliver [1942] 1 All ER 378
Facts: The Company received an offer from one of its subsidiaries to sell shares. The company did not buy them but four of its directors subscribed for the shares personally and sold later them for a profit. All the transactions were *bona fide.* The company claimed that the directors were accountable for their profit.
Ratio: "The rule of equity, which insists on those, who by use of a fiduciary position make a profit, being liable to account for that profit, in no way depends on absence of bona fides; or upon such questions or considerations as whether the profit

would or should otherwise have gone to the plaintiff, or whether the profiteer was under a duty to obtain the source of the profit for the plaintiff, or whether he took a risk or acted as he did for the benefit of the plaintiff, or whether the plaintiff had in fact been damaged or benefited by his action. The liability arises from the mere fact of a profit having, in the stated circumstances, been made. The profiteer, however honest and well intentioned, cannot escape the risk of being called upon to account" (per Lord Russell).**

Application: Company directors must not take advantage of their position to make personal profit. Trustees may retain directors' fees if they are appointed trustee independently of their shareholding capacity or if they were a director before they were trustee.

General principle: Courts have discretion to approve the purchase of trust property by a trustee in advance or retrospectively.

Holder v Holder [1968] Ch 353

Facts: V was appointed one of the executors in the deceased's will and had signed a few cheques for small amounts before renouncing his executorship. This meant that his renunciation was ineffective and he technically remained an executor and trustee, but he never actually assumed the duties of executor, and it was the other 2 executors who actually administered the will. V had wanted to renounce executorship because - as was known to all the beneficiaries - he intended to bid at public auction for the farmland of which he was tenant and which formed part of the deceased's estate. He took no part in instructing the auctioneers and acquired no special knowledge as trustee. He never actually acted as executor and took no part in the sale. His bid was the highest and the land was conveyed to him at a fair price. One of the beneficiaries sought to overturn the purchase.

Ratio: The Court held that that there was no conflict of interest on V's part in the special circumstances of the case, as he had never acted as executor and so was not selling to himself. Therefore, the sale was approved. In this case, the Court underlined that the beneficiary had accepted the sale by receiving his shares of the proceeds (in fact, at one stage, he had been pressing the trustee to complete the purchase).

Application: When determining if there is a breach of fiduciary duty, the acceptance of the sale from the beneficiary, being *sui juris*, is a crucial factor.

The "self-dealing" rule

There must be no conflict of interest, so a trustee should not purchase property from the trust of which he is a trustee, nor may he become a tenant of such property. The "self-dealing rule" is a strict rule that applies no matter how fair the price and other terms of the contract. For example, the trustee cannot sell the trust property to himself, whatever the price: See **Ex. P. James (1803) 8 Ves 337.**

General principle: A trust property cannot be sold to a company in which the trustee has a controlling interest such as a position of managing director or majority shareholder.

Re Thompson's Settlement [1986] Ch 99
Facts: A trustee sold a trust property to a company in which he was managing director and a majority shareholder.
Ratio: The Court decided to set aside the sale. In this case, the court will treat the trustee as effectively selling to himself.
Application: The controlling interest is a major factor to determine the application of the self-dealing rule.

General principle: Where the trustee was a minority shareholder, and there is a conflict of interest and duty and the beneficiary challenges or impeaches the sale, the onus is on the company to show that the trustee has taken all reasonable steps to obtain the best price.

Farrars v Farrars Ltd (1888) 40 Ch D 395
Facts: In this case, three mortgagees were in possession of a mortgaged property. One of the mortgagees, Mr Farrars, was also a solicitor to the mortgagees. The property was sold to a company in which Mr Farrars had a small shareholding.

Ratio: The beneficiary intended an action to set the sale aside, the Court held that if failed because it was sale by a person to himself. As Lindley LJ stated: "A sale by a person to a corporation of which he is a member is not, either in form or in substance, a sale by a person to himself. To hold that it is, would be to ignore the principle which lies at the root of the legal idea of a corporate body, and that idea is that the corporate body is distinct from the persons composing it."

Application: When determining if the self-dealing rule applies, the fact that the trustee is a minority shareholder of the company does not constitute a controlling interest that would set aside the sale.

When the trustee sales the trust property for himself, the transaction is voidable at the instance of any beneficiary. If the trustee has already resold the property, he must account to the trusts for his profits. If he has not resold, the property will be ordered to be re-conveyed, or the court may order a resale. However, this rule will not apply in all circumstances. For example, when the trust instrument or all the beneficiaries, being *sui juris* authorize it (See **Holder v Holder [1968]** Ch 353 above). Another exception is if the purchase is pursuant to a contract or option agreed or granted before the trusteeship arose.

General principle: The self-dealing rule cannot be evaded by a trustee retiring so as to make the purchase.

Wright v Morgan [1926] AC 788

Facts: In this case, a trustee resigned and bought trust property at a price fixed by independent valuers; the transaction was set aside because the arrangements were made while he was still trustee. Here the trustee as acted has an executor at some point.

Ratio: The Court held that the trustee's retirement was driven by the intention to purchase the trust property and therefore the sale was set aside.

Application: Here the trustee's intention of frauding by retiring to evade the self-dealing rule is crucial. Conversely, note that if a bona fide retirement is followed independently by the purchase, it should be acceptable.

The "fair-dealing" rule

The fair-dealing rule is an exception to the prohibitory self-dealing rule.

General principle: The fair dealing rule enables a trustee to purchase the beneficial interest of a beneficiary if the trustee can prove he acted fairly, there was no undue influence, and he gave full value.

Coles v Trescothick (1804) 9 Ves 234

Facts: In this case, the trustee purchased a trust property in the best interests of a beneficiary, without any fraud or advantage taken on the basis of a distinct contract.

Ratio: The Court recalled that the sale can be set aside unless the trustee can prove that they did not profit from the advantage of their position as trustee. Therefore, the sale in the present case did not raise any breach of fiduciary obligations. In this case, Eldon LC said: "[244]...a purchase by a trustee from the *cestui que* trust I agree, the *cestui que* trust may deal with this trustee, so that the trustee may become the purchaser of the estate. But, though permitted, it is a transaction of great delicacy, and which the Court will watch with the utmost diligence... [246]... at trustee may buy from the cestui que [247] trust, provided that there is a distinct and clear contract, ascertained to be such after a jealous and scrupulous examination of all the circumstances, proving, that the cestui que trust intended, the trustee should buy, and there is no fraud, no concealment, no advantage taken, by the trustee of information, acquired by him in the character of trustee."

Application: In contrast to the self-dealing rule, which prohibits a trustee from buying the trust property, the fair dealing rule, enables the trustee who acted in good faith to purchase the property.

<u>Summary</u>

- Trustees have a variety of duties, namely on first being appointed. However, in addition to those duties, a trustee is said to have overarching fiduciary duties to the beneficiaries. These do not stem from the trust instrument or terms of the trust itself, but rather from the special relationship of trust he is in. Fiduciary duties are essentially duties of good faith, to act solely in the interests of the other party.

- A fiduciary is generally not entitled to make a profit by taking advantage of his position (See **Bray v Ford [1896]** AC 44 at 51)

- English law does not provide a comprehensive list of the types of relationships that are fiduciary. Some relationships have come to be recognized as fiduciary *per se* for example trustee to beneficiary, solicitor to client, company director to company, business partner to co-partners, principal to agent, mortgagee to mortgagor.

- Hence it can be seen that in most cases a fiduciary duty is imposed where there is a pre-arranged relationship of trust and confidence, in which one party is expected to act in the interests of another.

- The main rule is that a trustee may not profit from his trust. He is taken to accept office gratuitously and is not entitled to remuneration for his services. This rule has been applied rigorously, so that a trustee who ran a business on behalf of the trust was not entitled to remuneration for doing so (**Barnett v Hartley** (1866) LR 2 Eq 789).

- Bribes and other "secret profits" obtained in breach of a fiduciary duty. A bribe exists when property is received by a fiduciary in order to perform a service that betrays the trust bestowed on him by his principal.

- Where a trustee gains a directorship of a company from a trust, he is obliged to hand over to the beneficiaries any directors' fees he receives.

- Some trustees' profits are authorized by the or by all the beneficiaries being *sui juris*.

- In addition to this, the rule in **Cradock v Piper (1850)** 1 Mac & G 664 permits a solicitor- trustee to be remunerated for court work undertaken for himself (as trustee) and his co-trustees, as long as this does not increase his costs over and above the costs he would have charged if he had not been a trustee.

- The courts have developed a rule prohibiting trustees and other fiduciaries, without authority, from purchasing the trust property. If the purchase takes place the transaction is treated as voidable at the instance of the beneficiary.

- There must be no conflict of interest, so a trustee should not purchase property from the trust of which he is a trustee, nor may he become a tenant of such property. The "self-dealing rule" is a strict rule that applies no matter how fair the price and other terms of the contract.

- Nevertheless, the fair dealing rule enables a trustee to purchase the beneficial interest of a beneficiary if the trustee can prove he acted fairly, there was no undue influence, and he gave full value.

Chapter 14 - Tracing

Introduction

Tracing is an equitable means that allows a person to track an asset that has been taken by fraud, misappropriation or mistake. If the beneficiary loses the property due to breach of trust, he is entitled to bring an action against the trustee for the restitution of the property. This action will be an action in personam, personally against the trustee. If the trustee will be found insolvent, the beneficiary's right to recover the property will rank with the claims of the other unsecured creditors of the trustee.

Tracing represents an alternative process the beneficiary may adopt to recover the property of the trust. The concept encompasses two processes: following and tracing. By adopting this type of claim, the beneficiary will be able to follow and trace the property in the hands of the trustee or third party (that is not bona fide transferees of the legal estate for value without notice). Following and Tracing allows the beneficiary to have priority over the trustees' creditors to recover the property. The claim is in rem so that it provides the recovery of the property itself. The best definition of tracing comes from the case of **Boscawen v Bajwa** [1996] 1 WLR 328 where Millett LJ:

"Tracing is neither a claim nor a remedy but a process. It is the process by which the plaintiff traces what has happened to his property, identifies the persons who have handled it or received it, and justifies his claim that the money which they handled or received can properly be regarded as representing his property."

Advantages of the proprietary remedies over personal remedies

The proprietary remedy has a number of advantages over the personal remedy, namely:

- The effectiveness of the claimant's action is not depending on the defendant's solvency; it is rather based on an assertion of ownership of the asset in question.

- The claimant may be able to take advantage of the increase in the value of the property.

- The limitation periods for commencing claims are not applicable to claimants who seek to trace and recover their property in the possession of the trustee.

Tracing in Common Law

Tracing is a proprietary right that enables the Claimant to follow an asset into the hands of the Defendant. The right to trace is recognised at both common law and equity, but common law tracing has certain disadvantages which usually make it advisable to trace in equity. The major disadvantage of the Common Law right is that, although it recognises the right to trace where an asset has been exchanged for another asset or even an identifiable sum of money it is not available where the original asset or its proceeds have become mixed with other property, such as placed in a bank account mixed with the Defendant's own money. Equity has no such difficulty and has developed rules to identify the asset claimed out of the mixed fund.

A further problem with common law tracing is that the Claimant must have a legal title to the asset claimed: a beneficial or equitable title is insufficient. In equity, the Claimant must have an equitable interest in the asset and there must be a fiduciary relationship between the Claimant and Defendant or another person who originally transferred the asset.
So, for these reasons, tracing is generally sought in Equity.

A proprietary claim against assets identified by the rules of tracing will usually be preferred over a personal claim only where it is advantageous. There are three advantages that a proprietary claim may have over a purely personal claim:

(i)   insolvency: the plaintiff gains priority over general creditors in the event of the   insolvency of the person against whom they would have had a personal claim;

(ii)   increase in value: in tracing, where an asset increases in value, the plaintiff is entitled to take advantage of the profit; and

(iii)   where a personal claim is barred: in unusual circumstances, such as in the trust instrument.

Note that tracing in equity only applies where the legal and beneficial interests have been separated and only the equitable interest itself falls to be traced.

General Principle: For a property to be traceable in common law, the property must be identifiable.

Taylor v Plumer (1815) 3 M&S 562
Facts: The Defendant gave his stockbroker £22,200 to invest in Exchequer bills. Mr. Walsh, the stockbroker, bought American investments and bullion with the intention of escaping to North America, via Portugal. The Defendant's attorney and police officer caught him before the escape and the Defendant recovered the property. Later, Mr. Walsh was adjudicated bankrupt. His assignee in bankruptcy sued the Defendant on the basis that he had no right in the property since the property was changed. Instead of the £22,200 there were now American investments and bullion.
Ratio: If the nature of the substitute property follows the nature of the original property, it can be considered ascertained.
Application: The court found in favor of the Defendant because the property was still ascertainable and traceable.

General Principle: The legal owner of a property may seek a tracing order (proprietary claim), provided that the property is indeed identifiable.

Lipkin Gorman v Karpnale Ltd [1991] 3 WLR 10
Facts: Lipkin Gorman is the owner of a firm of solicitors where Mr Cass was on the partner. He was a compulsive gambler. Unbeknown to the firm, he drew cheques on the client account to use for gambling. He withdrew money and used them at the gaming tables of the club, owned by the Defendant. Part of the money was proffered to the club for chips. 154,695 were still in possession of the club. When Mr Cass was convicted for theft, the law firm sued the gambling club to recover the stolen money. The club tried to argue that they accepted the money in good faith, unaware that Mr Cass was using unauthorised money.
Ratio: When giving judgement, Lord Goff explained that if the Claimant had sought a tracing order, he might have been successful. The Claimant is entitled to trace his property in its unconverted form or in its substituted form when the property is still identifiable. Nevertheless, the Claimant did not seek a tracing order.
Application: The House of Lords held that the club as recipient of stolen money was under the obligation to return the equivalent to the law firm. The club unjustly enriched at the expense of the law firm.

Tracing in Equity

In equity tracing is a proprietary right, and means the right of the beneficiaries to recover the trust property itself from the trustees or from any third party, except a *bona fide* purchaser for value without notice. This right is against the trust property either in its original form or in a converted form, provided the original property can be "traced" into the new property.

This is a secondary remedy exercisable by a beneficiary so long as she has (in theory) a primary personal right of action for the money against the trustees. If the beneficiary is seeking to recover trust property she is said to be "following" it, whilst if the property has been sold and the proceeds are in a bank account she is said to be "tracing" it.

To be able to trace trust property in equity, the beneficiary must show three aspects:

(a) The existence of an initial fiduciary relationship

It must be possible to trace the trust property into the hands of the trustee (or other fiduciary) who is holding it in breach of his obligations or into the hands of such a person's successor in title other than a *bona fide* purchaser for value without notice, in which case it may be possible to trace into the proceeds of sale.

General Principle: Once an initial fiduciary relationship is established, it does not matter that the person who is in possession of the trust property is in no such relationship to the beneficiary.

Re Diplock [1948] Ch 465
Facts: Caleb Diplock left the residue of his estate on trust for such charitable or benevolent purposes as his executors should in their absolute discretion select. A sum in excess of £200,000 was distributed to 139 charities before the validity of the gift was successfully challenged by his next of kin. They sought (*inter alia*) to trace the monies into the hands of the charities and were held by the Court of Appeal to be entitled to do so. **Ratio: Equity, it was said, "*may operate on the conscience not merely of those who acquire a legal title in breach of some trust, express or constructive, or of some other fiduciary obligation, but of volunteers provided, because of what has gone before some equitable proprietary interest has been created and attaches to the property in the hands of the volunteer.*"**
Application: Whilst a beneficiary under a deceased's estate is not the equitable owner of the assets in an non-administered estate (unlike a beneficiary under a trust) the "equitable proprietary interest" was in this case found in the equitable claim by the next

of kin against the executors – which gave them the right to trace against the charities.

(b) The property must be in a traceable and identifiable form

The property needs not be in the same form as it was when it left the trust. The remedy pre-supposes "the continued existence of the money either as a separate fund or as part of a mixed fund or as content in property acquired by means of such a fund. If…such continued existence is not established, equity is as helpless as the common law itself" – **Re Diplock** [1948] Ch 465. Tracing cannot, therefore, be used if the trust funds have been consumed or dissipated – such as spent on a cruise or lavish party.

Profits

If the trust property is still in the hands of the trustee, the beneficiary can take it back; if the trustee has used the trust property to buy something specific the beneficiary can take that, even though it may now be more valuable than the original property. Now, if a person in possession of trust property makes a profit on it, whether he will be liable to account for such profits depends on his relationship to the beneficiary:

o Trustee – such an individual is in a fiduciary relationship and he will be liable to account for any profits made on the trust property. For example, if the trustee used trust property to buy shares in his (the trustee's) own name, he will have to account not only for the trust monies but also any dividends paid on the shares bought with the trust money.

o Innocent volunteer – If the person is an innocent volunteer and the fund is unmixed, then **Re Diplock** [1948] Ch 465 suggests that the innocent volunteer is entitled to keep any profits made on the trust property. However, in **Re Tilley's Will Trusts** [1967] Ch 1179 it is suggested that in fact he should account to the trust for such profits, which means the beneficiaries are entitled to the profits.

o   Where the property of the beneficiary has been mixed with that of an innocent volunteer then both **Re Diplock** [1948] Ch 465 and **Re Tilley's Will Trusts** [1967] Ch 1179 suggest that the innocent volunteer should only account for a proportion of the profits; that is, they will share *pari passu* (in the proportion that each has contributed).

Payments of debts

If trust property or its proceeds are used to discharge a specific debt, the trust property will not be traceable: **Re Diplock** [1948] Ch 465. If trust property is paid into an overdrawn account, the trust property will not continue to be traceable – **Bishopsgate Investment Management Ltd v Homan** [1994] EWCA Civ 33. The account will be charged with the amount of money paid in. The charge will extend to any properties purchased with the assistance of the overdraft, but the beneficiaries cannot claim the properties themselves – they are regarded as having been purchased with the sums advanced.

Mixed funds

The mixing of funds usually takes place within bank accounts where there are complications of monies being paid in and withdrawals over a period of time. The rules differ depending on whether the trust monies are mixed with either those of a trustee or fiduciary or an innocent third party (which may be either another trust or an innocent volunteer).

- **Mixed fund** – no third party involved

If the trust money is mixed with the trustee's own money, then the presumption is that the trustee draws out his own money first and does not draw on money subject to the trust until all his own money is exhausted – no matter what order the money was paid in. The amount that remains in the account is trust money.

General Principle: When the trust fund is mixed with the trustee's money, the trustee will simply draw on his money and the remaining will be the trust property.

Re Hallett's Estate (1880) 13 Ch D 696
Facts: Hallett, a solicitor, was trustee of his own marriage settlement. He paid some of the money into his own bank account, into which he also paid money entrusted to him by a client for him to invest. He made various payments in and out of the account.

On his death, the account contained sufficient funds to meet the claims of his trust and his client, but not those of his ordinary (personal) creditors. **Ratio: The principle is that trustees are presumed to have acted properly. Beneficiaries are in a preferential position to general creditors.**

Application: The Court of Appeal held that both trust and client were entitled to a priority charge on the money; the various payments out of the account were treated as Hallett's own money.

General Principle: The above rule does not operate where a trustee purchases assets with withdrawals and then dissipates the balance. Here the beneficiary is entitled to a first charge on a mixed fund.

Re Oatway [1903] 2 Ch 356

Facts: The trustee had withdrawn money from a mixed account and invested it in shares, leaving a balance which at that time was ample to meet the claims of the beneficiaries. Subsequently the trustee dissipated the balance further. The issue was whether the trustee could withdraw his own money first (so that the shares would be treated as his own property)

Ratio: The beneficiaries' claim must be satisfied out of any identifiable part of the fund before the trustee could set up his own claim.

Application: The beneficiaries were entitled to the shares in priority to the general creditors. The trustee's allegation that he could have withdrawn the money first was rejected. The beneficiaries have a charge not only over the funds in the bank account but also any assets purchased with the shares.

General Principle: The beneficiary is entitled to recover the rise in value of the share of the premiums in those circumstances where the trust fund has been mixed with another asset.

Re Tilley's Will Trusts [1967] Ch 1179

Facts: An executrix mixed trust money in her bank account and used the account for purchases of real property. The purchases were speculative deals which were highly successful so that on her death her estate was worth £94,000. The claim on behalf of the trust was for a share of the profits made on the properties purchased with the mixed fund in the same proportion as the trust monies bore to the other monies in the account at the time of mixing.

Ratio: If the trust fund and trustee's estate have been mixed, the beneficiary is entitled to every portion of the blended property that the trustee cannot prove to be his own.

Application: The beneficiaries were only entitled to the return of their trust money with interest. Ungoed-Thomas J considered that if the trustee had used the trust money in the purchase of the property (or other assets, such as shares), then the beneficiaries would be entitled to the property and any profits to the extent that it had been paid for with trust property.

- **Comments in relation to cases involving mixed funds**

The judge reasoned that the rule in **Re Hallett's Estate** (1880) 13 Ch D 696 required that any purchase should initially be made with the trustee's own money; therefore, the trustee is entitled to the whole of the asset bought and any profits accruing to it. If the trustee goes further and dissipates the remaining balance, the beneficiaries will have a charge on the property bought – as in **Re Oatway** [1903] 2 Ch 356. This charge, per **Re Tilley's Will Trusts** [1967] Ch 1179, will be for the trust money and a proportionate part of the increased value and not merely for the original amount of the trust property.

If all money belonging to the trustee has been withdrawn, so that further withdrawals must necessarily take place out of trust monies, the beneficiaries cannot claim that any further monies paid in are intended to replace trust property, unless the trustee has shown an intention to make such a repayment. There is no presumption that later payments into the account are to repair any breach of trust that has been committed. The right to trace here is limited to the lowest balance of the account in the period between the trust fund monies being paid into the account and the time when the remedy is sought. For example: A trustee mixes £1000 of his own money into £3000 of trust money. Later the trustee withdraws £2000. Here the right to trace does not go beyond the £2000 left in the account – even if the trustee pays in further sums of his own money. The beneficiaries will have a right of personal claim against the trustee for the outstanding amounts. This is sometimes referred to as the "lowest intermediate balance rule".

- **Bank accounts** – third part involved

The rule here is the same as for mixing of two trusts: that is, where property belonging to two or more trusts are mixed, their claims rank *pari passu*: *Sinclair* v. *Brougham*. The rule also applies where trust money is paid into a bank account of an innocent volunteer where the competing interests of the beneficiaries and the volunteer have to be decided. The rule in *Clayton's Case* (1816) 1 Mer 572 is applied – it only applies in the context of a current bank account. The rule is to the effect that withdrawals out of the account are presumed to be made in the same order as payments in: the principle may be summed up as "first in, first out". Where the account is exhausted and the money or part of it is used for the purchase of assets such as shares then the competing sets of beneficiaries take *pari passu* under the principle in *Sinclair* v. *Brougham*.

General Principle: Where property belonging to two or more trusts is mixed, their claims rank *pari passu*.

Sinclair v Brougham [1914] AC 398
Facts: This case concerned a company that launched a banking business that was, admittedly, *ultra vires.* Customers deposited money until the society was wound up few years later. The assets were claimed at the same time by the ordinary shareholders and the depositors, each group claiming property over the other.
Ratio: Two innocent beneficiaries may be allowed to share the balance in the account, rateably. The amount will be calculated in proportion to the sums originally placed in the account from two trusts.
Application: Where there are insufficient funds to satisfy both claims, the rule in *Clayton's* case applies. That is, withdrawals are

made in the order of payments in, using the first trust money paid in first, where the mixing occurs in an active current account at a bank.

Action in Personam against a Recipient of Trust Property - Innocent volunteer

This remedy may be a possibility where the proprietary tracing remedy against an innocent volunteer has failed.

Remember that in *Re Diplock* executors distributed large sums of money to numerous charities under the terms of a residuary bequest which was subsequently held to be invalid. The misapplied money belonged, therefore, to the testator's next of kin, who wanted it back. They claimed, and the House of Lords agreed, that a direct action *in personam* lay against the innocent recipients in equity ~ that is, against the charities to whom the money was wrongfully distributed. The remedy is available to underpaid beneficiaries of a deceased person's estate against overpaid beneficiaries where a personal representative has wrongly distributed the estate or part of it, or to underpaid creditors or the next of kin of a deceased person.

It is of a purely personal nature and has no connection with tracing – it has no application against a *bona fide* purchaser without notice. Further, it is important to note that this action only lies against an innocent volunteer to the extent that the beneficiary has attempted and failed to recover from the trustee.

If judgement is given against an overpaid beneficiary, the overpaid beneficiary must find some means of satisfying the judgement. The fact that they have dissipated the funds is no defence since the action is against them personally, not simply against the assets. This remedy arose out of **Re Diplock** [1948] Ch 465 (CA), [1950] 2 All ER 1137 (HL). The remedy of tracing was found to be largely unsatisfactory in this case because large proportions of the money had already been spent and was unidentifiable, as the money had been used to improve the charities' property and therefore tracing was not available. The court held, however, that subject to the next of kin first pursuing their claim against the defaulting personal representatives (who were liable even though completely innocent), they would have a personal action for the difference between that claimed and the amount recovered for the personal representatives against the charities.

It should be noted that the beneficiaries must have first pursued the action against the personal representatives. Secondly, the overpaid beneficiaries are only liable for the difference (as explained above) – they are not liable for an interest on the amount claimed.

Limitations

There are some limits surrounding the right to trace for a claimant:

- **No Inequitable Results**

A court will not grant the relief, even if tracing is possible, where it will be inequitable to do so. Thus if an innocent volunteer has used trust monies to make improvements to her house, the court will not enforce a sale of the house in order to realise trust property since this would cause hardship to the volunteer - **Re Diplock.**

Recall that tracing is not possible or ceases to be possible if you can't identify the trust monies – for example, where the money has been used to pay off debts or where trust property comes into the hands of "equity's darling" – the *bona fide* purchaser for value without notice.

- **The equitable remedy does not affect rights obtained by a *bona fide* transferee of the legal estate for value without notice.**

All equitable claims are extinguished against such person. The beneficiary may be able to recover the proceeds of sale from the trustee if those funds are identifiable.

General Principle: The right to claim is extinguished if the claimant's property is no longer identifiable.

Re Diplock [1948] Ch 465

Facts: Caleb Diplock left the residue of his estate on trust for such charitable or benevolent purposes as his executors should in their absolute discretion select. A sum in excess of £200,000 was distributed to 139 charities before the validity of the gift was successfully challenged by his next of kin. They sought (*inter alia*) to trace the monies into the hands of the charities and were held by the Court of Appeal to be entitled to do so.

Ratio: As Lord green MR has put it : *" The equitable remedies presuppose the continued existence of the money either as a separate fund or as part of a mixed fund or as latent in property acquired by means of such a fund. If, on the facts of any individual case, such continued existence is not established, equity is as helpless as the common law itself."*

Application: For example, if the trust moneys have been spent on a dinner or a cruise or in paying off a loan, the courts will reject claims seeking to trace property.

General Principle: It is essential that the claimant proves that the property was held by another on his behalf in a fiduciary or quasi-fiduciary capacity in order to attract the jurisdiction of equity.

Agip (Africa) Ltd v Jackson and others (1991) 3 WLR 116

Facts: A company was victim of a fraudulent payment of £518, 522.

Ratio: The company was entitled to trace in equity a fraudulent payment since it has proved that it has been held by the defendant on its behalf. According to Fox LJ *"In the present case, there is no difficulty about the mechanics of tracing in equity. The money can be traced through the various bank to Baker Oil and onwards.* **It is however a perquisite to the operation of the remedy in equity that there must be a fiduciary relationship which calls the equitable jurisdiction into being. There is no difficulty about that in the present case since Mr. Zdiri must have been in a fiduciary relationship with**

Agip. He was the chief accountant of Agip and was entrusted with the signed drafts and orders. "

Application: There is no difficulty to prove that an employee of a company is in a fiduciary relationship with the latter.

Backward Tracing

The High Court concluded in **Serious Fraud Office v Hotel Portfolio II UK Ltd [2021]** EWHC 1273 (Comm) that assets acquired via a loan could not be tracked when the loan was repaid using money obtained in breach of trust because those assets were acquired prior to the breach of trust. That would be pure 'backwards tracing,' which was not permitted, and the circumstances did not fit into any of the exceptions to that rule.

Tracing and subrogation

On the one hand, tracing institutes appropriate remedy to secure property for a claimant which can prove that an identifiable interest is in the hands of a defendant. Subrogation, on the other hand, is an equitable remedy that substitutes one claimant for another. Millet LJ, in **Boscawen and Others 1995,** perfectly explaining the difference between tracing and subrogation: *"subrogation is a remedy, not a cause of action"*.

The rationale for the creation of this remedy is based on principles that bind the conscience of the defendant. In short, the underlying basis of subrogation is the reversal of unjust enrichment.

General Principle: Where there is a contract of indemnity, anything which reduces or diminishes the lost reduces or diminishes the amount which the indemnifier is bound to pay.

Burnand v Rodocanachi, Sons and Co (1882) 7 App Cas 333
Facts: A Co Ltd insured B's car under a comprehensive insurance policy and C, another motorist, negligently caused damages to B's car. A Co Ltd could have compensated B for the damage but decided to bring proceedings against C, albeit in B's name,

claiming that it was entitled to the rights of B to sue C in negligence and recover its loss.

Ratio: As Lord Blackburn has put it in this case "the general rule of law (and it is obvious justice) is that where there is a contract of indemnity … and a loss happens, anything which reduces or diminishes that loss reduces or diminishes the amount which the indemnifier is bound to pay; and if the indemnifier has already paid it, then, if anything which reduces or diminishes the loss comes into the hands of the person to whom he has paid it, it becomes an equity that the person who has already paid the full indemnity is entitled to be recouped by having that amount back".

Application: In an insurance contract, the insurer is entitled to bring proceedings against the person who negligently caused damages to the person who is protected by the insurance contract.

Summary

- The proprietary remedy has a number of advantages over the personal remedy, namely:

  - The effectiveness of the claimant's action is not depending on the defendant's solvency

  - The claimant may be able to take advantage of the increase in the value of the property

- Once an initial fiduciary relationship is established, it does not matter that the person who is in possession of the trust property is in no such relationship to the beneficiary.

- When the trust fund is mixed with the trustee's money, the trustee will simply draw on his money and the remaining will be the trust property. This rule does not operate where a trustee purchases assets with withdrawals and then dissipates the balance. Here the beneficiary is entitled to a first charge on a mixed fund.

- The beneficiary is entitled to recover the rise in value of the share of the premiums in those circumstances where the trust fund has been mixed with another asset.

- Where property belonging to two or more trusts is mixed, their claims rank *pari passu*: **Sinclair v. Brougham.**

- Action in personam against a Recipient of Trust Property may be a possibility where the proprietary tracing remedy against an innocent volunteer has failed.

- A court will not grant the relief, even if tracing is possible, where it will be inequitable to do so.

- The right to claim is extinguished if the claimant's

property is no longer identifiable.

- It is essential that the claimant proves that the property was held by another on his behalf in a fiduciary or quasi-fiduciary capacity in order to attract the jurisdiction of equity.

- Subrogation is an equitable remedy that substitutes one claimant for another.

- The rationale for the creation of this remedy is based on principles that bind the conscience of the defendant.

Chapter 15 - Equitable Remedies

Introduction

Prior to the Judicature Acts 1873/1975 Equity created new remedies that did not exist in Common law such as Specific Performance, Injunction, Rescission, Rectification and Account. Common law only provides damages. Equity provides more and its remedies are granted at the discretion of the court after fairly balancing the facts. The court looks at all the elements of the peculiar case in order to assess whether or not it is important to grant an equitable award. Usually courts provide equitable remedies in the following circumstances:

- when damages are not adequate,
- the Claimant has behaved in an inequitable way,
- there are severe delays in the claim
- if there is risk of undue hardship to the Defendant.

Thanks to the introduction of the Common Law Procedure Act 1854 and the Judicature Acts, common law courts may award equitable remedies. Both injunctions and specific performance will be examined in turn.

Injunctions

An injunction is an order of the court directing a party to the proceedings to do or refrain from doing a specified act. There are several types of injunctions: prohibitory, mandatory, perpetual etc. These types of injunctions will be examined specifically on the next section, but we need first to address general considerations applying to all of them.

Since the Judicature Acts 1873/75 both legal and equitable remedies have been available in the same court. Nowadays, the Senior Courts Acts 1981 confers this power to the High Court. The power of the County Court to issue injunctions is now contained in the County Courts Act 1984. Its jurisdiction is similar to the High Court, except in some exceptions.

The case law established a couple of general principles that will apply to all types of injunctions.

General Principle: The claimant shall prove the infringement or potential infringement of right which is recognized either in equity or at common law as a precondition for the grant of an injunction.

Day v Brownrigg [1878] 10 Ch D 284 (CA)
Facts: The claimant brought legal proceedings to seek an injunction preventing a neighbour to name his house by a certain appellation that he was already using for 60 years.
Ratio: The Court considered that the claimant did not prove any infringement or potential infringement of his rights, therefore it rejected the claim. As James L has put it in this case: "This Court can only interfere where there is an invasion of a legal or equitable right. No such legal or equitable right exists … I think it right to add that the power given to the Court by the judicature act 1873, to grant an injunction in all cases in which it shall appear to the Court to be "just or convenient" to do so, does not in the least alter the principles on which the Court should act".
Application: In order to seek an injunction, the claimant has to previously prove that one of his rights has been or will be infringed.

General Principle: The injunction will not be granted where damages will provide an equitable remedy.

Pride of Derby and Derbyshire Angling Association v British Celanese [1963] Ch 14
Facts: An injunction was granted, on behalf of the claimant, restraining the defendant from polluting a river due to his business activities.
Ratio: The Court considered that an injunction had to be added to damages since the behaviour of the defendant could trigger other infringements of the claimant's rights. According to Harman J: "The question arises whether there should be any injunction in the circumstances or whether the

plaintiffs, should content themselves with some less relief? Prima facie, a plaintiff, whose rights have been invaded ... Is entitled to relief from this court by way of an injunction."
Application: In practice, where damages have been awarded to repair a damage that is not likely to be repeated, an injunction may not be granted. However, if the claimant has shown that the defendant intends to continue with such conduct infringing his rights, he will *prima facie* be entitled to an injunction.

General Principle: An injunction will not be granted where the injury to the claimant's rights is trivial and an alternative remedy, such as declaration, is available.

Lladudno UDC v Woods [1899] 2 Ch 705
Facts: In this case the claimant sought both an injunction to restrain the defendant to preach on a beach and a declaration that he was a trespasser. **Ratio: The Court decided that the claim was too "trivial" to justify the grant of an injunction but the claimants were entitled to a declaration to the effect that the defendant was a trespasser. Cozens-Hardy J stated: "I cannot refuse to make a declaration that the defendant is not entitled, without the consent of the plaintiffs, to hold meeting or deliver addresses, lectures, or sermons on any part of the forshore in lease from the Crown. But I decline to go further. I decline to grant an injunction. That is a formidable legal weapon ought to be reserved for less trivial occasions".**
Application: An injunction is a serious remedy that cannot be granted for trivial complaints, specifically when a more appropriate remedy, such as declaration, is available. Claimants may seek injunctions where serious infringement of their right might be triggered.

General Principle: The Court, when deciding to grant an injunction, will take into consideration general equitable principles such as hardship of the parties, inordinate delay of the claimant imitating proceedings and whether the claimant comes to the court with "clean hands".

Jaggard v Sawyer [1995] 1 WLR 269

Facts: The defendants were breaching a covenant prohibiting them to trespass the claimant's property to build on the plot. The claimant delayed by about two years in seeking an injunction preventing the defendants of building a house on the plot, and he finally did it. When the claimant brought legal proceedings the building was at an advanced stage and cost already a significant amount of money.

Ratio: The Court refused to grant an injunction because it would have been unduly oppressive on the defendants. The court took into account the conduct of both the defendant and the claimant but also the nature of the trespass and the land in question. The Court considered that damages, being the most appropriate remedy available, had to be awarded in lieu of an injunction. As Millet LJ puts it : "In considering whether the grant of an injunction would be oppressive to the defendant, all the circumstances of the case have to be considered. (...) The case was a difficult one, but in an exemplary judgement the judge took into account all the relevant considerations, both those which told in favour of granting an injunction and those which told against."

Application: The general equitable principles and their relative importance will vary on a case-by-case basis. The oppressive nature of the order on the defendant is required to be judged on the date of the application for the grant.

Perpetual and interim injunctions

A perpetual or final injunction is one that is granted at the occasion of the final judgement. Conversely, an interim injunction is granted before the hearing and is intended to last only until the trial. In this case, the claimant will generally be required to give an undertaking in damages.

General Principle: The judge, when granting an interim injunction, assesses the balance of convenience based on his

exercise of discretion, determining if the case went to a trial with same evidence than that currently available the claimant would be entitled to a permanent injunction.

American Cyanamid Co v Ethicon Ltd 1975 2 WLR 316

Facts: In this case, an American company owned a patent on a specific type of surgical sutures, claimed that another company that was about to launch a similar product on the British market infringed its patent. Therefore, the claimant implied for an interim injunction to restrain the company to launch its product on the market. An interim injunction with undertaking in damages was granted at first instance. The Court of appeal reversed this decision invalidating the injunction.

Ratio: The House of lords allowed the claimants' appeal considering that the judge had a power of discretion when assessing the balance of convenience. Lord Diplock presented the new principles on which an interim injunction may be granted:

- **There must be a serious question to be tried, frivolous claims must be excluded;**
- **Is injunction a more adequate remedy than damages?**
- **Does the undertaking in damages are sufficient and will the claimant be able to honour it?**
- **Can the status quo be maintained?**
- **The Court can take into consideration other social or economic factors**
- **At a last resort if the decision is not taken, the judge may take into consideration the strength of the parties' cases.**

Application: When granting an interim injunction, the judge should proceed to balance of convenience taking into account a couple of factors that are laid down in this case.

However, important critics have been made to the last factor of the strength of the parties' cases. **In Series 5 Software Ltd v Clarke** (1996) 1 All ER 853, Laddie J suggested that this factor was not a matter of last resort but should be avoided in cases involving difficult dispute sin law or facts. An important number of exceptions to the **American Cyanamid** have been recognized by the case law:

- Where the injunction will finally dispose of the matter. In those cases the claimant has to present a strong *prima facie* case.
- Where the defendant has no arguable defence, there is no need to go through the **American Cyanamid** test, the Court can directly consider the strength of the parties' cases.

- In cases opposing private and public interests, the court will take into account the public interest in the balance of convenience (see, **Lewis v Heffer 1978** 1 WLR 106).

- In cases involving freedom of expression, the claimant has to prove that publication of information should not be allowed, according to section 12 of the Human rights act and article 10 of the European Convention on Human Rights.

Prohibitory injunction

A prohibitory injunction is granted to prevent the defendant of acting in a certain way. This is generally easier to obtain than a mandatory injunction that requires a positive action.

General Principle: Prohibortory injunction may be granted to restrain a breach of a negative term of a contract, once it is satisfied that there has been a breach of the term.

Doherty v Allman (1878) 3 App Cas 709
Facts: Between the claimant and the defendant, two leases of land were granted under covenants to maintain the premises in good order. No reservation of a power of re-entry for breaches of the covenants was agreed but the defendants proposed to act in breach of the covenant. Thus, the claimant sought a prohibitory injunction to restrain them acting in such a way.

Ratio: The Court rejected the prohibitory injunction claim in the exercise of its discretion and left the claimant pursue its claim for damages. In this case, Lord Cairns explained that in such cases there was no need to consider the balance of convenience since the parties had already agreed to not act in a particular way. However, the Court exercise its discretion when awarding such injunctions considering different factors such as whether the performance of such conduct will effectively produce an injury to the claimant, whether this injury is capable of being remedied by damages that can and finally if they must be sought in successive suits or could be obtained once for all.

Application: The main condition for a prohibitory injunction to be granted in such cases is that the defendant must have already acted in infringement of the negative term of the contract. Then, the court exercises its discretion while determining the articulation of the claim with damages.

Mandatory injunction

A mandatory injunction orders the defendant to perform a specified act. Here, there is an obvious proximity with specific performance that we will examine later in this Chapter. However, mandatory injunction will be useful where specific performance will not be granted for certain contracts leaving the claimant to his common law rights of damages. The order must be very clear and specific in order for the defendant to know exactly what he has to do since the disobedience to an injunction is a contempt of court. For example, mandatory injunctions have been granted to enforce contracts for the supply of goods where the failure to supply would have put the claimants out of business (see **petroleum Ltd v VIP Petroleum Ltd 1974** 1 WLR 576).

General Principle: When granting a mandatory injunction, the factor of hardship to the defendant and public interest may have a significant importance.

Wrotham Park Estates Ltd v Parkside Homes Ltd [1974] 3 All ER 321

Facts: In this case, the claimant applied to the court for a mandatory injunction seeking to order the defendant to demolish houses which have been built in breach of a restrictive covenant. **Ratio: The Court, exercising its discretion, refused to grant a mandatory injunction since the order of demolition would have been "an unpardonable waste of much needed houses". As a substitute, the Court awarded damages as a quid pro quo for relaxing the covenants. As Brightman J puts it : "The erection of the houses, whether one likes it or not is a** *fait accompli* **and the houses are now the homes of people. No damage of a financial nature has been done to the plaintiffs by the breach of the layout stipulation".**

Application: When awarding a mandatory injunction would be contrary to public interests or would be too hard to the defendant, the courts may substitute this remedy to damages repairing the loss.

Quia timet injunction

Quia timet literally means "because he fears", it is an injunction available to be granted before the occurrence of an apprehended injury, intended to prevent it. It serves as deterrence for the defendant. It is generally used where a defendant threatens to demolish a building. This injunction is an exception to the general principle that requires the applicant to prove an injury. In **Redland Bricks v Morris** (1970) AC 652 Lord Upjhon gives an explanation of *quia timet* injunction:

"My lords, quia timet actions are broadly applicable to two types of cases: first, wherethe defendant has as yet done no hurt to the plaintiff but is threatening and intending to do works which will render irreparable harm to him or his property if carried to completion. Secondly the type of case where the plaintiff has been fully recompensed both at law and in equity for the damage he has suffered but where he alleges that the earlier actions of the defendant may lead to future cause of action."

General Principle: A mandatory *quia timet* **injunction requires the claimant to show a strong possibility of damage**

occurring for which damages will be inappropriate and for which the cost to the defendant will not be disproportionate.

Redland Bricks v Morris (1970) AC 652 Lord Upjhon
Facts: The defendant was implied with the claimant in a business of gardeners. As a result of excavations carried out by the defendant, the claimant applied for an injunction ordering the defendant to restore support to the claimant's market garden.
Ratio: The House of Lords rejected the injunction on the grounds that the action expected to be taken was not clear, the defendant did not act unreasonably and that the cost of restoring support was out of all proportion to the value of the claimant's land.
Application: The granting of mandatory *quia timet* injunction is restricted to exceptional cases where the claimant will have to show that it is the only available adequate remedy to prevent an irreparable harm to happen.

<u>Specific Performance</u>

Underlying principles for specific performance

Before breach of contract, when the remedy of damages at common law is inappropriate, the court may prefer to impose the wronged party to perform the obligation he promised to do. This remedy will be appropriate in cases where there is a contract for the sale of land and the claimant might strongly want the land for its unique value and would regard damages as a poor substitute. It can also concern cases where paintings, shares in a private company or unique goods are involved.

The burden to show the existence of a valid contract between the parties lies on the side of the claimant. Once the validity of the contract is established and the defendant has been found in breach of his positive obligation, specific performance becomes available. If the defendant does not comply with the court order, this will constitute a contempt of court, for which the defendant may be punished by imprisonment or fine.

Before deciding whether or not awarding specific performance, the court will look at the adequacy of the remedy of damages at common law and at the potential unfair hardship on the defendant that may arise from the imposition of this equitable remedy.

General Principle: Specific performance, because it is an equitable remedy, is discretionary. Accordingly, when granting such a remedy, the Court will take into account various factors including laches, the conduct of the claimant and the question of hardship to the defendant.

Patel v Ali [1984] 1 All ER 978
Facts: The parties stipulated an agreement for the sale of a land. Since the sale was delayed, the Claimant brought an action requiring specific performance. After contracting to sell the house, the Defendant took cancer and she underwent amputation of the leg. The husband was in prison and she had three children to look after.
Ratio: The court does not grant specific performance of a contract if the defendant may suffer hardship from it, even though the hardship is not caused by the claimant and it is a consequence of something happened after the date of the contract.
Application: The court refused to grant specific performance on the ground that of hardship. The delay of the sale could not be attributed to the conduct of the Defendant. The Claimant had a remedy in damages.

General Principle: Courts may grant specific performance in exceptional circumstances, for example when the claimant is in serious danger of being forced out of the business.

Sky Petroleum Ltd v VIP Petroleum Ltd [1974] 1 WLR 576
Facts: The claimant entered into a contract stipulating that he will be supplied all the petrol he needed. However, the defendant purported to suspend the contract for a certain period. The claimant, without the supply of petrol from the defendant, because he could not continue running his business activities, would be forced out of business.

Ratio: The Court granted specific performance with an interim injunction prohibiting the defendant to refuse supplying the petrol. As Goulding J has put it in this case: "There is, in my judgement, so far as I can make out on the evidence before me, a serious danger that unless the court interferes at this stage the plaintiff company will be forced out of business."

Application: Courts will generally be reluctant to grant specific performance unless it is to avoid a greater harm.

For long, it was taught that mutuality, implying that the remedy will be granted only if it is available to either party, was strictly required for the granting of specific performance. This approach was based on the old case **Flight v Boland** (1882) 4 Russ 298. More recently, in **Price v Strange (1977)** 3 All ER 371, it was held that mutuality was a mere factor to be considered in the discretionary decision of the court.

Specific performance will only be granted where damages are inadequate. Conversely, specific performances will not be granted where damages would appropriately compensate the claimant. This is particularly the case where contracts concern goods that are freely available on the open market. In this situation, the claimant, after being awarded damages will be free to purchase the good elsewhere.

Contracts requiring supervision

Contracts that require continuous supervision by the court do not usually justify the award of specific performance. This is to avoid successive applications seeking to secure compliance with the contract.

General Principle: Difficulties of enforcement and supervision of an order for specific performance may restrain the court in adopting it.

Co-operative Insurance Society Ltd v Argyll Stores (Holdings) Ltd [1997] 3 All ER 297 **Facts:** A covenant in a shop lease required the tenants to keep the premises open as a supermarket during the usual hours of business. However, the shop had been closed because it was losing money. The Court of Appeal made an order for specific performance of the covenant.

Ratio: If the court realises that there are difficulties in drawing an order of specific performance with precision, it should avoid wasteful litigations.

Application: The House of Lords allowed the appeal against the decision achieved by the Court of Appeal.

Nevertheless, the awarding of specific performance will depend on a degree of supervision that the contract will require. For instance, the continuity of the obligation sought to be ordered will not necessarily render the granting of specific performance impossible for excessive supervision provided that it is quite clear what the defendant is required to do. For instance, in **Beswick v Beswick** (1958) AC 58 specific performance was granted although it required the defendant to pay an annuity continuously to the claimant.

Contracts for personal services

The same reasoning is applied to contracts for personal services. In order to award specific performance in these circumstances, the court will incur in constant supervision. Furthermore, it would be against public policy to compel the parties involved to continue the working relationship.

In **Lumley v Wagner** (1852) 42 ER 687 the Court refused to grant specific performance that would force the defendant to sing only at the claimant's theatre during a certain period of time. This could have been considered as infringing Article 4 on the European Convention of Human Rights on the prohibition of forced labour. However, the courts have drawn a line between contract for personal services and contract to achieve a common goal. In the latter cases, the courts are less reluctant to grant specific performance.

General Principle: Specific performance could be granted in cases involving contracts to achieve a common goal.

Eskine Macdonald Ltd v Eyles (1921) 1 Ch 631
Facts: The claimant signed a copyright agreement offering the defendant, an authoress, a publishing contract to write her next three books subject to royalty terms. The defendant tried to sell one of her books to a rival publisher.
Ratio: The Court an order of specific performance on the ground that such agreements were not contract to render personal services, but contracts to sell the products of the labour or industry of the contracting party.
Application: The courts, when assessing whether or not they should order specific performance, will take into consideration the nature of the contract.

Agreements that are futile

The famous maxim says: "Equity does nothing in vain". Therefore, specific performance will not be granted where it would be either futile or impossible. For example, applications for specific performance will be rejected in cases of agreements which are not for a fixed term as the partnership could be terminated anyway at will (see **Hercy v Birch** (1804) 9 Ves 357).

Mistake and Misrepresentation

Mistake and misrepresentation usually gives the parties the right to rescind the contract. In addition to this, it seems that it also has a role to play in specific performance actions since the Court will generally refuse to grant in such circumstances.

General Principle: Mistake and misrepresentation may be used as a defence to an action for specific performance.

Co-operative Insurance Society Ltd v Argyll Stores (Holdings) Ltd [1997] 3 All ER 297
Facts: When the contract was concluded, the defendant believed that it included "three fine elm trees" whereas in fact it did not.

This mistake was attributable to a misleading report provided by the claimant. The claimant sued for specific performance and the defendant invoked a mistake.

Ratio: The Court refused to grant specific performance as it would have been inequitable. The Court also noticed that mistake not induced by the claimant might be a ground for refusing specific performance.

Application: When the contract is not clear about certain obligations, the defendant should invoke mistake and misrepresentation to counter the claimant's application for specific performance.

General Principle: A unilateral mistake not induced by the claimant might be a ground for refusing personal performance although it would not entitle the defendant to rescind the contract.

Co-operative Insurance Society Ltd v Argyll Stores (Holdings) Ltd [1997] 3 All ER 297

Facts: The defendant bid for property at an auction, believing that it included "three fine elm trees", whereas in fact it did not. His mistake was attributable to a plan provided by the claimant. The defendant subsequently wished to withdraw from the contract and the claimant sued for specific performance.

Ratio: The Court refused the claimant's application as it was felt that granting specific performance would be inequitable. The Court also noted that a unilateral mistake not induced by the claimant might be a ground for refusing personal performance although it would not entitle the defendant to rescind the contract.

Application: In general, it seems that courts may be more willing to refuse a decree of specific performance by accepting mistake as a defence than to grant rescission.

Summary

- Initially, Common Law only provided damages as a remedy. However, it happened that in some cases damages were not an appropriate remedy. Therefore,

Equity was based on justice and fair play to the parties. Injunctions and specific performance have been recognized. Any willingly attempt to not comply with these court orders will constitute a contempt to Court.

- An injunction is an order of the court directing a party to the proceedings to do or refrain from doing a specified act. The claimant shall prove the infringement or potential infringement of right which is recognized either in equity or at common law as a precondition for the grant of an injunction.

- The injunction will not be granted where damages will provide an equitable remedy.

- The Court, when deciding to grant an injunction, will take into consideration general equitable principles such as hardship of the parties, inordinate delay of the claimant imitating proceedings and whether the claimant comes to the court with "clean hands".

- A perpetual or final injunction is one that is granted at the occasion of the final judgement. Conversely, an interim injunction is granted before the hearing and is intended to last only until the trial. In this case, the claimant will generally be required to give an undertaking in damages.

- The judge, when granting an interim injunction, assesses the balance of convenience based on his exercise of discretion, determining if the case went to a trial with same evidence than that currently available the claimant would be entitled to a permanent injunction.

- A prohibotory injunction is granted to prevent the defendant of acting in a certain way. This is generally easier to obtain than a mandatory injunction that requires a positive action.

- A mandatory injunction orders the defendant to perform a

specified act. When granting a mandatory injunction, the factor of hardship to the defendant and public interest may have a significant importance.

- *Quia timet* literally means "because he fears", it is an injunction available to be granted before the occurrence of an apprehended injury, intended to prevent it.

- Before breach of contract, when the remedy of damages at common law is inappropriate, the court may prefer to impose the wronged party to perform the obligation he promised to do.

- Specific performance, because it is an equitable remedy, is discretionary. Accordingly, when granting such a remedy, the Court will take into account various factors including laches, the conduct of the claimant and the question of hardship to the defendant.
- Difficulties of enforcement and supervision of an order for specific performance may restrain the court in adopting it.

- Mistake and misrepresentation may be used as a defence to an action for specific performance.

Chapter 16 – Liability of Strangers

An introduction to Liability of strangers

In the context of equity and trusts law, a stranger is someone related to a trust although not appointed by a trustee. Strangers who committed faults may be liable to account to the beneficiary for breach of trust.

On the one hand, strangers may be held liable when they knowingly receive or deal with the trust property in breach of trust. This is traditionally referred to as "knowing receipt". For instance, such behaviour includes the refusal for the recipient to return the property to its rightful owner, the beneficiary, even though he or she was aware that it should be returned.

On the other hand, strangers may dishonestly assist or procure a breach of trust. The Privy Council in **Royal Brunei Airlines v Philip Tan Kok Ming [1995]** 2 AC 378 UKPC 22, mentioned it as "dishonest assistance". However, the regime of liability for such behaviour is slightly different and is generally referred to as "accessory liability". It should be noted that dishonesty in this civil sphere extends beyond the subjective dishonesty required in criminal law.

The distinction between recipient and accessory liability is of fundamental importance for the purposes of this chapter. The distinction has been explained by Lord Millett in **Twinsectra v Yardley [2002]** UKHL 12, [105], [107]: "Liability for "knowing receipt" is receipt-based. It does not depend on fault. (…) The accessory's liability for having assisted in a breach of trust is quite different. It is fault-based, not receipt-based. The defendant is not charged with having received trust moneys for his own benefit, but with having acted as an accessory to a breach of trust".

The personal liability of stranger was extended by the courts beyond trust property to property in respect of which fiduciary duties exist. For example, personal liability of strangers was upheld to company directors' duties in respect of company property.

Traditionally, stranger's liability makes a distinction between knowing receipt or dishonest assistance. This classification is derived from **Barnes v Addy (1874) LR 9 Ch App 244 at 251–252**, where Lord Selborne LC stated: "Strangers are not to be made constructive trustees merely because they act as the agents of trustees in transactions within their legal powers, transactions, perhaps, of which a court of equity may disapprove, unless those agents receive and become chargeable with some part of the trust property, or unless they assist with knowledge in a dishonest and fraudulent design on the part of the trustees".

Knowing Receipt

Personal liability for knowing receipt

As a general rule, where a person receives property misappropriated from a trust, the recipient (unless a *bona fide* purchaser for value without notice) will be obliged to return the property or its proceeds as soon as they become aware of the position. However, in terms of personal liability in equity to pay compensation, a fault has to be proven in the defendant's behaviour, such as the knowledge of the existing equitable interest.

General principle: An innocent volunteer recipient of money which is the product of a breach of trust, without having previously acquired knowledge of the existence of the trust, cannot be held personally liable to account for the trust property.

Independent Trustee Services Ltd v GP Noble Trustees Ltd [2012] EWCA Civ 195
Facts: Under a consent order in ancillary relief proceedings on divorce, H paid a lump sum of around £1.4 million to W from trust assets liquidated from nine pension schemes by the then trustees in breach of trust. Subsequently, the consent order was partially

set aside on W's application. The question of her personal liability as a stranger was raised by the plaintiff.

Ratio: The Court refused to hold the stranger liable. Millett J held that a volunteer who has received trust property is not liable to account for the trust property if he has parted with it without having previously acquired knowledge of the existence of the trust. Thus, it is clear that, if the proprietary claim against the respondent is justified, it only extends to money (or its traceable proceeds), which was in the defendant's hands at the time she was given notice of the trustee's claim.

Application: The recipient cannot be held personally liable for innocent actions.

Conversely, a recipient of property, however, will be under a personal liability to account to the beneficiaries for the loss to the trust if they dissipated the trust property (or its proceeds) after becoming aware that it was trust property. Therefore, knowledge is crucial to determine the recipient's liability in this context. In those cases, the defendant is sometimes characterized as a constructive trustee, in order underline that even though they are not real trustees, they should be treated as if they were, and therefore be liable to make good any losses to the beneficiaries resulting from the trustee's breach of trust. As Lionel Smith wrote: *"to say that a defendant is "liable as a constructive trustee" is just to say that he is liable even though he is not actually a trustee; it says exactly nothing about what makes someone liable."*

Levels of knowledge

When the courts' case law drew the distinction between knowing receipt and dishonest assistance, what has concerned the legal community in relation to both these forms of personal liability is the degree of "knowledge" which the third party has when acting in relation to the trust and whether dishonesty is necessary.

General principle: Common Law devised five levels of knowledge to determine whether the recipient was personally liable.

Delvaux and Lecuit v Société Générale pour Favoriser le Développement du Commerce et de l'Industrie en France SA [1983] BCLC 325

Facts: The plaintiffs were liquidators of the Luxembourg Mutual Investment Fund and claimed that *Société Générale* owed them $4,009,697.91, which it held for its customer, the Bahamas Commonwealth Bank Ltd in a trust account. On 10 May 1973, it followed BCB's instructions, in arrangement with Algemene Bank, Amsterdam, transferred the money to Banco Nacional de Panama, to a non-trust account in BCB's name. This, claimed Baden, made *Société Générale* a constructive trustee, and so had a duty to account.

Ratio: The court looked to various forms of knowledge which could be attributed to a party when considering a rectification and divided it into five types:

1. Actual knowledge;

2. Wilfully shutting one's eyes to the obvious;

3. Wilfully and recklessly failing to make such inquiries as an honest and reasonable man would make;

4. Knowledge of circumstances which would indicate the facts to an honest and reasonable man (but not a morally obtuse man); and

5. Knowledge of circumstances which would put an honest and reasonable man on inquiry.

In an attempt to define knowledge in further details, Peter Gibson J explained: "Again, however, I do not think it need be knowledge of the whole design: that would be an impossibly high requirement in most cases. What is crucial is that the alleged constructive trustee should know that a design having the character of being fraudulent and dishonest was being perpetrated. Further he must know that his act assisted in the implementation of such design".

Application: It seems that the knowledge test requires that the defendant is aware that a fraudulent design is being prepared and that his assistance will help to implement it.

General principle: A person with knowledge in categories (ii) and (iii) will be taken to have actual knowledge while a person

in categories (iv) or (v) has constructive notice only. Constructive notice can suffice for the protection of proprietary interests.

Baden case and Agip (Africa) Ltd v Jackson [1990] Ch 265
Facts: An Agip Ltd employee, changed the name on a payment order of $518,000 to Baker Oil Services Ltd, acting on clients' instructions. All but $43,000 was then paid on to unknown parties. Agip Ltd sued Mr Jackson for return of the money.
Ratio: The Court held that the claimant had actual knowledge. According to Millet J: "If a person did suspect wrongdoing yet failed to make inquiries because he did not want to know or because he regarded it as none of his business - he is dishonest, and he will be treated as if he had actual knowledge. In contrast, if a man does not draw the obvious inferences or make the obvious inquiries because, however foolishly, he did not suspect wrongdoing or, having suspected it, had his suspicions allayed, however unreasonably, would not be guilty of dishonest conduct".
Application: In this case, the test focuses mainly on the defendant's good faith or intention when exposed to suspicions of breach of trust, rather than looking at the reasonableness of whether or not he should have suspected anything. It should be noted that this case should be taken in conjunction with other cases adopted later, namely the case **Royal Brunei Airlines v Tan [1995]** 2 AC 378 which enshrined, five years later, a different solution.

These principles have been questioned in later cases. Confusion has prevailed for many years after the adoption of contradictory views in several cases. However, the development of the concept of dishonest assistance has clarified the situation.

Dishonest Assistance (Accessory Liability)

The following cases clarified the law relating to an accessory's liability for a trustee's breach of trust. What has perplexed the courts is what level of knowledge is required, how to define dishonesty but also whether a fraudulent third party would be liable if the trustee was not dishonest. In such cases, in order to hold the defendant personally liable, it has to be demonstrated that he or she was dishonest but also that he has assisted the third party in the breach of trust.

Dishonesty

General principle: The accessory's knowledge is not the key question to determine their liability, it is rather their knowledge of the circumstances which would indicate the facts to an honest and reasonable man (but not a morally obtuse man) and knowledge of circumstances which would put an honest and reasonable man on inquiry. Therefore, categories (iv) and (v) if the Baden test will suffice for personal liability for dishonest assistance in a breach of fiduciary position.

Royal Brunei Airlines v Tan [1995] 2 AC 378
Facts: Royal Brunei Airlines appointed Borneo Leisure Travel, directed by Mr Tan, for booking passenger flights and cargo transport. The money was agreed to be held on trust in a separate account until passed over. But Borneo Leisure Travel, with Mr Tan's knowledge and assistance, paid money into its current account and used it for its own business. Borneo Leisure travel failed to pay on time, the contract was terminated, and it went insolvent. Royal Brunei claimed the money back from Mr Tan. The Judge held Mr Tan was liable as a constructive trustee to Royal Brunei. The Court of Appeal of Brunei Darussalam held that the company was not guilty of fraud or dishonesty, and so Mr Tan could not be either. The case was appealed to the Privy Council.
Ratio: The Privy Council held that: "liability in equity to make good resulting loss attaches to a person who dishonestly procures or assists in a breach of trust or fiduciary obligation". Giving the advice of the Privy Council, Lord Nicholls held it was the dishonest assistant's state of mind which matters: "Whatever may be the position in some criminal or other contexts (see, for instance, R v Ghosh [1982] QB 1053), in the context of the accessory liability principle acting dishonestly, or with a lack of probity, which is

synonymous, means simply not acting as an honest person would in the circumstances. This is an objective standard. At first sight this may seem surprising. Honesty has a connotation of subjectivity, as distinct from the objectivity of negligence. (…) Carelessness is not dishonesty. Thus for the most part dishonesty is to be equated with conscious impropriety. However, these subjective characteristics of honesty do not mean that individuals are free to set their own standards of honesty in particular circumstances. The standard of what constitutes honest conduct is not subjective. Honesty is not an optional scale, with higher or lower values according to the moral standards of each individual. If a person knowingly appropriates another's property, he will not escape a finding of dishonesty simply because he sees nothing wrong in such behaviour" [at 389].**

Application: Although the state of the accessory's knowledge is no longer the core element of their liability, their knowledge of the circumstances is relevant in determining whether they acted honestly or not.

General principle: In addition to the test laid down in Royal Brunei Airlines v Tan [1995] to determine dishonesty, there is a subjective element to take into account. Not only must the defendant have acted dishonestly according to the ordinary conception of reasonable and honest people, he must have been aware that they would so view his conduct.

Twinsectra Ltd v Yardley & Others [2002] 2 AC 164

Facts: Twinsectra had loaned Yardley approximately £1 million that he gave to Sims, Yardley's initial solicitor. Sims then gave a written undertaking to Twinsectra that the money was to be used solely for acquiring property for Yardley and for no other purpose. Yardley ordered Sims to transfer the money to his other solicitor, Leach, who knew of Sims' undertaking. Leach then used the money, on Yardley's instructions, for other purposes than acquiring property. Leach knew that he was allowing the money to be used for an unauthorised purpose, but thought that Sims was merely under a contractual obligation to Twinsectra.

Ratio: The House of Lords confirmed that the money was held on trust, only to be used for acquiring property, but held that Leach, the stranger, was not liable, given that he was not himself subjectively aware that his conduct was something that the ordinary reasonable person would consider dishonest. Application: In order to determine a stranger's liability, one should look at the test laid down in **Royal Brunei Airlines v Tan [1995]** combined with the subjective element upheld in the present case, which implies to take into account the defendant's awareness that his or her conduct would be seen dishonest by ordinary and reasonable people.

The approach upheld in the case **Twinsectra Ltd v Yardley & Others [2002]** created an important controversy. Firstly, Lord Millet strongly dissented in this case considering that this approach departed from the rather objective test laid down in **Royal Brunei Airlines v Tan [1995]**. In addition to this, in **Barlow Clowes International v Eurotrust International Ltd [2005] UKPC 37, [2005]** 1 WLR 1476, Lord Hoffmann, delivering the advice for the Privy Council, conceded an element of ambiguity in remarks made in **Twinsectra** by himself and Lord Hutton in relation to the defendant's knowledge that his conduct was dishonest. In this respect, Lord Hoffmann developed in **Barlow** that by dishonest state of mind, him and Lord Hutton meant: "consciousness of those elements of the transaction which make participation transgress ordinary standards of honest behaviour. It did not also require (…) thought about what those standards were". This question can be considered as settled by the **Abou-Rahmah** case.

General principle: The test for dishonesty remains primarily objective: it is sufficient if the defendant knows of the elements of the transaction which make it dishonest according to normally accepted standards of behaviour.

Abou-Rahmah v Abacha [2006] EWCA Civ 1492 at [59 and 69] **Facts:** The appellants were victims of a fraud conducted via the respondent bank by one of their clients. This case concerned particularly a claim brought by the claimants against a bank into which a two payments totalling US$625,000, which had been taken from the claimants as part of the scam in Benin, had been paid. A first instance decision held that the bank was not liable to the victims either in the equitable tort of knowing or dishonest assistance in a breach of trust.

Ratio: The Court of Appeal dismissed the appeals and confirmed that the defendant was not personally liable. Arden LJ affirmed that the test for dishonesty was primarily an objective one: "It is unnecessary to show subjective dishonesty in the sense of consciousness that the transaction is dishonest. It is sufficient if the defendant knows of the elements of the transaction which make it dishonest according to normally accepted standards of behaviour".

Application: This case can be considered as settling the controversy over the test for dishonesty since its findings have been applied in subsequent case-law (see **Aerostar Maintenance International Ltd v Wilson [2010]** EWHC 2032 (Ch) at [183], [198] and **Starglade Properties Ltd v Nash [2010]** EWCA Civ 1314 at [30] where it is reaffirmed that the subjective understanding of the person concerned as to whether his conduct is dishonest is irrelevant).

General principle: The relevant standard to assess dishonesty is the ordinary standard of honest behaviour, it is irrelevant that there may be a body of opinion which regards the ordinary standard of honest behaviour as being set too high.

Starglade Properties Ltd v Nash [2010] EWCA Civ 1314 at [32]
Facts: The defendant, Mr Nash, was the director of a company, Larkstore, which owed money to Starglade Properties. The debt arose as a result of an agreement under which Larkstore agreed to share the money it received as damages in litigation against a third party. Starglade had originally assigned its rights in the litigation to Larkstore, and by a side letter Larkstore agreed to hold on trust any moneys it received from the third party.

Mr Nash subsequently paid the money to other creditors (not Glancestyle) to deliberately frustrate Starglade's attempts to recover the money.

Mr Nash then applied for Larkstore to be dissolved and taken off the Companies Register.

Starglade sued Mr Nash, claiming that he was liable for dishonest assistance in a breach of trust by Larkstore.

Ratio: The Court of Appeal concluded that the defendant had therefore dishonestly assisted in a breach of trust and found him personally liable. Morritt C recalled, after having thoroughly analysed the case law on the question of dishonesty that: "The relevant standard is the ordinary standard of honest behaviour. Just as the subjective understanding of the person concerned as to whether his conduct is dishonest is irrelevant so also is it irrelevant that there may be a body of opinion which regards the ordinary standard of honest behaviour as being set too high".

Application: Accordingly, in order to be considered honest, the correct approach would have been for the defendant to put Larkstore into liquidation or administration and to allow the moneys to be distributed in the ordinary way.

Assistance

The second requirement to hold the defendant liable consists on demonstrating that the defendant assisted with the breach of trust or fiduciary duty. A sort of causative link has to be shown between the acts of the defendant and the breach.

General principle: The defendant is not liable for any loss suffered by the claimant, only those resulting from the breach of trust or fiduciary duty which has been dishonestly assisted.

Grupo Torras SA v Al-Sabah (No 5) [1999] CLC 1469

Facts: The plaintiff, GT, was incorporated in Spain and was controlled by the Kuwait Investment Office (KIO) in London. The key facts were that the first defendant (F) had been chairman of GT and of KIO, and was accused, together with 55 other defendant individuals and companies, as a result of complex transactions, of being at the heart of very large-scale fraud upon GT. The claims were made on the basis of conspiracy, dishonest assistance and knowing receipt.

Ratio: The defendants liable for dishonest assistance were identified. In this case, Mance LJ, clarified the limited liability of defendants under dishonest assistance: "The starting point is that the requirement of dishonest assistance relates not to any loss or damage which may be suffered, but to the breach of trust or fiduciary duty. The relevant enquiry is what loss or damage resulted from the breach of trust or fiduciary duty which has been dishonestly assisted".

Application: This case limited the defendant's liability in cases of dishonest assistance. The reasoning behind this rule stems from a traditional conception of liability which implies that a defendant can only be held responsible for the losses resulting from his or her conduct.

General principle: Whilst there has to be some form of causative impact between the breach and the assistance, the claimant does not have to show that the defendant's actions "inevitably had the consequence that a loss was suffered".

Delvaux and Lecuit v Société Générale pour Favoriser le Développement du Commerce et de l'Industrie en France SA [1983] BCLC 325

Facts: The plaintiffs were liquidators of the Luxembourg Mutual Investment Fund and claimed that *Société Générale* owed them $4,009,697.91, which it held for its customer, the Bahamas Commonwealth Bank Ltd in a trust account. On 10 May 1973, it followed BCB's instructions, in arrangement with Algemene Bank, Amsterdam, transferred the money to Banco Nacional de Panama, to a non-trust account in BCB's name. This, claimed Baden, made *Société Générale* a constructive trustee, and so had a duty to account.

Ratio: According to Peter Gibson's ruling in this case: "the claimant does not have to show that the defendant's actions, inevitably had the consequence that a loss was suffered".

Application: The causation threshold between the defendant's actions and the loss suffered is quite low.

General principle: The defendant does not need to know precisely the nature of the breach of fiduciary duty, so long as

they have some appreciation that they are helping someone who is up to no good before the occurrence of the breach and its cover-up.

Ultraframe (UK) Ltd v Fielding [2005] EWHC 1638 (Ch)
Facts: The parties had engaged in a bitter 95 day trial in which allegations of forgery, theft, false accounting, blackmail and arson. A company owning patents and other rights had become insolvent, and the real concern was the destination and ownership of those rights.
Ratio: The Court held the defendant had not dishonestly assisted with breach of trust. Lewison J clarified the key elements of assistance: "The defendant does not need to know precisely the nature of the breach of fiduciary duty, so long as they have some appreciation that they are helping someone who is up to no good". The main point is whether defendants acted *a priori* and somehow participated to the planning of the breach or if they intervened after the breach and subsequent cover-up. In the first situation, the defendant has assisted whereas it is not the case in the second situation.
Application: The standard for proving assistance is not very high, as far as one can demonstrate that the defendant assisted before the occurrence of the breach.

Finally, it should be noted that, when the fiduciary and the assistant were not acting in a joint venture, the accessory cannot be held liable for profit made by the fiduciary. In other words, assistants are only liable for any profit that they made (see **Novoship (UK) Ltd v Nikitin [2014]** EWCA Civ 908).

Recipient Liability

Traditionally, three requisite elements are required to engage a recipient liability under knowing receipt claims. It should be respectively demonstrated that there has been (i) a disposal in breach of trust or fiduciary duty (ii) a beneficial receipt by the defendant of assets which are traceable to the claimant and that (iii) the defendant knew that the assets are traceable to a breach of trust or fiduciary duty. This three-limb-test has been identified by

Hoffmann LJ in **El Ajou v Dollar Land Holdings plc [1994]** 2 All ER 685 at 700.

Beneficial receipt

General principle: The recipient is only liable when he beneficially received assets which are traceable to the claimant. Where the recipient acted in a ministerial capacity (as a solicitor or a banker) they can only be held liable if the agent lawfully receives property but then deals with it for his own benefit knowing this to be inconsistent with the relevant fiduciary duty.

El Ajou v Dollar Land Holdings plc [1994] 2 All ER 685 at 700
Facts: Mr Murad, an investment manager held El Ajou's money but was bribed to invest in fraudulent share selling operations perpetrated by three Canadians. The proceeds got invested in Dollar Land Holdings plc, and El Ajou sought restitution on the basis of knowing receipt in equity.
Ratio: In this case, the Court insisted on the importance of beneficial receipt, as being a requirement for holding a recipient liable. Where receipt was not beneficial but in a ministerial capacity on behalf of a client to pass it on as directed by the client there can be no liability for knowing receipt if they pass it on, except if they dishonestly assisted a third party (accessory liability).
Application: It should be noted that the receipt has to be personally beneficial to the recipient for the purposes of engaging his personal liability for knowing receipt.

Knowledge

General principle: Recipient's liability requires knowledge on the part of the defendant that the assets are traceable to a breach of trust or fiduciary duty. A recipient, who innocently receives property in breach of the transferee's equitable duties as a fiduciary is under duties to restore the property to its rightful owner but cannot be held personally liable. Recipients

will only be held liable if they had knowledge that another person has a better right to the property.

El Ajou v Dollar Land Holdings plc [1994] 2 All ER 685 at 700
Facts: Mr Murad, an investment manager held El Ajou's money but was bribed to invest in fraudulent share selling operations run by three Canadians. The proceeds got invested in Dollar Land Holdings plc, and El Ajou sought restitution on the basis it was a knowing recipient in equity. The court was asked whether, for the purposes of establishing a company's liability under the knowing receipt head of constructive trust, the knowledge of one of its directors can be treated as having been the knowledge of the company.
Ratio: The Company was fixed with the knowledge of its part-time chairman and a non-executive director, because he had acted as its directing mind and will for the particular purpose of arranging its receipt of the tainted funds. It was sufficient that the director had management and control so far as the receipt of the fraud was concerned, having made arrangements for the receipt and disposal of the money, even though he had no general managerial responsibility in the company. Nourse LJ said: "The doctrine attributes to the company the mind and will of the natural person or persons who manage and control its actions. (He concluded, quoting Lord Millet): "Their minds are its mind; their intention its intention; their knowledge its knowledge".
Application: It seems that the knowledge test requires that the defendant is aware that a fraudulent design is being prepared and that his assistance will help to implement it.

The standard for appreciating the requirement of knowledge gave rise to an important discussion when Nourse LJ, in **Bank of Credit and Commerce International (Overseas) Ltd and another v Akindele [2000]** 4 All ER 221, first presented it as "problematic". Before this case, there had been contradictory case-law on this issue.

General principle: The test of whether a recipient had knowledge of the breach of trust in order to determine if he or

she is a constructive trustee is whether he or she had knowledge of circumstances which made it unconscionable to hold the property and to deal with it without taking steps to restore it to its rightful owner.

Bank of Credit and Commerce International (Overseas) Ltd and another v Akindele [2000] 4 All ER 221

Facts: The liquidators of Bank of Credit and Commerce International (Overseas) Ltd (BCCI) sued Akindele, a Nigerian businessman, for moneys that he got in divestiture payments with an interest rate of 15%. Akindele did not know this was part of a fraud scheme to enable BCCI Holdings to buy its own shares. The liquidator argued that Akindele was a constructive trustee, for knowing receipt on the basis of artificially arranged loan transactions and his unusually high interest rate of 15%.

Ratio: The High Court refused recovery and upheld that the knowledge requirement was not satisfied. The court considered the following: "just as there is now a single test of dishonesty for knowing assistance, so ought there to be a single test of knowledge for knowing receipt. The recipient's state of knowledge must be such as to make it unconscionable for him to retain the benefit of the receipt. A test in that form, though it cannot, any more than any other, avoid difficulties of application, ought to avoid those of definition and allocation to which the previous categorisations have led. Moreover, it should better enable the courts to give common sense decisions in the commercial context in which claims in knowing receipt are now frequently made".

Application: In this case, the **Baden** test of levels of knowledge is considered irrelevant and replaced by the concept of unconscionability. However, regarding the different types of knowledge laid down in **Baden**, it seems that the unconscionability test covers types (i), (ii) and (iii) for sure, that type (iv) of knowledge will suffice for liability (see **Belmont Finance Corporation v Williams Furniture Ltd (No 2) [1980]** 1 All ER 393), but that negligent conduct of type (v) cannot give rise to liability.

However, when the **BCCI v Akedele** case was adopted, the unconscionability test raised several questions to the extent of the clarity of then definition of what unconscionability is. Some academics have commented that this might lead to misinterpretation and misapplication of the test by other judges in future decisions. In an attempt to clarify the situation, the Privy Council held that unconscionability is "conduct amounting to equitable fraud" (see **Arthur v A-G of the Turks and Caicos Islands [2012]** UKPC 30 at [40]).

Regarding the later application of the unconscionability test, Nicholas Strauss QC in **Starglade Properties Limited v Roland Nash [2009]** EWHC 148 (Ch) held that the test was a flexible one that was of a lower standard than dishonesty in dishonest assistance.

As a conclusion, if the recipient had knowledge that the property or assets received are traceable to a breach of trust or fiduciary duty, such as to make it unconscionable for them to deal with the property by doing anything other than taking steps to restore the property to its rightful owner, they are personally liable to account as a constructive trustee.

The High Court found in **Byers v Samba [2021]** EWHC 60 (Ch) that a claim in knowing receipt failed if the beneficiary's equitable interest lost priority as against the receiver at the time of receipt (for example, if the transferee was awarded a good, clean title by law). The case is still being appealed.

Summary

- In the context of equity and trusts law, a stranger is someone related to a trust although not appointed by a trustee.

- On the one hand, strangers may be held liable when they knowingly receive or deal with the trust property in breach of trust. This is traditionally referred to as "knowing receipt".

- On the other hand, strangers may dishonestly assist or procure a breach of trust.

- The personal liability of stranger was extended by the courts beyond trust property to property in respect of which fiduciary duties exist.

- An innocent volunteer recipient of money which is the product of a breach of trust, without having previously acquired knowledge of the existence of the trust, cannot be held personally liable to account for the trust property.

- Conversely, a recipient of property, however, will be under a personal liability to account to the beneficiaries for the loss to the trust if they dissipated the trust property (or its proceeds) after becoming aware that it was trust property.

- Common Law devised five levels of knowledge to determine whether the recipient was personally liable…cont.

1. Actual knowledge;

2. Wilfully shutting one's eyes to the obvious;

3. Wilfully and recklessly failing to make such inquiries as an honest and reasonable man would make;

4. Knowledge of circumstances which would indicate the facts to an honest and reasonable man (but not a morally obtuse man); and

5. Knowledge of circumstances which would put an honest and reasonable man on inquiry.

- A person with knowledge in categories (ii) and (iii) will be taken to have actual knowledge while a person in categories (iv) or (v) has constructive notice only. Constructive notice can suffice for the protection of proprietary interests.

- The accessory's knowledge is not the key question to determine their liability; it is rather their knowledge of the circumstances which would indicate the facts to an honest and reasonable man (but not a morally obtuse man) and knowledge of circumstances which would put an honest and reasonable man on inquiry.

- The second requirement to hold the defendant liable consists on demonstrating that the defendant assisted with the breach of trust or fiduciary duty.

- The reasoning behind this rule stems from a traditional conception of liability which implies that a defendant can only be held responsible for the losses resulting from his or her conduct.

- Traditionally, three requisite elements are required to engage a recipient liability under knowing receipt claims. It should be respectively demonstrated that there has been (i) a disposal in breach of trust or fiduciary duty (ii) a beneficial receipt by the defendant of assets which are traceable to the claimant and that (iii) the defendant knew that the assets are traceable to a breach of trust or fiduciary duty.